The *New*
Boston Globe Cookbook

The *New*
Boston Globe Cookbook

More than 200 Classic New England Recipes,

From Clam Chowder to Pumpkin Pie

Edited by Sheryl Julian

The Boston Globe

ThreeForks®

GUILFORD, CONNECTICUT
HELENA, MONTANA

AN IMPRINT OF THE GLOBE PEQUOT PRESS

Text design by Sheryl P. Kober

Photos on pages: iii, viii, x, 3, 5, 8, 9, 11, 12, 15, 19, 21, 24, 30, 32, 37, 40, 43, 44, 45, 50, 53, 55, 58, 64, 66, 67, 73, 79, 83, 86, 89, 90, 94, 98, 109, 115, 117, 119, 125, 132, 137, 141, 147, 148, 154, 156, 161, 165, 166, 170, 173, 174, 187, 193, 198, 203, 222, 227, 229, 232, 237, 239, 249, 252, 263, 264, 267, 272, 277, 281, 284, 287, 288, 291, 292, 293, 296, 298, 301, 308, 311, 312 © *The Boston Globe*

Photos on pages: i, ii, vi, 7, 22, 27, 29, 34, 39, 57, 74, 80, 88, 105, 111, 120, 122, 127, 129, 130, 138, 139, 145, 150, 152, 153, 178, 183, 197, 206, 209, 213, 214, 218, 221, 241, 243, 244, 247, 248, 256, 273, 285 © Shutterstock

Photos on pages: 61, 62, 65, 69, 70, 81, 113, 163, 224, 258, 269, 278, 295, 303, 305 © Photos.com

Library of Congress Cataloging-in-Publication Data

Julian, Sheryl.
  The new Boston globe cookbook : more than 200 classic New England recipes, from clam chowder to pumpkin pie / edited by Sheryl Julian.
    p. cm.
  Includes bibliographical references and index.
  ISBN 978-0-7627-4988-1 (alk. paper)
  1. Cookery, American—New England style. I. Title.
  TX715.2.N48J85 2009
  641.5974—dc22

                                                                          2009013813

Printed in China

10 9 8 7 6 5 4 3 2 1

Contents

Acknowledgments

The community of cooks and chefs in Boston is a spirited and generous group of men and women who are willing to share recipes, vendors, and kitchen experiences. We thank those professionals who let us watch them cook and taught us their recipes. We're also grateful to the writers who regularly contribute recipes to *The Boston Globe*. They hear about outstanding dishes, call the cooks who made them, and go into their own kitchens to figure out streamlined versions.

Among those writers are Karoline Boehm Goodnick, who also styled many of the photographs in this book, and Jonathan Levitt, who photographs everything he makes, and who is represented often in these pages. Other *Globe* contributors who have been writing about food for many years include Jane Dornbusch, Keri Fisher, Christine Merlo, Andrea Pyenson, Julie Riven, Tony Rosenfeld, Debra Samuels, Jill Santopietro, Rachel Travers, Lisa Yockelson, and Lisa Zwirn.

Janice Page, who oversees book projects on the *Globe* staff, is quick, graceful, and amusing, and production assistant Liberty McHugh Pilsch works the computer like a talented pianist running over the keyboard. Ann Luisa Cortissoz, a longtime food copy editor, and friend to all contributors, also pitched in. Among the *Globe* photographers who contributed to this book are John Blanding, Wendy Maeda, Wiqan Ang, Michele McDonald, Joanne Rathe, Essdras M. Suarez, Aram Boghosian, Dina Rudick, John Tlumacki, Pat Greenhouse, Vincent DeWitt, George Rizer, Jonathan Wiggs, David L. Ryan, and Erik Jacobs.

You have to really love food to be excited by just reading recipes. And you have to be really dedicated to go home and spend your free time at the stove. We're lucky to have so many writers and editors who are both.

Thank you all.

Introduction

When this volume was first published in 1948, it was called *The Boston Globe Cook Book for Brides*. Where were the grooms? They certainly weren't anywhere near the pots and pans. Whether you were new to cooking or an old hand in the kitchen, everyone knew that only women were at the stoves.

Thank goodness all that has changed. But sixty years later, something about the original book still feels familiar. Those pages celebrated the spirit and tastes of the New England table, as these updated recipes do. You can imagine the fishermen bringing their catch into the docks, growers spreading out their produce at the markets, eager consumers shopping for traditional, hearty fare whose main ingredients have hardly varied in all these decades.

The recipes in the first book came from an unusual source. *The Boston Globe* had a forum in the newspaper for good cooks who wanted to share their recipes with other readers. If you were looking for something in particular or had a dish you liked, you could write it down and mail it—remember when we all carefully copied down recipes and mailed them to each other?—to the newspaper for a daily column called "Confidential Chat." That popular reader exchange (it offered household tips, health remedies, and assorted other advice, too) started in 1884 and ran for more than one hundred years. "Chat" readers used code names such as "Suburban Secretary," "A Fireman's Wife," "White Moonflower," "Jessica's Polonaise." The recipes they sent in were largely family heirlooms, dishes that might have graced their tables for two generations.

Here's how it often worked: A reader headed for a summer picnic, for instance, might request a baked bean recipe. In a week or two, that reader could pick up the newspaper and find one recipe, sometimes several, submitted by other readers. In other instances, someone might send in a recipe that turned out particularly well, or a new dish learned from a friend.

The idea behind the *Book for Brides* was that all the Chatters (as they were called) were essentially a community of seasoned cooks. Their favorite dishes were collected in one place to offer to the newest cooks among them.

All of this, of course, was a precursor of the food chat rooms on the Internet, complete with pseudonyms. But now men are welcome in the kitchen, as are young adults, teenagers, and tots. So this volume is for everyone who wants a flavor of New England, including anyone who has ever rented a cottage on Cape Cod, climbed a mountain in New Hampshire, or driven through western Massachusetts during fall's glorious leaf-changing season.

Recipes have been updated for modern tastes. Where our sauces were once thick and floury, contemporary cooks prefer thinner sauces. There are more salads and interesting things to do with vegetables (and make for vegetarians). Entertaining is less formal now, so there are dishes you can serve to large gatherings, bring to potlucks, or leave to simmer on the stove top for guests to help themselves.

For this new edition, recipes are culled from the cooks who have been writing for *The Boston Globe* food pages for the last decade. Many have families to make dinner for every night, most have a practical streak, and all understand that home cooks want things that are generally simpler than restaurant chefs offer.

Sometimes our writers do go to restaurants for recipes, then go home to their own kitchens and adapt the dish so any complicated techniques are streamlined. There are also recipes from people who are known for a particular specialty or confection, cooking teachers and caterers we have interviewed, and formulas for some dishes that are so traditional, we couldn't offer a New England cookbook without them.

To that end, here are seafood chowders, those prized baked bean dishes, old-fashioned pots of pasta and sauce, simmered meats and vegetables, and the best versions of cookie-jar cookies. You'll also find breakfast eggs from a Brazilian cook, Vietnamese pot-fried rice, and the Greek spinach pie spanakopita. In the years since the *Book for Brides*, many immigrant groups have settled in Boston, changing the culinary landscape dramatically. Some of their dishes are represented here.

Every time you pick up this volume, we hope you'll find recipes that make you want to head for the kitchen and start cooking. We think the best gatherings are at home, where generations of voices can be heard and you can laugh all you want because there's no one at the next table. And with every meal, you'll refill your house with the heady aromas of a time gone by.

That's still the best way to welcome friends and family to your table.

—Sheryl Julian
Food Editor, *The Boston Globe*

Appetizers

Because they're the first thing you serve, appetizers are almost more important than the rest of the meal. What guests drink and eat at the beginning of the night often sets the tone for the whole evening.

You can offer substantial appetizers as a way to get people to mingle. Half a dozen guests sitting around nibbling small pizzas or sticky glazed chicken wings may make a little mess, but it will certainly relax everyone and get previously unacquainted guests talking. But if your dinner is more formal and everyone arrives dressed up, you probably want to avoid complicated things and begin with simple marinated olives, a white bean-olive spread, or homemade crackers.

Appetizers generally fall into three categories. There are the hors d'oeuvres you serve in the living room so guests have a little something with their drinks. Other appetizers, also served in a sitting area, are more substantial and perhaps presented together. These heftier nibbles might include *gourgeres*, the little French cheese puffs, deviled eggs, or a Middle Eastern hummus. If the array is hearty enough, you can skip a first course at the table.

That first course or appetizer also varies greatly. For an elegant dinner, offer baked eggs topped with a dot of caviar or thin potato slices draped with smoked salmon. A festive family meal might begin with the Greek spinach pie spanakopita, baked stuffed clams, or steamed mussels. If a few friends have gathered to celebrate, you might make shrimp ceviche or country pâté.

There are no rules, except that you should offer *something* right at the beginning. If you're pressed for time, a bowl of roasted almonds or a nice local cheese is just right. If you have a moment a few days ahead of time, tuck homemade cheese crackers into the freezer or grill eggplant for poor man's caviar.

But whatever you decide, remember this: If you have a reputation as a good cook, your guests will eat lightly that day. They're counting on dining well at your table. So you owe them a fine nibble when they walk in the door.

Rye Crackers

Thin and crisp, these rye crackers go well with cheese, a spread, or on their own. Roll them out, prick the dough with a fork, then use a pastry or pizza cutter to make professional-looking rectangles.

MAKES 24

1 cup rye flour

½ cup all-purpose flour

1 teaspoon salt

6 tablespoons butter, cut into
  pieces

6 tablespoons cold milk

Butter (for the baking sheet)

Extra all-purpose flour (for
  rolling)

1 egg white, beaten with 1
  teaspoon water

1. In a food processor fitted with the metal blade, combine the rye flour, all-purpose flour, and salt. Work the machine in on-off motions for 5 seconds. **2.** Add the butter and process until the mixture resembles sand. With the machine running, pour in the milk. Mix just until the dough forms a ball. **3.** Turn the dough out onto a lightly floured board and shape it into a smooth, flat cake. Wrap it in foil and refrigerate for several hours. **4.** Set the oven at 400°F. Have on hand a large, rimless baking sheet. Butter it lightly. **5.** Remove the dough from the refrigerator and place it in the center of the baking sheet. Press it with the heel of your hand to make a 6-inch cake. **6.** Lightly flour the dough and, with a rolling pin, roll it into a rectangle about 12 by 14 inches. If the edges are jagged and the sides not quite even, that's OK. **7.** With the tines of a fork, pierce the dough all over the surface. Using a pastry or pizza cutter, make 3 vertical cuts and 5 horizontal cuts to form 24 crackers. **8.** Brush the dough with the egg-white mixture. **9.** Bake the crackers for 15 to 20 minutes or until they are brown. If the crackers on the edges get too brown, remove them early and transfer them to a wire rack to cool. **10.** When the crackers are done, transfer all of them to the rack. Let them cool completely. Store in an airtight container for up to 1 week.

Ingrid Lysgaard

Cheese Crackers

Cheese Crackers

A simple dough, made like a pastry crust, but with lots of cheese, is rolled into logs and sliced for baking. The rounds are very cheesy and flaky.

MAKES 40

1 cup flour

¼ teaspoon baking powder

½ teaspoon salt

Pinch of cayenne pepper

½ cup (1 stick) unsalted butter, at room temperature

½ pound cheddar cheese, grated (to make 2 cups)

1. In a bowl, combine the flour, baking powder, salt, and cayenne pepper. Whisk to blend them. **2.** In a food processor, combine the butter and cheese. Pulse the mixture until blended. **3.** Add the flour mixture and pulse again until the dough comes together to form moist clumps. **4.** Lay two long sheets of plastic wrap on the counter. Divide the dough between the sheets. Working with one sheet at a time, roll the pastry up in the sheet to form a log shape. Roll it under your palms to form a log that is about 7 inches long and about 1½ inches in diameter. Wrap completely in the plastic wrap, securing the ends. **5.** Do the same with the other dough and sheet. **6.** Refrigerate the logs for at least 3 hours or for up to 2 days. **7.** Set the oven at 375°F. Line two baking sheets with parchment paper. **8.** Using a straight-bladed knife, cut the logs into ⅓-inch thick slices. Arrange them on the baking sheets. **9.** Bake for 15 to 18 minutes or until golden. Cool on the baking sheets. Transfer to a wire rack to cool completely.

Ellen Forst

Thin-Crusted Individual Pizzas

Making pizza with store-bought dough couldn't be easier, and so many places offer good dough. In fact, most pizzerias like to sell their dough at the end of each day—and it's often not expensive. Ask your neighborhood place if they do.

MAKES FOUR 7-INCH PIZZAS

1 pound store-bought pizza
    dough, at room temperature
Flour (for shaping)
2 tablespoons olive oil, plus
    more for sprinkling
1 clove garlic, thinly sliced
1 can (14 ounces) crushed
    tomatoes
1 teaspoon salt
1 teaspoon sugar
½ cup fresh basil leaves,
    coarsely chopped
Coarse semolina flour or
    cornmeal (for sprinkling)
10 ounces fresh mozzarella,
    torn into 16 thin pieces

1. Set the oven at 550°F. Place a pizza stone in the top third of the oven. Let it heat for 45 minutes. **2.** Punch down the dough. Divide it into 4 equal balls. Dust each lightly with flour and cover 3 of them with a clean towel. **3.** Using a rolling pin, roll the remaining ball of dough firmly and evenly, flattening it to a 5-inch disk. Dust with flour when the dough becomes sticky. Using your palms and fingertips, stretch the dough, shaping it into a 7-inch round. Slip it under the towel and shape the remaining rounds. Let them rest under the towel for 15 minutes. **4.** In a medium saucepan, heat 2 tablespoons of the olive oil with the garlic over medium heat. Cook the garlic for 2 minutes or until it is fragrant but not colored. Add the tomatoes, salt, and sugar. Simmer gently for 20 minutes. Add ¼ cup of the basil leaves and set the sauce aside. **5.** Scatter coarse semolina or cornmeal onto the surface of a wooden pizza peel, cutting board, or rimless baking sheet. Place one piece of dough on it. With the back of a spoon, spread about 2 tablespoons of tomato sauce on the round, then add 4 small pieces of mozzarella. Sprinkle with extra oil. **6.** Slide the pizza off the board or sheet onto the hot stone. Bake for 3 minutes or until the crust is firm and golden. Remove the pizza from the oven with a wide spatula and transfer it onto a plate. Sprinkle a few of the remaining basil leaves on top. Repeat with the other 3 rounds of dough.

Jonathan Levitt

Thin-Crusted Individual Pizza

Marinated Olives

You can buy marinated olives everywhere, but they're always more expensive than ordinary olives. So make your own. The important step is to rinse off the excess salt before you add olive oil and seasonings. Ideally, you should let the olives sit for a week. Store them in the refrigerator for up to 3 weeks. (If not storing, use the olives without rinsing.)

SERVES 8

1 quart mixed black and green
   olives in brine

¼ cup olive oil

Pared rind of ½ orange

¼ cup fresh thyme leaves

1 bay leaf

5 dried hot peppers

½ teaspoon ground cumin

1. Drain the olives, rinse them in a colander, then transfer them to a bowl and cover with plenty of cold water. Soak for 10 minutes. Rinse thoroughly, then leave them in a colander to drain completely. **2.** In a large plastic container combine the oil, orange rind, thyme, bay leaf, peppers, and cumin. Add the olives and toss them thoroughly in the marinade. Cover tightly and refrigerate for at least 3 days and as long as 3 weeks, tossing the olives in the marinade several times. **3.** If the olives seem dry, add a few more spoonfuls of oil to the container. Let the olives sit at room temperature for several hours before serving. Serve them in their marinade.

Sheryl Julian

Edamame in the Pods

Edamame (ed-ah-MAH-may) are fresh green soybeans that are sweet and nutty, with a texture similar to fava beans. They grow in fuzzy green 2½-inch-long pods, with two or three beans packed into each one. They also happen to be extremely nutritious. This is the way Japanese restaurants serve the popular edamame, right in the pods. Nibble them with wine. If you can resist the urge to eat them all at once, cooked edamame can be refrigerated for up to 5 days.

SERVES 4

1 pound fresh or frozen
    edamame in the shell
Coarse salt, to taste

1. Place the edamame in a large saucepan fitted with a steamer insert and several inches of water. Cover and bring to a boil. Steam for 10 to 12 minutes or until they are tender. **2.** Remove the edamame from the pan and transfer to a large plate to cool. Sprinkle with salt.

Andrea Pyenson

Glazed Chicken Wings

Sticky, messy, delicious chicken wings are everyone's favorite football game food. Supply plenty of napkins.

SERVES 8

3 pounds chicken wings
1 tablespoon vegetable oil
1 can (15 ounces) whole
    tomatoes, crushed in a bowl
½ cup chicken stock
½ cup cider vinegar
¼ cup brown sugar
2 tablespoons Worcestershire
    sauce
1 tablespoon honey
2 teaspoons dry mustard
¼ teaspoon crushed red
    pepper (optional)
Salt and black pepper, to taste

1. Turn on the broiler. With kitchen scissors, cut the chicken wings in half to separate the drumettes from the slender two-bone part. Snip off the pointy tips (use them for soup). **2.** Place the wings in a roasting pan large enough to hold them in one layer. **3.** Place the pan in the oven about 10 inches from the broiler. Broil the chicken wings for 10 minutes, turning them halfway through cooking. They should not be charred; if necessary, move the rack farther from the broiling unit. **4.** Meanwhile, in a saucepan, heat the oil and stir in the tomatoes, stock, vinegar, brown sugar, Worcestershire sauce, honey, mustard, red pepper (if using) and salt and black pepper. Bring to a boil and simmer, stirring often, for 10 minutes. **5.** Turn the oven to 375°F. **6.** Pour the sauce over the wings. Cook the wings for 40 minutes or until they are glazed, turning several times during cooking.

Julie Riven

Pork Spare Ribs

Many cooks maintain that the best ribs are cooked first in a low oven, then glazed in a much hotter oven (or over a hot grill) with sauce.

SERVES 10

5 pounds pork spare ribs, cut in half crosswise

Salt and pepper, to taste

1 cup tomato sauce

2 tablespoons cider vinegar

2 tablespoons brown sugar

1 tablespoon Dijon mustard

2 tablespoons Worcestershire sauce

2 tablespoons lemon juice

1. Set the oven at 300°F. Line a roasting pan with a rack. Lay the ribs on the rack. Sprinkle with salt and pepper. Cook the ribs for 2 hours or until they are cooked through. **2.** Meanwhile, in a saucepan, combine the tomato sauce, vinegar, sugar, mustard, Worcestershire sauce, and lemon juice. Bring to a boil and simmer for 10 minutes or until the sauce reduces slightly. Set aside. **3.** Turn the oven temperature up to 450°F. **4.** Brush the ribs with the sauce. Cook them for 30 minutes, basting often with the sauce, or until they are glazed and sticky. Cut the ribs into individual fingers.

Goat Cheese Croquettes

Goat Cheese Croquettes

The Japanese bread crumbs called panko, *available at most specialty markets, make a crisp exterior for these pan-fried croquettes. You can also use plain white bread crumbs. Serve with a simple salad.*

MAKES 8

1 pound fresh goat cheese

1 cup panko

2 tablespoons olive oil

Salt and pepper, to taste

1. Form the goat cheese into 8 balls. Flatten them slightly. **2.** Sprinkle the panko on a shallow plate. Roll the cheese in the crumbs. **3.** In a nonstick skillet, heat the olive oil over medium-low heat. When it is hot, add the croquettes. Sprinkle them with salt and pepper. Cook for 2 minutes on a side or until they are lightly browned all over.

Jonathan Levitt

Deviled Eggs

Deviled Eggs

At one time, you couldn't go to a picnic without seeing a plate of deviled eggs. Then they went out of style. Now deviled eggs are back and often on menus where bar food nibbles are popular. At Hungry Mother restaurant in Cambridge, Massachusetts, the cooks render good smoky bacon, then break off pieces and pop them vertically into the yolks, so they look like they have flags (pictured here). You can add bacon flags to this recipe, if you like.

SERVES 12

12 eggs, hard cooked
  (see page 108)
½ cup mayonnaise
4 scallions, finely chopped
1 tablespoon sweet pickle relish
2 teaspoons Dijon mustard
⅛ teaspoon cayenne pepper
Salt and black pepper, to taste

1. Halve the eggs horizontally. Using a teaspoon, tip the yolks into a bowl. **2.** Add the mayonnaise, scallions, relish, mustard, cayenne, salt, and black pepper. Cut a tiny slice off the rounded sides of the halves, so they sit flat on a platter. Spoon the yolk mixture into the halves. Cover tightly with plastic wrap and refrigerate until ready to serve.

Sheryl Julian & Julie Riven

Eggs Stuffed with Tuna

More substantial than deviled eggs, these tuna-stuffed eggs became popular when local chef and restaurant owner Ana Sortun began offering them on her Oleana menu as a nibble.

SERVES 6

6 eggs, hard cooked
   (see page 108)
6 tablespoons unsalted butter,
   at room temperature
1 can (6½ ounces) tuna in
   olive oil
1 tablespoon capers
¼ teaspoon salt, or to taste
⅛ teaspoon cayenne pepper
About 1 teaspoon paprika
2 tablespoons chopped fresh
   parsley

1. Halve the eggs horizontally. Transfer the yolks to a food processor. **2.** Add the butter, tuna, capers, salt, and cayenne pepper. Pulse the mixture to form a puree. With a pastry bag fitted with a small plain tip or a small spoon, stuff the egg whites with the tuna mixture. Sprinkle sparingly with paprika, then with parsley.

Oleana restaurant,
Cambridge, Massachusetts

Baked Eggs with Caviar

Although this sounds ordinary—eggs cooked in individual baking dishes until the whites are just set and the yolks runny—topping each one with a dot of black caviar turns them into an elegant presentation. The tiny straight-sided pleated dishes called ramekins are ideal for baking and serving.

SERVES 6

Butter (for the dishes)
Salt and pepper, to taste
6 eggs
¾ cup heavy cream
1 jar (1 ounce) black caviar

1. Set the oven at 350°F. Have on hand six ramekins or custard cups (½-cup capacity) and a small roasting pan. Bring a kettle of water to a boil. **2.** Butter the ramekins or cups generously. Sprinkle them with salt and pepper. Break an egg into each cup and add 2 tablespoons of cream to each. Set the dishes in the roasting pan. Pour enough boiling water to come halfway up the sides of the dishes. **3.** Bake for 15 to 20 minutes or until the tops are just firm to the touch (the whites should set, and the yolks will be runny). Top each egg with a spoonful of caviar and serve with toast.

Sheryl Julian

Roasted Potato Planks

Very thin, incredibly crisp, and golden brown, these long slices of potato are roasted in a hot oven and can be served as an accompaniment to steak, roast chicken, or as an appetizer on their own.

SERVES 4

3 tablespoons olive oil

3 large russet potatoes, scrubbed and dried

Salt and pepper, to taste

1. Set the oven at 400°F. Have on hand two rimmed baking sheets. Brush them with some of the oil. Set the sheets in the oven while you slice the potatoes. **2.** Using a mandoline or straight-bladed chef's knife, cut the potatoes lengthwise into ¼-inch pieces. Carefully remove the baking sheets from the oven and set them on a heatproof surface. **3.** Arrange the potato slices on the baking sheets. Brush with oil and sprinkle with salt and pepper. Roast the potatoes for 12 minutes or until they brown on top. Use a wide metal spatula to turn them and roast the other side for 12 minutes more or until the potatoes are golden brown and very crisp. If the potatoes at the edges brown earlier, turn them over when they are brown. Drain the potatoes on paper towels.

Sheryl Julian

Roasted Potato Planks

Potato Crisps with Smoked Salmon

Potato Crisps with Smoked Salmon

Holly Safford, owner of The Catered Affair in Hingham, Massachusetts, offers a first course of layered potatoes and smoked salmon, a riff on the crisp French mille-feuille pastry.

SERVES 8

Olive oil (for the pan and for
  sprinkling)
2 large russet potatoes
Salt, to taste
¼ cup sour cream
1 tablespoon chopped fresh
  parsley
1 scallion, finely chopped
6 ounces thinly sliced smoked
  salmon

1. Set the oven at 450°F. Generously oil two large rimmed baking sheets. **2.** Using a mandoline or another handheld slicing machine, thinly slice the potatoes lengthwise. Set the slices on the baking sheets without overlapping. Brush with olive oil and sprinkle with salt. Turn and brush with oil, then sprinkle with salt. **3.** Roast the potatoes for 10 minutes. Remove from the oven and let them cool in the pan for 2 minutes. Use a metal spatula to dislodge them. Carefully turn them. Continue roasting for 10 minutes or until golden, checking that they do not burn. Remove the slices from the pan as they brown. **4.** In a bowl, whisk the sour cream, parsley, scallion, and salt. **5.** Cut the salmon into pieces about the size of the potato slices. Arrange the potatoes on a platter. Set a piece of salmon on each one. Add a dollop of the sour cream mixture and pass the rest separately.

The Catered Affair,
Hingham, Massachusetts

Smoked Bluefish Pâté

Use smoked trout when bluefish is not available. This is the spread made by Amanda Lydon and Gabriel Frasca at Straight Wharf restaurant in Nantucket, Massachusetts.

MAKES 2 CUPS

6 ounces boneless smoked
   bluefish
8 ounces cream cheese,
   softened
1/2 medium red onion, finely
   chopped
Generous dash of hot sauce
2 tablespoons Worcestershire
   sauce
1 tablespoon lemon juice
1 tablespoon finely chopped
   parsley
1/4 cup chopped fresh chives
   (for garnish)

1. Remove and discard the skin, any bones, and darkest flesh from the bluefish. Flake the fish into a medium bowl. **2.** In a food processor, combine the fish, cream cheese, onion, hot sauce, Worcestershire sauce, and lemon juice. Pulse the mixture until it is smooth. Taste for seasoning and add more hot sauce, Worcestershire, or lemon juice, if you like. **3.** Transfer to a serving bowl and cover with plastic wrap. Refrigerate for at least 2 hours or overnight (maximum). Serve at room temperature with toasts or crackers. **4.** Sprinkle with parsley and chives.

Straight Wharf restaurant,
Nantucket, Massachusetts

Clam Dip

Popular since the 1940s, this clam dip was first made with canned clams. Make it with steamed, chopped fresh clams (also available frozen in fish markets).

SERVES 6

1 package (8 ounces) cream
   cheese, at room temperature
1 cup chopped cooked fresh
   clams
1 tablespoon lemon juice, or to
   taste
1 teaspoon Worcestershire
   sauce, or to taste
Dash hot sauce, or to taste
Salt and pepper, to taste

1. In a bowl, combine the cream cheese, clams, lemon juice, Worcestershire sauce, hot sauce, salt, and pepper. Stir well. **2.** Taste for seasoning and add more lemon juice, Worcestershire, or hot sauce. Serve with crackers.

Country Pâté with Pistachios

This begins like an ordinary meat loaf but turns into an elegant pâtè. Mix equal quantities of ground beef and pork, add plenty of allspice and cloves, and stud the mixture with pistachios. After the loaf is cooked, press it with weights while it cools, and the texture will change from a meat loaf to a pâtè. Serve it with a small bowl of grainy mustard and toast, along with cornichons, the tiny unsweetened French pickles.

SERVES 8

½ Spanish onion
2 slices stale sandwich bread,
    crusts removed
⅓ cup whole milk
1 egg, lightly beaten
1 pound lean ground beef
1 pound ground pork
¼ cup shelled unsalted
    pistachios
⅛ teaspoon ground allspice
½ teaspoon ground cloves
½ teaspoon salt
½ teaspoon pepper
Toasted sandwich bread, crusts
    removed (for serving)
Cornichons (for serving)
Grainy mustard (for serving)

1. Set the oven at 350°F. Have on hand an 8½ x 4½-inch glass loaf pan. In the bowl of a food processor fitted with the steel blade, work the onion in on-off motions until it is grated. Remove it from the processor and transfer to a bowl. **2.** Add the bread to the processor. Work the bread in on-off motions until it is coarse crumbs. Transfer to the bowl of onion. Pour in the milk and stir well. Set aside for 5 minutes. **3.** Add the egg, beef, pork, pistachios, allspice, cloves, salt, and pepper. With a large spoon or clean hands, knead the mixture until it is well combined. **4.** Transfer the mixture to the loaf pan. Bake it for 75 minutes. **5.** Remove the meat loaf from the oven. You'll see lots of juices at the edges of the pan of meat, so set the loaf pan in a small roasting pan to catch the overflow. Cover the meat loaf with foil. Place a second loaf pan right side up on top of the meat loaf. Fill the pan with heavy cans so that it presses down on the loaf as it cools. Set the meat loaf aside for 1 hour. Remove the cans and foil and pour off the juices that have accumulated around the meat. **6.** Cover the loaf, still in its pan, with the foil and place the second loaf pan on top. Fill with the cans again. Refrigerate the loaf for 1 to 2 days. **7.** Remove the loaf pan from the refrigerator. Lift off the second loaf pan, along with the cans and foil. Place the meat loaf on a cutting board. Using a serrated knife, slice the loaf ½-inch thick. Slice each piece in half on the diagonal. Arrange the slices on a platter and serve with toasts, pickles, and mustard.

Sheryl Julian

Spanakopita (Greek spinach pie)

Spanakopita (*Greek spinach pie*)

The layered Greek spinach pie, made with phyllo dough, is a crisp, buttery wonder. Serve as a first course or set squares beside roast meats.

SERVES 10

¼ cup (½ stick) butter, melted, or more if needed

2¼ pounds fresh spinach, stems removed

1 onion, grated

Salt and pepper, to taste

1 teaspoon dried mint

3 eggs, lightly beaten

1 tablespoon olive oil

½ pound imported feta cheese, crumbled

1 package phyllo dough, at room temperature

1. Set the oven at 375°F. Use some of the melted butter to butter a 10 x 15-inch baking dish. Rinse and dry the spinach, removing as much moisture as possible (use paper towels, if necessary). Tear the leaves into small pieces. **2.** In a large bowl, mix the spinach, onion, salt, pepper, mint, eggs, olive oil, and feta. **3.** Lay the phyllo dough on the counter. Have the melted butter and a brush nearby. Working quickly, lift off 1 sheet from the stack of phyllo and lay it in the bottom of the baking dish. Don't worry if the sheet has a small tear or two. Scrunch any excess dough into the sides of the pan, forming a thicker wall around the edges. Using a pastry brush, lightly brush the top sheet with melted butter. Lay another sheet on top and brush again with butter. Repeat until you've used about 10 sheets. **4.** Spread the spinach filling evenly over the sheets, pressing lightly to compact it slightly. Smooth the top. **5.** In the same way you made the bottom layer, make the top crust, brushing butter between each sheet. Continue until you have used about 8 more sheets. **6.** Cut two slits through the top crust for steam to escape. Using your fingers, sprinkle the top lightly with cold water. Bake the pie for 45 to 60 minutes or until it is golden brown. Serve hot or warm, cut into squares.

Bette Novicki

Tabbouleh

In the middle of winter, when Italian flat-leaf parsley is one of the freshest-looking greens in the market, make this Middle Eastern bulgur salad. Serve it with roast chicken or lamb.

SERVES 4

1 cup medium bulgur (available at a Middle Eastern market)

Juice of 1 lemon

Salt and pepper, to taste

¼ cup olive oil

2 pickling cucumbers, halved lengthwise, seeded, and chopped

½ pint cherry tomatoes, cut into quarters

1 bunch scallions, trimmed and chopped

½ cup chopped fresh parsley

1. In a large bowl, combine the bulgur and enough water to cover it. Set aside for 2 hours. **2.** In a bowl, whisk the lemon juice, salt, and pepper. Whisk in the oil a little at a time. **3.** Tip off any water that the bulgur grains have not absorbed. Stir the dressing into the bulgur with the cucumbers, cherry tomatoes, scallions, and parsley. Taste for seasoning, and add more salt, if you like.

Sheryl Julian

Cheese Spread

Based on an old English dish, this blend of sharp cheddar and butter was invented as a way to use up scraps of cheese left from making other dishes. If you add blue cheese, the mixture will turn grayish. Add a little Camembert or goat cheese to make a buttery color. The spread keeps well in the refrigerator and is an inexpensive nibble to offer with crackers.

SERVES 6

¾ pound sharp cheddar cheese, grated (to make 3 cups)

¼ pound goat, feta, or Camembert, crumbled or cut up (about ¾ cup)

2 tablespoons butter, at room temperature

1 heaping tablespoon Dijon mustard

⅛ teaspoon cayenne pepper, or to taste

1. In a food processor, combine the cheeses, butter, mustard, and cayenne. **2.** Pulse the mixture until it is smooth and spreadable. Taste for seasoning and add more cayenne, if you like. Pack into a crock or bowl, cover with plastic wrap, and refrigerate for at least 1 day for the flavors to mellow.

Sheryl Julian

Poor Man's Caviar (*grilled eggplant spread*)

Most vegetables change character from the smokiness of grilling; eggplant is completely transformed. In this spread, the chopped eggplant is mixed with garlic, lemon juice, cayenne pepper, cumin, and black olives. It's best made a day in advance for the flavors to mellow. Serve as an hors d'oeuvre with pita bread or as an accompaniment to roast leg of lamb.

SERVES 6

2 large eggplants

Salt and black pepper, to taste

2 tablespoons olive oil

1 clove garlic, finely chopped

Juice of 1 lemon

1/8 teaspoon cayenne pepper, or to taste

1/8 teaspoon ground cumin, or to taste

1/2 cup black olives, coarsely chopped

4 small rounds pita bread, cut into triangles

1. Light a charcoal grill, or turn a gas grill to medium. Remove and discard the stems from the eggplants. Halve the eggplants lengthwise and score the flesh with the tip of a knife. Sprinkle the cut sides with salt and leave the eggplants on a plate, tipping each one slightly for 20 minutes. Rinse them, pat them dry with paper towels, and rub the eggplants all over with oil. **2.** When the coals are hot, set the eggplants, cut sides down, on the grill and cook them, turning often, for 15 to 20 minutes or until they are cooked through. Move charred eggplant halves to the edges of the fire and continue cooking until they soften. **3.** Remove the eggplants from the grill and leave them to cool completely. With a spoon, scrape the flesh from the skin. Discard the skin. **4.** On a board, coarsely chop the eggplant. Transfer to a bowl. **5.** Add the garlic, lemon juice, black pepper, cayenne pepper, cumin, and olives. Cover and refrigerate for at least 1 hour or for up to 1 day. **6.** Let the eggplant mixture return to room temperature and taste it for seasoning. Add more salt or red pepper, if you like. **7.** Mound the eggplant on a platter and serve with pita.

Sheryl Julian

Hummus

You can find many versions of hummus, which is served all over the Middle East. This is the Armenian version, which is especially creamy and lemony. Tahini is a puree of sesame seeds with the consistency of thin peanut butter.

MAKES 2 CUPS OR ENOUGH TO SERVE 6

1 can (15 ounces) chickpeas

1/2 cup sesame tahini

Juice of 1 lemon, or to taste

1/4 teaspoon salt, or to taste

1 tablespoon olive oil

1. Set a strainer over a bowl. Tip the chickpeas into it; reserve the liquid. In a food processor, combine the chickpeas, 1 tablespoon of their liquid, tahini, lemon juice, salt, and oil. Pulse the mixture until it is smooth and creamy. **2.** Add enough of the remaining chickpea liquid, 1 tablespoon at a time, to make a mixture that just holds its shape. **3.** Taste for seasoning and add more lemon juice or salt, if you like. Serve with pita bread or crackers.

Emeline Aroush

Baked Stuffed Clams

Gerri Sullivan of Boston and Osterville, Massachusetts, on Cape Cod, grew up on these clams. Her mother, Rose Colella, made her own bread crumbs from the stale pieces that she collected in the bread drawer. These were sprinkled over the chopped sea clams that her husband and children found at the beach after a storm. Sullivan makes her own bread crumbs, but you can also buy them, along with the clams.

SERVES 4

1 pound fresh clams, chopped

½ cup fresh or bottled clam broth

¼ cup chopped fresh parsley

½ cup grated Parmesan

½ cup fresh bread crumbs

Pepper, to taste

2 tablespoons butter

1. Set the oven at 375°F. In an 8-inch baking dish, place the clams and broth. **2.** In a bowl, mix the parsley, Parmesan, bread crumbs, and pepper. Sprinkle the mixture on top of the clams and dot with the butter. **3.** Bake the clams in the hot oven for 25 to 30 minutes or until the juices are bubbling at the edges. **4.** Turn the oven to broil. Slide the dish under the broiler and cook it for 30 seconds. Watch it very carefully. The top should be browned but not burnt. Spoon onto plates and serve at once.

Gerri Sullivan

Broiled Scallops and Bacon

Another version of angels on horseback, one of the smoky nibbles made by wrapping bacon around oysters, these bacon-wrapped scallops cook in minutes and are best hot. Arrange them on a rack on a broiling tray and make them just before you serve them.

SERVES 4

2 tablespoons honey

2 tablespoons soy sauce

2 tablespoons lemon juice

1 pound sea scallops

8 slices bacon, cut in half

1. In a bowl, combine the honey, soy sauce, and lemon juice. Add the scallops, cover, and refrigerate for several hours. **2.** Remove the scallops from the marinade. Wrap each scallop with a half slice of bacon. Secure with toothpicks. **3.** Turn on the broiler. Set the scallops on a rack in a broiling pan. Broil the scallops about 8 inches from the element, turning them often, for 5 minutes or until the bacon is golden brown and crisp.

Shrimp Ceviche with Capers

Shrimp Ceviche with Capers

Ceviche is a method of "cooking" fish by marinating it in citrus juice. In this recipe, the shrimp are actually simmered for 1 minute, then marinated for an hour or two in a vinaigrette. Spear the shrimp on small bamboo skewers or serve with toothpicks.

SERVES 6

Salt and pepper, to taste

2 pounds large shrimp, shelled

1/8 teaspoon dry mustard

1/8 teaspoon ground ginger

1/4 cup white wine vinegar

1/4 cup olive oil

1/2 sweet onion, halved and thinly sliced

4 scallions, finely chopped

2 tablespoons large capers

2 tablespoons chopped fresh parsley

4 leaves romaine lettuce (for serving)

1. Bring a large pot of salted water to a boil. Drop in the shrimp and cook for 1 minute or until the shrimp just begin to turn pink. Do not let them cook until they're done. Drain into a colander and transfer the shrimp to a large bowl. **2.** In another bowl, whisk the salt, pepper, mustard, ginger, and vinegar until the salt dissolves. Whisk in the oil a little at a time until the dressing emulsifies. Pour the mixture over the shrimp and toss to coat it. Let it cool completely. **3.** Cover the shrimp with plastic wrap and refrigerate for 1 to 2 hours. Add the onion, scallions, capers, and parsley and toss well. Add more salt and pepper if you like. **4.** Arrange the lettuce on a platter, and set the shrimp on the lettuce leaves.

Fancy's Market,
Osterville, Massachusetts

Gougeres

Gougeres are small French cheese puffs made from a savory cream-puff dough. They need to be beaten vigorously, which you can do by hand or in a heavy-duty electric mixer. To pipe them onto a baking sheet, use a pastry bag or a heavy plastic zipper bag with a hole cut in one corner. Jacky Cattani is the American-born chef to French consul general Francois Gauthier in Boston, Massachusetts, who nominated her for the Merite Agricole *(France's oldest civil award). Cattani makes these savory puffs for consul receptions.*

MAKES ABOUT 3 DOZEN

1 cup water

½ cup (1 stick) unsalted butter, cut up

1 cup flour

Pinch of salt

4 or 5 eggs

1¼ cups finely shredded Gruyere cheese

1 egg yolk, beaten with ¼ cup heavy cream (for the glaze)

1. Set the oven at 425°F. Line two baking sheets with parchment paper. In a medium saucepan, combine the water and butter. Bring to a boil. Remove from the heat and with a wooden spoon, stir in all of the flour and the salt. Mix vigorously until the dough is smooth. **2.** Return the pot to medium heat and continue cooking the mixture, stirring constantly, until almost no steam rises from it. Continue folding it over onto itself and moving it from side to side in the pan. Cook for about 5 minutes, but make sure not to scorch the dough. **3.** Remove the pan from the heat. Stir the dough for a few more seconds to cool it slightly. **4.** Continue stirring with a wooden spoon or transfer the dough to a heavy-duty mixer that has a paddle attachment. Add 1 egg, beating the dough until it is very smooth. Continue adding 3 more eggs, one at a time, beating well after each addition, until the mixture is smooth, shiny, and has a "flowy" quality. When you pick it up on the spoon, the dough should drop easily. If the mixture is still stiff, break the 5th egg into a bowl, beat it lightly, then add it 1 teaspoon at a time to the batter. The dough should not be too runny or too stiff. **5.** Stir in the cheese and mix well. **6.** Use a large pastry bag with a ¼-inch plain round tip, or a gallon zipper bag with one of the bottom corners clipped. Set either one in a cylindrical container and fold over half the top. Spoon in one-third of the dough, pressing it down, then fold the unfilled cuff up and twist. Hold the bag tightly in the middle so the dough does not escape from the top; this also keeps the air out. **7.** Pipe the dough into golf-ball-size rounds. Refill the bag and continue piping until all the dough has been used. Brush the rounds lightly with the beaten egg glaze. **8.** Bake the *gougeres* for 10 minutes. Turn the oven temperature down to 350°F. Continue baking for 25 minutes (total baking time is 35 minutes), or until the mounds are golden brown and firm. Cool slightly before serving.

Jacky Cattani

Gougeres

Steamed Mussels

A pot of mussels cooked in white wine tastes like much more was involved in the cooking. Serve them with toasted or grilled bread sprinkled with olive oil.

SERVES 6

½ cup white wine

1 shallot, finely chopped

½ bunch fresh thyme

6 pounds mussels, cleaned and
  debearded

1. In a stockpot, combine the wine, shallot, and a few sprigs of thyme. Bring to a boil. Add the mussels, cover the pot, and steam over high heat, shaking the pot gently, for about 8 minutes or until the mussel shells all open. Very gently stir the contents once or twice during cooking. **2.** Meanwhile, chop the remaining thyme leaves. **3.** Using a slotted spoon, divide the mussels among six large deep bowls. Sprinkle with thyme.

Sheryl Julian

Chicken Liver Mousse

Only a few ingredients go into a pâtè that tastes like it was made by a French chef. Pack it into a dish lined with plastic wrap, then unmold it and surround with crackers or French bread.

SERVES 12

1 tablespoon olive oil

1/2 cup plus 6 tablespoons (14 tablespoons) unsalted butter, at room temperature

1 pound chicken livers

1/2 cup pale dry sherry

2 packages (8 ounces each) cream cheese, at room temperature

1. Have on hand a 1-quart serving bowl. Line it with plastic wrap so the wrap hangs over the edges; set aside. **2.** In a skillet, heat the oil. When it is hot, add 2 tablespoons of the butter. Add the chicken livers and sherry. Cook over medium heat, stirring occasionally, for 5 minutes or until the livers are cooked through. **3.** With a slotted spoon, remove the livers from the pan. Simmer the liquid in the pan until it reduces by half. **4.** In a food processor, combine the warm livers, cream cheese, and remaining butter. Pulse the mixture, adding the reduced cooking liquid, until it is smooth and creamy. **5.** Use a spatula to transfer the mousse to the bowl. Fold the excess plastic wrap over the mousse to cover completely. Refrigerate overnight. **6.** Unwrap the mousse. Set a large platter upside down on the bowl. Turn both over together so the platter is right side up. Lift off the bowl. Peel off the plastic wrap.

From 224 Boston Street Restaurant,
Boston, Massachusetts

Artichoke Dip

This is an example of what we call a "community recipe," which means that at some point—we think around 1960—everyone in the neighborhood was making it. It begins with mayonnaise, feta, canned sliced artichoke hearts, and pimiento, which are baked together until they're hot. The ingredients don't sound like they'll come together to make something terrific, but they do.

SERVES 4

1 can (15 ounces) artichoke
    hearts (not marinated)
1 jar (2 ounces) pimiento
1 cup mayonnaise
4 ounces feta, crumbled
½ cup grated Parmesan
1 clove garlic, crushed
Salt and pepper, to taste

1. Set the oven at 350°F. Have on hand a 6-inch baking dish. **2.** Drain the artichokes and pimiento. Slice both and set aside. **3.** In a bowl, stir the mayonnaise, feta, Parmesan, garlic, salt, and pepper. Stir in the artichokes and pimiento. **4.** Transfer the mixture to the baking dish. Bake for 20 to 25 minutes or until the mixture is bubbling at the edges. Serve with melba toasts or warm pita bread triangles.

Elizabeth Carvalho

White Bean-Olive Spread

Smooth and garlicky, this spread begins with canned white beans, which are pureed with a little olive oil and crushed red pepper, then mixed with black olives.

SERVES 6

1 can (1 pound) cannellini or
    other white beans
1 small garlic clove, chopped
2 tablespoons olive oil
Pinch of crushed red pepper
Salt and black pepper, to taste
½ cup pitted black olives,
    coarsely chopped

1. Set a strainer over a bowl. Drain the beans without rinsing them; reserve the liquid from the can. **2.** In a food processor, combine the beans, garlic, olive oil, red pepper, salt, and black pepper. Pulse the mixture until it is smooth. **3.** Add enough of the liquid from the beans, 1 tablespoon at a time, to make a moist puree that holds its shape. Transfer the mixture to a bowl. **4.** Stir in the olives and taste for seasoning. Add more salt and pepper, if you like. Serve with crackers.

Sheryl Julian

Yogurt-Feta Dip

Imported feta is usually creamier and tastier than domestic varieties. Serve this herb-flecked dip with chunks of fresh bread, wedges of pita, or vegetables.

SERVES 6

½ pound imported feta, crumbled

1 cup plain whole-milk yogurt

1 tablespoon lemon juice

Salt and pepper, to taste

3 tablespoons chopped fresh chives

1 tablespoon chopped fresh oregano

1. In a food processor, combine the feta, yogurt, lemon juice, salt, and pepper. Pulse the mixture until it is smooth. **2.** Add the chives and oregano and pulse again just to mix them well. **3.** Spread the mixture in a shallow bowl.

Lisa Zwirn

Soups and Chowders

The Colonists cooked over an open fire and everything in the pot was soupy, so perhaps our love of soup has been passed down. Or maybe the brief months of fine weather and endless cold winters have made us embrace hot bowls of broth. Whatever the reason, New Englanders sip soup in all seasons.

Beloved fish and clam chowders head the list, but if you can grow it, it can go into a simmering pot. That includes butternut squash, mushrooms, corn, tomatoes, potatoes, and all kinds of other vegetables. Add alphabets so kids can find them and spell their own names. Puree the vegetables into smooth bowls for serving as a first course to guests. Chill them for summer dining at the beach.

Great soups are nourishing and loaded with flavor. Whatever the commercials say about tipping a can of soup into a pot and getting to eat a fine meal, those broths are nothing compared to something ladled from your heart into the bowl.

All-Purpose Soup Stock

After the stock has been cooked and strained, it should almost look like it has gelatin added—it will jiggle.

MAKES ABOUT 1½ QUARTS

5 pounds chicken bones (backs and necks)
2 onions, quartered
2 carrots, quartered
2 stalks celery, cut into 2-inch pieces
1 bay leaf
6 peppercorns
1 teaspoon salt

1. In a soup pot, combine the chicken bones, onions, carrots, and celery. Add water to cover the bones by 2 inches. Bring to a boil. With a large metal spoon, skim the scum from the surface. Continue skimming until the surface is clear. **2.** Lower the heat, and add the bay leaf, peppercorns, and salt. Cover the pan and simmer the bones for 1½ hours. Skim the surface every 15 minutes during simmering. **3.** Strain the soup into a large plastic container. Leave to cool. **4.** Cover the container and refrigerate the soup overnight. **5.** With a slotted spoon, skim off and discard the fat from the soup. Use the stock as directed.

Sheryl Julian

Split Pea Soup

Split green peas, knockwurst, and a ham hock make a meaty bowl.

SERVES 6

3 tablespoons canola oil
1 pound knockwurst or other cooked sausage, cut into 2-inch slices
1 smoked ham hock (½ pound)
1 large onion, coarsely chopped
1 pound dried split peas
6 cups water, or more if necessary
3 large carrots, cut into 2-inch pieces
Salt, to taste
1 teaspoon freshly ground pepper

1. In a large pot, heat the oil over medium heat. Add the knockwurst slices and cook, stirring often, for 5 minutes. With a slotted spoon, remove the meat from the pan; set it aside. **2.** Add the ham hock and cook, stirring often, for 3 minutes more, to brown the hock on all sides. Remove it from the pan. **3.** Add the onion and cook, stirring often, for 3 minutes. Add the split peas, and stir to coat them with the oil. Return the ham hock to the pan. **4.** Pour in the water and bring to a boil. Cover the pan and cook the mixture for 10 minutes on medium heat. Remove the lid and use a spoon to skim the foam from the surface of the soup. **5.** Reduce the heat to low and add the carrots. Set on the cover slightly askew and simmer for 45 minutes. Stir occasionally to keep the soup from burning on the bottom as it thickens. **6.** Remove the lid and add the knockwurst. Simmer for 15 minutes more, stirring occasionally, or until the split peas have dissolved into a smooth, thick puree. **7.** Remove the ham hock and set the meat aside. When it is cool enough to handle, discard the fat and bone. Cut the meat into strips. Add them to the soup with salt and pepper. Return to a boil.

Debra Samuels

Quick Black Bean Soup with Turkey Sausages

Turkey sausages, widely available in supermarkets, are browned with onion and bell pepper, then simmered with canned black beans in this soup.

SERVES 4

2 cans (15 ounces each) black beans

5 cups chicken stock

1/2 tablespoon olive oil

2 links fresh turkey sausage, pricked well all over

1 medium onion, chopped

1 red bell pepper, seeded and chopped

2 cloves garlic, finely chopped

1/2 teaspoon ground cumin

1/2 teaspoon crushed red pepper, or to taste

Salt and black pepper, to taste

1. In a soup pot, combine the beans and stock. Set them over medium heat. **2.** Meanwhile, in a skillet, heat the oil over medium-high heat. Add the sausage, onion, and bell pepper. Cook, stirring often, for 10 minutes or until the sausage browns and the vegetables soften. **3.** Stir in the garlic, cumin, red pepper, salt, and black pepper. Cook, stirring, for 2 minutes more. **4.** With a slotted spoon, remove 1 cup of the black beans from the pot and transfer to a shallow bowl. Mash them and return them to the pot. **5.** Add the sausage mixture to the beans. Bring the soup to a boil, lower the heat, and simmer, stirring often, for 20 minutes. **6.** Taste for seasoning and add more salt or red pepper, if you like.

Lisa Zwirn

Curried Butternut Squash Soup

Some soups become so popular that you'll find versions in many restaurants. This curried squash soup is one of them. Here, the peeled butternut is simmered with onion, apples, curry powder, ginger, and a hint of cayenne pepper. Butternut squash is sold already peeled.

SERVES 6

3 large peeled butternut squash
Olive oil (for sprinkling)
Salt and black pepper, to taste
2 tablespoons butter
1 large Spanish onion, coarsely
    chopped
2 Cortland apples, peeled,
    cored, and coarsely chopped
2 teaspoons curry powder
1 teaspoon ground ginger
Pinch of cayenne pepper, or to
    taste
7 cups chicken stock

1. Set the oven at 450°F. Place the squash, cut side up, on a rimmed baking sheet. Sprinkle sparingly with oil, salt, and black pepper. Cover with foil, shiny side down, and transfer to the hot oven. Roast the squash for 30 minutes. **2.** In a large flameproof casserole, melt the butter. Cook the onion and apples over medium heat, stirring often, for 8 minutes or until they soften. **3.** Add the curry, ginger, and cayenne. Cook, stirring constantly, for 2 minutes. **4.** Use a spoon to transfer soft pieces of squash to the pot. Cook, stirring, for 2 minutes. **5.** Pour in the stock and bring the mixture to a boil. Set the cover on askewed and cook over low heat, stirring occasionally, for 20 minutes. **6.** In a blender, puree the soup in batches. Return it to the pot. **7.** Reheat the soup over medium heat. Taste for seasoning and add more salt and cayenne pepper, if you like.

Sheryl Julian

Easy Alphabet Soup

You can ladle six children's-size bowls from this pot of soup. The kids will enjoy finding letters in their soup. Ask them to spell out their own names.

SERVES 4

3 tablespoons butter
2 medium carrots, diced
1 medium onion, diced
1 small russet potato, diced
Salt and pepper, to taste
1 can (15 ounces) tomato sauce
4 cups chicken or vegetable
    stock
1 cup alphabet pasta, or other
    very small pasta shape (such
    as stars)
1 cup frozen peas
1 cup frozen corn

1. In a medium pot, melt the butter. Add the carrots, onion, potato, salt, and pepper. Cook over medium heat, stirring often, for 5 minutes or until the vegetables soften. **2.** Add the tomato sauce and stock. Bring to a boil, lower the heat, and partially cover the pot. Simmer for 8 minutes, or until vegetables are almost tender. **3.** Turn the heat to high. Stir in the pasta. Simmer, stirring often, for 5 minutes or until the pasta is tender but still has some bite. **4.** Add the peas and corn. Cook for 2 minutes, stirring occasionally, or until they are heated through. **5.** Taste for seasoning and add more salt and pepper, if you like.

Keri Fisher

Chicken Soup

This is the traditional chicken soup, the one known as Jewish penicillin. It (almost) cures the common cold.

SERVES 8

1 broiler chicken, quartered, or
   1 large package of chicken
   thighs (3 pounds total)
2 pounds chicken bones
1 medium onion, quartered
1 small sweet potato, peeled
   and cut into chunks
2 parsnips, cut into thirds
1 pound carrots, cut into
   chunks
2 celery stalks, cut into fourths
1 tablespoon chopped fresh
   parsley or fresh dill or both
1 bay leaf
Salt and pepper, to taste

1. Rinse chicken and remove excess fat and skin (it's okay to leave a little skin). In a large soup pot, place chicken and bones. Add cold water to cover and bring to a boil over medium-high heat, skimming any scum that rises to the top as it boils. **2.** Add the onion, sweet potato, parsnips, carrots, celery, parsley or dill, and bay leaf. Return to a boil, lower the heat, and cover the pot. Simmer, stirring occasionally, over medium-low heat for 3 hours. **3.** Turn off heat and let pot stand on stove for 1 hour. With a slotted spoon, transfer chicken, bones, and vegetables to a large bowl. Discard bones and celery. Set a large strainer over another soup pot. Strain the broth, removing any remaining solids. Set aside the cooked chicken. **4.** Press some of the cooked carrots, sweet potatoes, onions, and parsnips through the strainer into the soup. Scrape mashed vegetables from the bottom of the strainer and add to the soup. **5.** Strain the soup a second time. Add salt and pepper to taste. Slice some of the cooked carrots into ½-inch pieces and return to the soup. Allow soup to cool, then refrigerate. **6.** When cold, skim fat from top of soup. Return to a soup pot and bring to a boil. Serve with matzo balls (see recipe next page) and some of the cut-up cooked chicken, if you like.

Mady Donoff

Chicken Soup with Matzo Balls

Matzo Balls

Many people think that traditional Jewish matzo balls are an art. It's easy to make them hard and chewy, rather than light and feathery. A technique many cooks use is to keep the pot closed while the matzo balls are simmering.

MAKES ABOUT 20

4 eggs

½ cup water

⅓ cup vegetable oil

1 teaspoon salt, and more for cooking

Dash of pepper

1 cup matzo meal

1. In a bowl, beat the eggs with water, oil, 1 teaspoon salt, and pepper. Mix well. Add the matzo meal and stir thoroughly, but do not overmix. Cover mixture and refrigerate for at least 20 minutes. **2.** Bring a large pot of salted water to a boil. Remove matzo mixture from the refrigerator and stir once to make sure all liquid has been absorbed. Using a large soup spoon, scoop up the mixture and form it into free-form balls. With wet fingers, lightly shape them by pressing into the spoon, handling the dough as little as possible. Slide the matzo balls off the spoon into the boiling water. Repeat, using all the matzo mixture. **3.** When the water has returned to a boil, lower the heat and cover the pot. Simmer for 20 minutes. With a slotted spoon, remove the cooked matzo balls from the water and transfer to bowls of hot chicken soup.

Mady Donoff

Fish Chowder

Cod, haddock, pollock, or another plain white fish form the base of chowder. This one is made with water. If you live near a good fish market, ask for fish frames. Simmer them separately and use the broth instead of water.

SERVES 6

1½ pounds fresh cod

6 cups water

Salt and pepper, to taste

3 medium russet potatoes, cut into 1-inch chunks

3 strips bacon

1 large onion, chopped

2 cups light cream

1. In a soup pot, combine the cod, water, and a generous pinch each of salt and pepper. Bring barely to a boil, lower the heat, and simmer the fish for 5 minutes or until it is cooked through. **2.** Meanwhile, in another saucepan, combine the potatoes with enough water to cover them. Add a pinch of salt. Bring to a boil, lower the heat, cover the pan, and simmer for 12 minutes or until the potatoes are tender. **3.** In a dry skillet, render the bacon over medium heat until it is golden. Remove it from the pan and transfer to paper towels to drain. Crumble the bacon. Add the onion to the pan and cook, stirring often, for 10 minutes or until it softens. **4.** With a ladle, add half the potato cooking liquid to the pot of fish. Use a slotted spoon to add the potatoes to the pot. **5.** Add the onion mixture to the fish with the cream and bacon. Bring just to a boil. Taste for seasoning and add more salt and pepper, if you like.

Christine Merlo

Oyster Stew

A special winter holiday treat, oyster stew was once served in many homes. It consists of little else besides oysters, butter, milk, and cream. Serve with oyster crackers.

SERVES 4

¼ cup (4 tablespoons) unsalted butter

1 pint shelled fresh oysters and their liquor

3 cups whole milk

1 cup light cream

Salt and pepper, to taste

1. In a large saucepan, melt the butter. Add the oysters and their liquor. Heat just until the edges begin to curl. **2.** Meanwhile, in another saucepan, scald the milk and cream. **3.** Pour the milk mixture into the oysters. Add salt and pepper. Reheat without boiling.

Clam Chowder

Clam Chowder

Originally, clam chowder was made with diced salt pork, but it's too hard to find now, so use bacon instead. If you open and clean your own clams, strain the juice through cheesecloth to remove sand and bits of shells and use that instead of the bottled clam broth. Wash the clams well and chop them in a food processor (or buy chopped clams in a fish market).

SERVES 4

4 slices bacon, cut up

1 medium onion, finely
   chopped

1 tablespoon flour

2 cups (16 ounces) bottled
   clam broth

2 medium Yukon Gold or
   Yellow Finn potatoes, peeled
   and cut into 1/2-inch dice

Salt and pepper, to taste

2 cups whole milk

2 cups chopped clams

1. In a large flameproof casserole, render the bacon over medium heat until it is golden brown. Transfer the bacon to paper towels. **2.** Add the onion and cook, stirring often, for 8 minutes or until it softens. Stir in the flour and cook, stirring, for 2 minutes. **3.** Stir in the clam broth and let the mixture come to a boil. Add the potatoes, salt, and pepper. Cover the pan and simmer for 15 minutes or until the potatoes are tender. **4.** Stir in the milk and reheat it without boiling. **5.** Add clams and reheat again without boiling. Taste for seasoning and add more salt and pepper, if you like.

Rhode Island Clam Chowder

Evelyn's Drive-In in Tiverton, Rhode Island, makes this chowder and ladles hundreds of bowls. The main difference between clam chowder that Bostonians make and the Rhode Island version is that this one isn't milky.

SERVES 6

4 cups chopped sea clams

4 cups (32 ounces) bottled
  clam broth

2 cups water

¼ onion, finely chopped

4 tablespoons unsalted butter

1 bay leaf

1 teaspoon coarse salt, or more
  to taste

1 teaspoon black pepper

4 russet potatoes, peeled and
  cut into ¾-inch dice

1. In large flameproof casserole, combine the clams, clam broth, water, onion, butter, bay leaf, salt, and pepper. Set over high heat and bring to a boil. **2.** Add the potatoes and let the liquid return to a boil. Turn down the heat and simmer for 40 minutes or until the potatoes are tender but not falling apart. **3.** Use tongs to remove the bay leaf from the pot. **4.** With a slotted spoon, remove ½ cup of the potatoes and transfer them to a shallow bowl. With a fork, mash the potatoes to form a puree. Stir them back into the chowder. Taste for seasoning and add more salt, if you like.

From Evelyn's Drive-In,
Tiverton, Rhode Island

Corn Chowder

Use corn freshly cut from cobs (see page 157). Simmer the cobs first to make stock for the chowder.

SERVES 4

6 ears fresh corn, kernels
  removed from the cobs

3 cups water

Salt and pepper, to taste

2 medium Yukon Gold or
  Yellow Finn potatoes, cut
  into ½-inch dice

2 cups whole milk

2 tablespoons chopped fresh
  parsley

1. In a soup pot, combine the corn cobs (not kernels), water, and a generous pinch of salt. Bring to a boil, lower the heat, and simmer for 20 minutes. **2.** With tongs, remove the cobs from the pot. **3.** Add the potatoes and return the liquid to a boil. Lower the heat and simmer for 20 minutes or until the potatoes are tender. **4.** Add the milk, corn kernels, salt, and pepper. Simmer over low heat for 5 minutes or until the corn is cooked through. **5.** Ladle into bowls and sprinkle with parsley.

Sheryl Julian

New England Cioppino

Originally from San Francisco, the famous seafood stew cioppino adapts nicely to the East Coast. Serve with toasted slices of French bread rubbed with a garlic clove and sprinkled with salt and olive oil.

SERVES 4

2 tablespoons olive oil

1 medium fennel bulb, sliced into ½-inch pieces

Salt and black pepper, to taste

3 cloves garlic, chopped

½ cup white wine

1 can (28 ounces) whole peeled tomatoes, pureed with their juices in a food processor

6 tablespoons chopped fresh parsley

½ teaspoon crushed red pepper

½ pound large shrimp, peeled

1 pound skinless, boneless cod (about 1 inch thick), cut into 4 pieces

2 pounds mussels, scrubbed and debearded

1. In a large Dutch oven, heat the oil and cook the fennel with salt and black pepper over medium heat for 8 minutes or until the fennel softens. Add the garlic and cook, stirring, for 1 more minute. **2.** Add the wine and cook, stirring, until it almost evaporates; there should only be a couple of tablespoons of wine remaining in the pan. Add the tomatoes, 4 tablespoons of parsley, and red pepper. **3.** Bring the broth to a boil, lower the heat, cover the pan, and simmer the broth for 15 minutes. (If making ahead: At this point, cool and then refrigerate the broth for 1 to 2 days; reheat until hot.) **4.** Sprinkle the shrimp and cod with salt and black pepper. Increase the heat to medium. Add the mussels and shrimp to the broth and cover the pan. Cook, stirring occasionally, for 5 minutes or until the mussels open and the shrimp turn pink and firm to the touch. **5.** Reduce the heat to low, add the cod to the pan, ladle broth over the fish, and cover the pan. Cook the stew for 8 minutes or until the cod turns opaque and begins to flake. Sprinkle the remaining parsley over the stew.

Tony Rosenfeld

Mushroom Soup

Use a variety of mushrooms—button, shiitake, and portobello—to make this soup. Serve it as a first course for guests, or add a salad and fruit and turn it into a light supper.

SERVES 4

1½ pounds mixed mushrooms (if using portobello, use 1 cap)

¼ cup (½ stick) unsalted butter

2 shallots, finely chopped

Salt and pepper, to taste

2 tablespoons flour

4 cups chicken stock

½ cup light cream

2 tablespoons chopped fresh parsley

1. Trim and discard the ends of the mushroom stems. Coarsely chop the stems; slice the mushrooms, and coarsely chop the portobello cap. **2.** In a large saucepan, melt the butter. Add the mushrooms, shallots, salt, and pepper. Cook over medium heat, stirring often, for 10 minutes or until the mushrooms release their liquid. **3.** Turn up the heat and continue cooking, still stirring, until the mushroom liquid evaporates. **4.** Sprinkle flour into pan. Cook, stirring, for 2 minutes. **5.** Stir in the chicken stock and cook, stirring, until the mixture comes to a boil. Lower the heat, cover the pan, and simmer the soup for 20 minutes. **6.** In a blender, puree 1 cup of the soup and return it to the pan. Stir in the cream, reheat until the cream is hot, and taste for seasoning. Add more salt and pepper, if you like. **7.** Ladle into bowls and sprinkle with parsley.

Summer Tomato Soup

Bruised tomatoes, sometimes called "canners," or "seconds," or "grade B," are perfect for this simple soup. Use a variety—heirlooms and cherries are fine, too. Simmer the cut-up tomatoes with lots of fresh herbs and a little chicken stock. After half an hour, the tomatoes will collapse, but the skins and seeds give the mixture body. Work the soup through a food mill or coarse strainer.

SERVES 6

12 large tomatoes, cored

2 cups chicken stock

1 cup fresh basil leaves

½ cup fresh mint leaves

Salt and pepper, to taste

1. Cut up the tomatoes. If they're bruised, cut off and discard any soft spots. **2.** In a soup pot, combine the tomatoes, chicken stock, basil, mint, salt, and pepper. Bring to a boil, lower the heat, and simmer the mixture for 30 minutes or until the tomatoes have collapsed completely. **3.** Set a food mill or coarse strainer over a bowl and work the soup through it. Return the soup to the pot. Bring to a boil, taste for seasoning, and add more salt and pepper, if you like.

Sheryl Julian

Red Lentil Soup

In the pot, red lentils collapse into a beautiful smooth rosy puree.

SERVES 8

6 tablespoons olive oil

2 onions, finely chopped

2 cloves garlic, finely chopped

2 teaspoons ground cumin

2 tablespoons tomato paste

Salt and pepper, to taste

1/4 teaspoon chili powder, or
    more to taste

2 quarts chicken stock

3 cups water

1 pound red lentils, rinsed with
    cool water and sorted to
    remove any small stones

2 large carrots, cut into 1/4-inch
    dice

5 tomatoes, peeled and
    chopped, or 1 can
    (14 ounces) diced tomatoes

Juice of 1 lemon

1. In a soup pot over medium heat, heat the olive oil. When it is hot, add the onions and cook, stirring often, for 8 minutes. Add the garlic and cook 1 minute more. **2.** Stir in the cumin and cook, stirring, for 1 minute. Add the tomato paste, salt, pepper, and chili powder. Cook, stirring, for 1 minute more. **3.** Add the stock, water, lentils, carrots, and tomatoes. Bring to a boil, partially cover the pan, and turn the heat to medium-low. Simmer the soup for 30 to 40 minutes or until the lentils are soft. Add the lemon juice. Taste for seasoning and add more salt and chili powder, if you like.

Allison Boomer

Red Lentil Soup

Beef Pho

The hearty Vietnamese soup, pho, comes in many variations. This is the beef version, which begins with marrow bones and a piece of meat to make the broth, then strips of lean sirloin, rice noodles, and lots of crunchy vegetables go into the bowl.

SERVES 4

BROTH

5 pounds beef marrow bones

1 pound beef chuck or round, trimmed of excess fat and cubed

12 quarts water

3 star anise

2 whole cloves

1 stick cinnamon

1 teaspoon black peppercorns

1 whole cardamom pod, slightly crushed

1 large piece (3 inches) fresh ginger

2 onions, halved

5 tablespoons fish sauce, or to taste

Salt, to taste

GARNISH

1 pound boneless lean sirloin beef, very thinly sliced across the grain into 2-inch-long slices

3 scallions, thinly sliced on the diagonal

1 pound thin dried rice noodles, soaked in warm water for 15 minutes and drained

½ cup chopped fresh cilantro

3 shallots, thinly sliced

2 cups bean sprouts, rinsed

½ cup Asian basil or sweet basil leaves

2 serrano chili peppers, cored and thinly sliced

2 limes, cut into wedges

BROTH

1. In a large stockpot, combine the bones and beef chuck or round. Add 6 quarts of the water and bring to a boil. Boil vigorously for 5 minutes. Drain the meat into a colander. Rinse it well. Rinse out the pot. Return the meat and bones to the pot. **2.** Add the remaining 6 quarts of water to the pot. Bring to a boil. Skim the surface, if necessary. Turn the heat down. Add the star anise, cloves, cinnamon stick, peppercorns, and cardamom. **3.** Using tongs, hold the ginger and onion pieces over a gas flame or set them in a cast-iron skillet. Heat them until they char. Add them to the pot. **4.** Let the broth simmer gently, uncovered, skimming occasionally, for 1 hour. Add the fish sauce and continue simmering uncovered, for 2 hours. (Total cooking time is 3 hours.) **5.** Remove the soup from the heat. Remove and discard the bones and solids. Line a colander with a double layer of cheesecloth. Strain the soup into a clean bowl. Let the stock cool, then refrigerate, covered, for at least 2 hours. Skim off and discard the fat from the top. **6.** In a large pot, heat the broth until it is boiling. Again, line a colander with cheesecloth and strain the soup into a clean pot. Bring to a boil, add salt, and taste for seasoning. Add more fish sauce, if you like.

GARNISH

1. Divide the beef among four large soup bowls. Add scallions, noodles, cilantro, and shallots. **2.** Ladle boiling hot broth into the bowls. Serve with bean sprouts, basil, chili peppers, and lime.

Jonathan Levitt

Asparagus Soup

In the middle of New England's asparagus season—around the same time in early summer that strawberries ripen—there are enough spears at a reasonable price to make this bright green soup.

SERVES 6

2 pounds fresh asparagus

2 sprigs fresh thyme

4 parsley stems

1 bay leaf

6 cups water

2 tablespoons olive oil

2 onions, chopped

2 Yukon Gold or Yellow Finn
  potatoes, peeled and
  chopped

Salt and pepper, to taste

³/₄ cup crème fraiche or sour
  cream

1. Snap off and discard the tough ends of the asparagus. Cut the tips in half lengthwise. Roughly chop the tender stalks. **2.** Wrap the thyme, parsley, and bay leaf together with kitchen twine. **3.** In a saucepan, bring the water to a boil. Add the chopped asparagus stalks and herb bundle. Simmer for 5 minutes. Discard the herb bundle. **4.** Meanwhile, in a flameproof casserole over low heat, heat the oil and, when it is hot, cook the onions, stirring often, for 10 minutes. **5.** Set a colander over a large bowl. Tip the asparagus cooking water with the asparagus into the colander, reserving the water. Pour just the water into the onion mixture. Add the potatoes, salt, and pepper. Bring to a boil. Simmer gently for 15 minutes or until the potatoes are tender. **6.** Bring a small saucepan of water to a boil. Add the asparagus tips. Cook 2 minutes or until they are bright green. Drain and rinse with cold water. **7.** Add the asparagus stems to the potato mixture. In a blender, puree the soup in batches. Taste for seasoning and add more salt and pepper, if you like. **8.** Ladle the soup into bowls, garnish with a spoonful of crème fraiche or sour cream, and top with asparagus tips.

Jonathan Levitt

Cold Cucumber Soup

Yogurt isn't just a breakfast dish. In this bowl, yogurt is pureed with cucumbers and mint to make a cooling summer soup, then garnished with more crisp cucumbers.

SERVES 4

SOUP

1 pound slicing cucumbers, peeled, seeded, and cut into 1-inch pieces

Salt and pepper, to taste

1/4 sweet onion, cut into 6 pieces

1 bunch fresh mint, leaves only

1 cup chicken stock

1 tablespoon lemon juice

1/2 teaspoon Dijon mustard

Pinch of sugar

32 ounces plain low-fat yogurt

GARNISH

2 pickling cucumbers, unpeeled, seeded, and finely chopped

2 tablespoons chopped fresh mint

2 tablespoons chopped fresh parsley

SOUP

1. In a colander, sprinkle the cucumbers with salt and toss to coat them. Set the colander on a plate. Let the cucumbers sit for 30 minutes to draw out the liquid, then rinse the cucumbers and pat them dry with paper towels. **2.** In the bowl of a food processor, work the onion and mint in on-off motions until the mint is coarsely chopped. Add the cucumbers and pulse the machine several times until the cucumbers are finely chopped. **3.** Add the chicken stock, lemon juice, mustard, and sugar. Pulse again two or three times until the mixture is smooth. Scrape down the sides of the work bowl with a rubber spatula. **4.** Add the yogurt and work again just to mix it in. Add salt and pepper, to taste. Transfer the soup to a plastic container and refrigerate for at least 4 hours or as long as overnight.

GARNISH

In a bowl, combine the cucumbers, mint, and parsley. Stir the soup. Ladle the mixture into bowls and garnish with the cucumber mixture.

Sheryl Julian & Julie Riven

Gazpacho

Arlene Tofias of Wayland, Massachusetts, uses tomato juice instead of fresh tomatoes in her gazpacho. When they're in season, the fresh fruit gives the soup a more robust flavor.

SERVES 4

4 large tomatoes, cored

1 small sweet onion, cut into 2-inch pieces

2 cloves garlic, coarsely chopped

1 green bell pepper, cored, seeded, and cut into 2-inch pieces

1 red bell pepper, cored, seeded, and cut into 2-inch pieces

3 pickling cucumbers, peeled, seeded, and cut into 2-inch pieces

3 tablespoons chopped fresh herbs (thyme, basil, oregano)

Pinch of sugar

Pinch of crushed red pepper

1 teaspoon salt, or to taste

⅓ cup sherry vinegar, or more to taste

Generous dash of hot sauce

1 bunch scallions, coarsely chopped

1 tablespoon chopped fresh parsley

1. Have on hand a large bowl of very cold water. **2.** Bring a large saucepan of water to a boil. Add the tomatoes, count to 10, then transfer them to the cold water. When the tomatoes are cool, peel off the skins. Halve the tomatoes horizontally, squeeze the halves over a bowl so the seeds pop out, then discard the seeds. Coarsely chop the flesh. **3.** In the bowl of a food processor, pulse the onion, garlic, green and red bell peppers, cucumbers, herbs, sugar, and red pepper until very coarse. **4.** Add the tomatoes and salt. Pulse again just until the mixture is chunky. **5.** Transfer to a bowl. Stir in the vinegar and hot sauce. Taste for seasoning and add more salt, red pepper, or vinegar if you like. **6.** Cover and refrigerate the soup for 4 hours or until well chilled. Taste again for seasoning and adjust if necessary. Ladle the gazpacho into bowls or large cups and sprinkle with scallions and parsley.

Arlene Tofias

Vichyssoise

The chilled leek and potato soup called vichyssoise has been popular since Louis Diaz invented it at the beginning of the twentieth century. There are richer versions made with heavy cream, but this version is rich enough.

SERVES 4

4 leeks, white and light green
    parts only, thinly sliced

¼ cup (½ stick) butter

1 onion, chopped

Salt and pepper, to taste

3 medium Yukon Gold or
    Yellow Finn potatoes, peeled
    and cut into 1-inch pieces

3 cups chicken stock

1 cup light cream

1 tablespoon snipped fresh
    chives

1. Soak the leeks for 20 minutes to remove any sand. Drain them into a colander. **2.** In a large flameproof casserole, melt the butter. Add the leeks, onion, salt, and pepper. Cook, stirring often, for 10 minutes or until the leeks soften. **3.** Add the potatoes and chicken stock. Bring to a boil, lower the heat, and cover the pan. Simmer for 30 minutes. Let the soup cool. **4.** In a blender, puree the soup in batches until smooth. Return it to the pot. **5.** Add the cream and taste for seasoning. Add more salt and pepper, if you like. **6.** Transfer the soup to a plastic container and refrigerate. Serve cold; garnish with chives.

Steamer Clam Soup

Full of clam flavor, this soup combines plenty of steamers, salt pork, and a little cream. Common crackers, once sold everywhere in New England, are now only at specialty markets. They're small, round, and thick. Split, butter, and toast them for a real treat.

SERVES 4

2 ½ pounds medium steamer
   clams
2 cups water
½ teaspoon vegetable oil
2 ounces salt pork, coarsely
   chopped
1 tablespoon butter
2 stalks celery, finely chopped
1 teaspoon chopped fresh
   thyme
½ cup heavy cream
Salt and pepper, to taste
8 common crackers, split,
   buttered, and toasted, or 32
   oyster crackers
2 tablespoons chopped chives

1. Rinse clams in several changes of cold water to remove the sand. **2.** In a large pot, bring the water to a boil. Add the clams, cover, and steam for 8 to 9 minutes, stirring once gently, or until they are all open. Use a slotted spoon to remove the clams from the broth, discarding any that do not open; set aside. **3.** Line a strainer with cheesecloth. Set it over a bowl; strain the broth. **4.** Remove the clams from the shells. Peel away the skin on each clam. Cover and refrigerate. **5.** In a flameproof casserole, heat the oil and render the salt pork over low heat, stirring often, for 4 minutes. Turn the heat to medium and cook, stirring, until the salt pork is crisp and golden brown. Use a slotted spoon to remove it from the skillet and transfer to paper towels. **6.** Add the butter, celery, and thyme to the pan. Cook over low heat, stirring often, for 8 minutes or until the celery softens. **7.** Add the cream and 3½ cups of the clam broth (add water, if necessary, to make that amount). Heat, stirring, until you see bubbles at the edge of the pan. Lower the heat and simmer gently for 10 minutes. **8.** Add the clams, salt, and pepper. Serve garnished with crackers, salt pork, and chives.

Adapted from Victory restaurant,
Portsmouth, New Hampshire

Tomato-Bread Soup

Instead of tossing their day-old bread, Italian cooks make all sorts of dishes with it, including this pappa al pomodoro, *essentially fresh tomato sauce thickened with stale bread. The texture is a luxurious red mush and resembles a savory bread pudding. While tomatoes are in season, you'll find yourself letting the bread go stale on purpose, just to make this soup.*

SERVES 4

8 large tomatoes, cored

3 tablespoons olive oil

3 cloves garlic, crushed

1/2 loaf day-old, slightly stale, crusty bread, roughly torn or cut into cubes

1 cup basil leaves, coarsely chopped

Salt and pepper, to taste

Olive oil (for sprinkling)

1/4 cup freshly grated Parmesan

1. Place the tomatoes in a large heatproof bowl. Pour enough boiling water over them to cover them. Set aside for 10 seconds to loosen the skins. Drain the water. Peel off and discard the skins. Roughly chop the tomatoes. **2.** In a large skillet heat the olive oil over medium heat. Add the garlic and cook for 3 minutes until soft but not brown. Add the tomatoes and their juices and bring to a boil. Simmer for 5 minutes or until the tomatoes begin to soften and break down. **3.** Add the bread to the tomatoes. Continue cooking for 5 minutes or until the bread soaks up the sauce. **4.** Stir in the basil, salt, and pepper. Simmer 5 minutes more. Ladle into bowls, and sprinkle with more olive oil and Parmesan.

Jonathan Levitt

Escarole and Meatball Soup

The name of this soup, minestra maritata, *means "married soup," though it's often called "wedding soup." The bowls contain escarole, or curly bitter greens, and pork and beef meatballs simmered in chicken stock. Near the end of cooking add dried pasta—ditalini, bow ties, orzo—and top with Parmesan.*

SERVES 4 AS A MAIN COURSE
SOUP

8 cups chicken stock
2 carrots, thickly sliced
1 celery stalk, thickly sliced

MEATBALLS

½ pound ground beef
½ pound ground pork
2 eggs, lightly beaten
½ cup chopped parsley
½ cup grated Parmesan
2 cloves garlic, chopped
½ cup fresh white bread
    crumbs
1 teaspoon salt, and more to
    taste
½ teaspoon pepper, and more
    to taste
1 head escarole, rinsed and
    chopped
½ cup small pasta (ditalini,
    bow ties, orzo)
Extra shredded Parmesan (for
    sprinkling)

SOUP

1. In a soup pot over medium heat, bring the chicken stock to a boil.
2. Lower the heat and add the carrots and celery. Simmer for 30 minutes.

MEATBALLS

1. In a bowl, combine the beef, pork, eggs, parsley, Parmesan, garlic, bread crumbs, salt, and pepper. With your hands, shape small balls (about 1 tablespoon each). You should get about 40. **2.** Add the meatballs and escarole to the simmering soup. Cover and cook for 15 minutes. **3.** Add the pasta and cook, uncovered, for 10 minutes more, stirring occasionally, or until it is tender but still has some bite. Taste for seasoning; add more salt and pepper, if you like. Ladle into bowls and sprinkle with Parmesan.

Alice Taverna

Pasta, Beans, Grains, Legumes, and Rice

Long before it was known as "pasta," spaghetti and its kin were the backbone of the family table. Italian-American immigrants from the late nineteenth century taught us to love red sauce, meatballs, and layered lasagnas.

When the new Italian revolution hit restaurants nationwide in the 1980s—and pasta became the watchword of professional and home kitchens —commercial companies began bottling tomato sauce. That meant that even the most frazzled parents could produce a dinner of pasta and sauce with very little effort.

The pendulum is swinging back. Everyone knows there's nothing like homemade sauce. Simmer it Italian-grandmother-style for a couple hours or make one in 20 minutes. And the array of shapes now available makes the combinations of sauce, cheese, and pasta fun.

Pasta may be the reason why all grains, beans, and legumes are becoming popular on the nightly table. While New Englanders feasted on beans for centuries—at one time poor Colonists ate them for early morning, midday, and evening meals—the long soaking and simmering process put off modern cooks. Today's one-hour quick-soak method allows you to enjoy the nutritional benefits of bean cookery without the wait.

And on the heels of the movement to healthier forms of protein come quinoa, brown rice, bulgur, couscous, and lentils. They're fueling a generation of vegetarians and adding interesting elements to the side of the plate, the picnic table, and the holiday buffet.

Penne with Fresh Tomatoes and Basil

The busy task here is chopping fresh plum tomatoes, which make a light sauce for penne. Add a few leaves of torn basil, some Parmesan cheese, a link of roasted sausage for the hearty diners, and dinner is ready.

SERVES 4

½ teaspoon kosher salt, and more for the pasta water

3 tablespoons olive oil

3 cloves garlic, smashed

¼ teaspoon crushed red pepper

2 pounds plum tomatoes (about 10), cored and coarsely chopped

½ teaspoon black pepper

8 fresh basil leaves, torn into large pieces

1 pound dried penne

½ cup freshly grated Parmesan

1. Bring a medium pot of generously salted water to a boil. **2.** Meanwhile, in a large flameproof casserole over medium heat, heat the oil and add the garlic. Cook, stirring occasionally, for 2 minutes or until the garlic starts to brown lightly. **3.** Add the red pepper and cook, stirring, for 30 seconds. **4.** Add the tomatoes, salt, and black pepper, and cook, stirring occasionally, for 10 minutes or until the tomatoes cook down into a sauce. **5.** Stir in the basil and remove from the heat. **6.** When the pot of water comes to a boil, add the penne and cook, stirring occasionally, for 11 minutes or until it is tender but still has some bite. Drain the pasta into a colander and tip the pasta into the tomato mixture. Add half the Parmesan. **7.** Raise the heat under the pan to medium-high and cook the pasta, stirring, for 1 to 2 minutes so it absorbs some of the sauce. With tongs, remove the garlic cloves from the sauce, taste for seasoning, and add more salt and black pepper, if you like. Serve sprinkled with the remaining cheese.

Tony Rosenfeld

Basil Pesto

If you keep a container of pesto in the freezer, and plenty of pasta in the pantry, you only need a sprinkle of cheese to put a fine meal on the table in minutes. On a dreary winter day, pesto with penne is always welcome.

MAKES ABOUT 2 CUPS

½ cup pine nuts

2 big bunches fresh basil, leaves only

2 cloves garlic, quartered

½ teaspoon salt, or to taste

½ cup olive oil

¼ cup grated Parmesan

¼ cup grated pecorino cheese

1. Set the oven at 350°F. Place the pine nuts on a rimmed baking sheet. Toast them for 8 minutes or until lightly browned. Set aside to cool. **2.** In a food processor combine the basil, garlic, salt, and pine nuts. Pulse the mixture until it is finely chopped. **3.** With the machine running, pour the oil through the feed tube in a steady stream until the mixture forms a paste. **4.** Use a rubber spatula to transfer the pesto to a plastic container. Stir in the Parmesan and pecorino. Refrigerate until serving.

Note: To store pesto longer, spoon it into ice cubes trays and freeze until firm. Then pop the pesto cubes into a freezer zipper bag. To keep in the refrigerator, add a spoon of olive oil to the top of the pesto to keep it from discoloring.

Jonathan Levitt

Long-Cooked Short-Rib Ragu for Pasta

Satisfying and meaty, this ragu begins with short ribs, which are cooked with tomatoes for more than 2½ hours in the oven. The meat is removed from the bones and returned to the sauce. Toss with noodles, such as pappardelle.

SERVES 4

1 tablespoon canola oil

2 pounds bone-in beef short
   ribs, each about 3 inches
   long, cut crosswise

Salt and pepper, to taste

1 tablespoon olive oil

1 onion, chopped

¼ cup tomato paste

4 cloves of garlic, chopped

1 can (28 ounces) imported
   whole tomatoes, crushed in
   a bowl

1 cup water, or more if
   necessary

1. In a large heavy skillet, heat the canola oil over medium heat. Season the short ribs with salt and pepper on both sides and put them in the skillet. Adjust the heat so that the meat sizzles gently. Brown the meat thoroughly on all sides except the bone side. Remove the meat to a platter and set aside. **2.** Set the oven at 250°F. In a large, heavy pot with ovenproof handles, heat the olive oil over medium heat. Add the onion and tomato paste and cook, stirring often, for 10 minutes or until the onion softens but does not color. **3.** Add the garlic and cook for 2 minutes more. Add the crushed tomatoes and water. Stir well and cover with the lid. **4.** Transfer to the oven and cook for 2½ to 3 hours, or until the meat separates and falls off the bones when pierced with a fork. During cooking, add more water to the pan if the mixture seems dry. **5.** Remove the short ribs from the sauce and set aside to cool. **6.** Strip the meat from the short rib bones. Discard the bones and return the meat to the sauce.

Jonathan Levitt

20-Minute Tomato Sauce

If you have a couple of cans of imported Italian tomatoes on hand, crush them in a bowl and turn them into a quick sauce. You can, of course, simmer this longer. But the shorter cooking time is a light, refreshing red sauce for pasta, sausages, or broiled fish. Toss with spaghetti or angel hair pasta.

**MAKES 5 CUPS OR ENOUGH
TO SERVE 6**

2 tablespoons olive oil

2 cans (28 ounces each)
   imported whole tomatoes,
   crushed in a bowl

Pinch of crushed red pepper,
   or to taste

Salt and black pepper, to taste

1. In a large saucepan, heat the oil and when it is hot, add the tomatoes. Cook, stirring constantly, for 2 minutes. **2.** Add the red pepper, salt, and black pepper. Continue cooking, stirring often, for 20 minutes or until the sauce reduces slightly.

Sheryl Julian

Rigatoni with Tomato Sauce

Penne with Puttanesca

Puttanesca is a bold, spicy tomato sauce with capers, red pepper, and olives—a favorite of many cooks. The name comes from the Italian word for streetwalker, and the idea is that it's a sauce that's hot and takes only minutes to make. For a more substantial meal, grill chicken breasts, cut them into thin slices, set the chicken on penne tossed with puttanesca, and spoon a little sauce over the chicken. In that case, use pennette (small penne).

SERVES 4

¼ cup olive oil

4 anchovies, coarsely chopped

1 tablespoon capers

2 cloves garlic, chopped

½ teaspoon crushed red
   pepper

14 plum tomatoes, peeled and
   coarsely chopped

2 tablespoons tomato paste

Salt and black pepper, to taste

1 pound dried penne pasta

⅓ cup chopped imported
   black olives

¼ cup chopped fresh parsley

1. In a large, heavy skillet, heat the oil and cook the anchovies, capers, garlic, and red pepper over low heat, stirring often, for 5 minutes or until the anchovies begin to break down and the garlic softens. **2.** Add the tomatoes and tomato paste. Cook over medium heat, stirring occasionally, for 15 minutes or until the tomatoes make a sauce. **3.** Meanwhile, bring a large pot of salted water to boil. Add the penne and cook for 10 to 12 minutes or until the pasta is tender but still has some bite. Drain in a colander and transfer to a bowl. **4.** Stir the olives, parsley, salt, and black pepper into the tomato sauce. Taste for seasoning and add more red pepper, if you like. Toss with penne.

Sheryl Julian & Julie Riven

Turkey-Mushroom Ragu for Pasta

Timothy Chin was a high school student living in Wellesley, Massachusetts, when he came up with this low-fat alternative to beef ragu. His version is made with ground turkey and chopped portobello mushroom, which simmer with tomatoes, red wine, and chicken stock. Serve over pasta and sprinkle with Parmesan.

SERVES 4

1 tablespoon olive oil

1 pound ground dark-meat turkey

Salt and pepper, to taste

1 small onion, chopped

2 cloves garlic, crushed

½ teaspoon ground allspice

1 medium portobello mushroom cap, finely chopped

1 can (28 ounces) imported whole tomatoes, crushed in a bowl

½ cup red wine

¾ cup chicken stock

1. Heat a deep skillet over medium high heat. Add the olive oil and turn the pan to coat it. **2.** Add the turkey, salt, pepper, onion, garlic, and allspice. Cook, stirring often, for 5 minutes or until the turkey browns. **3.** Add the mushroom and continue cooking 5 minutes more. **4.** Add the tomatoes, wine, and stock. Bring to a boil, lower the heat, and simmer for 10 minutes.

Timothy Chin

Pasta and Lentils

Equal parts lentils and small pasta, this hearty Italian dish can be a main course. The mixture thickens as it stands. If you want to add something more filling, serve it with turkey sausages.

SERVES 4

8 cups water

Salt and pepper, to taste

2 cups green lentils

3 tablespoons chopped fresh parsley

2 cloves garlic, chopped

¼ cup olive oil

1 cup small pasta shells

1. In a large saucepan, combine the water and a large pinch of salt. Bring to a boil. Add the lentils, cover partially, and simmer for 15 minutes. **2.** Add the parsley, garlic, olive oil, and salt. Re-cover the pan and cook over low heat, stirring occasionally, for 10 minutes. Add more water to the pan if it seems dry; the mixture should be very soupy. **3.** Add the pasta and pepper. Continue cooking for 10 minutes or until the pasta is tender.

Donna Meuse

Rigatoni with Summer Squash, Basil, and Goat Cheese

Rigatoni with Summer Squash, Basil, and Goat Cheese

Cook the yellow squash slowly in plenty of olive oil. They'll turn sweet but stay moist and summery, and maintain their beautiful golden color. As you cook the sliced rounds, mash them against the sides of the skillet to break them up. Then toss the squash with rigatoni, leaves of fresh basil, and crumbled goat cheese.

SERVES 4

4 tablespoons olive oil

7 small summer squash, thinly
   sliced

20 fresh basil leaves, torn in
   half

1 pound rigatoni

Salt and pepper, to taste

¼ cup fresh goat cheese,
   crumbled

1. In a large skillet over low heat, heat 3 tablespoons of the olive oil. Add the squash and cook, stirring often, for 30 minutes or until the squash soaks up the oil and is not at all watery. As the squash cooks, use a wooden spoon to mash it against the side of the pan. Stir in half of the basil leaves. **2.** Meanwhile, bring a large pot of salted water to a boil over high heat. Add the rigatoni to the pot. Cook for 10 to 12 minutes or until the pasta is tender but still has some bite. Drain into a colander and transfer to a serving bowl. Add the remaining 1 tablespoon of olive oil, salt, and pepper; toss gently. **3.** Tip the squash mixture into the rigatoni and toss gently. Top with the goat cheese and remaining basil leaves.

Jonathan Levitt

Farm Stand Pasta

In the waterfront city of Belfast, Maine, the family-run cafe Chase's Daily offers dishes made from their own homegrown vegetables and herbs. It's a favorite stop for vegetarian diners.

SERVES 4

Salt and pepper, to taste

1 pound penne

4 tablespoons olive oil

1 onion, thinly sliced

20 cherry tomatoes, halved

½ pound small green beans, trimmed at stem ends

2 cups corn kernels (cut from 4 ears)

1 cup tightly packed fresh basil leaves

½ cup grated Parmesan

1. Bring a large pot of salted water to a boil. Add the penne. Cook, stirring often, for 10 minutes or until the pasta is tender but still has some bite. Drain into a colander. Return to the pot. Add 1 tablespoon of the olive oil and toss gently. **2.** In a large, deep skillet over medium-low heat, heat 2 tablespoons of the olive oil. Add the onion and cook, stirring often, for 10 minutes or until it softens. **3.** Add the tomatoes, green beans, and corn. Cover with a lid and cook for 5 minutes, tossing occasionally, or until the green beans are tender but still bright green and the tomatoes are beginning to burst. **4.** Add the tomato mixture to the pasta and toss well over low heat. **5.** Remove the pan from the heat. Add the basil, Parmesan, remaining 1 tablespoon olive of oil, salt, and pepper.

Chase's Daily, Belfast, Maine

Mac and Ricotta

Surprisingly light, this combination of ricotta, eggs, and fontina, tossed with pasta and mozzarella, turns golden brown and crusty on top after baking.

SERVES 6

Olive oil (for the dish)

Salt and pepper, to taste

1 pound penne, shells, or other medium-size pasta

1 tablespoon olive oil

1 cup fresh whole-milk ricotta

3 eggs, lightly beaten

¼ pound fontina, cut into ¼-inch cubes

1 cup grated mozzarella

1. Set the oven at 375°F. Oil a 9 x 13-inch baking dish. **2.** Bring a large saucepan of salted water to a boil. Add the pasta and stir several times as the water returns to a boil. Cook, stirring occasionally, for 8 minutes or until the pasta is not quite tender; it will cook more later. Drain the pasta and transfer to a large bowl. Add the oil and pepper. Toss well and set aside to cool slightly, stirring occasionally. **3.** In a bowl, cream the ricotta with salt and pepper. Add the eggs a little at a time. Pour the ricotta mixture into the pasta and stir gently but thoroughly. **4.** Add half the mixture to the baking dish. Scatter the fontina on top. Sprinkle with half the mozzarella. Add the remaining pasta mixture to the dish. Sprinkle with the remaining mozzarella. **5.** Bake the pasta for 30 minutes or until the top starts to brown and the dish is bubbling at the edges.

Sheryl Julian

Mac and Ricotta

Orecchiette with Broccoli Rabe and Toasted Bread Crumbs

Broccoli rabe is a hearty green that goes well with chewy pasta ears or orecchiette. Blanch the greens first, then saute them in plenty of garlic before tossing with the pasta.

SERVES 4

Salt, to taste

3 tablespoons olive oil

½ cup panko bread crumbs

5 cloves garlic, mashed to a
    fine paste

5 anchovy fillets, mashed to a
    fine paste

1 teaspoon crushed red pepper

1 bunch (about 1 pound)
    broccoli rabe, rinsed,
    trimmed, and cut into thirds

1 pound orecchiette pasta

1. Bring a large pot of salted water to a boil. **2.** Meanwhile, in a skillet over medium heat, heat 1 tablespoon of the olive oil. Add the bread crumbs and cook, stirring constantly, for 3 minutes or until the bread crumbs are golden. Transfer them to a bowl. Wipe out the pan. **3.** In the skillet over low heat, heat the remaining 2 tablespoons of olive oil. Add the garlic, anchovies, and red pepper. With a spoon, press the mixture into the oil. Remove the pan from the heat as soon as the garlic and anchovies have melted into the oil. **4.** When the water boils, add the broccoli rabe to the pot. Cook for 3 minutes. With a slotted spoon, remove the broccoli rabe from the water and drain it in a colander. Don't drain the cooking water. Add the broccoli rabe to the garlic mixture in the skillet. Toss the mixture and return it to a low heat. **5.** Return the cooking water to a boil. Add the orecchiette and cook, stirring occasionally, for 8 minutes or until the pasta is tender but still has some bite. Drain the pasta into a colander, shake well, and tip the pasta back into the pot. **6.** Add the broccoli rabe mixture to the pasta and toss well. Taste for seasoning, and add more salt and black pepper, if you like. Sprinkle with toasted bread crumbs.

Jonathan Levitt

Angel Hair Pasta with Cherry Tomato Sauce

For quick family suppers, especially during the summer, this angel hair dish, with a fresh, uncooked cherry tomato and olive sauce, couldn't be easier. Dress it up with crumbled goat cheese and fresh basil.

SERVES 4

1 pint cherry tomatoes, halved

½ cup kalamata olives, pitted and coarsely chopped

2 tablespoons large capers, coarsely chopped

1 clove garlic, finely chopped

1 tablespoon lemon juice

2 tablespoons olive oil

Salt and pepper, to taste

8 ounces angel hair or capellini pasta

4 ounces goat cheese, crumbled

½ cup fresh basil leaves, finely chopped

1. In a large shallow serving bowl, combine the tomatoes, olives, capers, garlic, lemon juice, oil, salt, and pepper. Toss gently. **2.** Bring a large pot of salted water to a boil. Add the pasta and cook, stirring occasionally, for 6 minutes or until the pasta is tender, but still has some bite. **3.** Drain the pasta into a colander and add it to the tomato mixture. Add the goat cheese. **4.** Use two large forks to lift the pasta to distribute the sauce and cheese. Divide the mixture among four shallow bowls, and spoon more sauce over the pasta. Sprinkle with basil.

Debra Samuels

Spaghetti Lasagna

A variation on the layers of wide noodles, this lasagna uses spaghetti, tomato sauce, and mozzarella. It can be transported, reheated, and frozen, all without harm, which makes it an ideal dish for taking to the beach, ski lodge, or potluck supper.

SERVES 8

Olive oil (for the dish)

2 teaspoons salt, and more to taste

1 pound spaghetti

4 tablespoons olive oil

1 large onion, coarsely chopped

2 cloves garlic

2 cans (28 ounces each) whole imported tomatoes, crushed in a bowl

1 teaspoon crushed red pepper

2 teaspoons dried oregano

1 tablespoon brown sugar

½ teaspoon black pepper, or to taste

1 pound shredded mozzarella

¼ cup grated Parmesan (for sprinkling)

1. Set the oven at 350°F. Oil a deep 9 x 13-inch baking dish. **2.** Bring a large pot of salted water to a boil. Add the spaghetti and cook, stirring occasionally, for 8 minutes or until the noodles are not quite tender. Strain into a colander and transfer to a bowl. With scissors, snip the spaghetti in several places. Sprinkle with 1 tablespoon of the olive oil. Toss well and set aside. **3.** In a large saucepan, heat the remaining 3 tablespoons of oil. Add the onion and garlic, and cook, stirring often, for 3 minutes. Add the tomatoes, red pepper, oregano, brown sugar, a generous pinch of salt, and black pepper. Bring the sauce to a boil. Lower the heat and simmer, stirring occasionally, for 20 minutes or until the mixture thickens. Taste for seasoning and add more salt and pepper, if you like. **4.** Ladle enough tomato sauce in the bottom of the baking dish to make a thin layer. With tongs, add a layer of spaghetti, using one-third of the mixture. Tuck spaghetti into the corners of the dish. Cover with sauce, one-third of the mozzarella, then continue layering like this, ending with Parmesan. **5.** Set the dish on a large rimmed baking sheet. Bake for 30 to 40 minutes or until sauce is bubbling at the edges and the top is brown.

Debra Samuels

Lazy Man's Lasagna

The dish contains all the elements of a layered lasagna without the work. It's actually baked rigatoni with ricotta cheese and tomato sauce. Use a commercial sauce, the 20-minute sauce on page 49, or the short-rib ragu on page 49.

SERVES 8

Butter (for the dish)

Salt and pepper, to taste

1 pound rigatoni

1 pound part skim-milk ricotta
    cheese

5 eggs

¼ cup grated Romano cheese

3 cups grated mozzarella

1 quart (4 cups) tomato sauce

1. Set the oven at 350°F. Butter a 9 x 13-inch baking dish. **2.** Bring a large saucepan of salted water to a boil. Add the rigatoni, stir well, and cook the pasta for 14 minutes or until it is tender but still has some bite. Drain it into a colander and shake the colander well to remove excess moisture. **3.** Meanwhile, in large bowl, combine the ricotta, eggs, Romano, 2 cups of the mozzarella, and plenty of pepper. Stir until well blended. **4.** Ladle a layer of tomato sauce into the baking dish. Add the rigatoni. Pour the cheese mixture on top. **5.** Add the tomato sauce (it should cover the cheese mixture). Sprinkle with the remaining 1 cup mozzarella. **6.** Bake the dish for 30 to 40 minutes or until it is bubbling at the edges.

Donna Meuse

American Chop Suey

Popular among the Boomer generation, this American chop suey was served everywhere. Moms made it—and so did the ladies in the school cafeteria.

SERVES 6

2 tablespoons olive oil

1 Spanish onion, finely chopped

2 cloves garlic, finely chopped

2 pounds lean ground beef

1 can (28 ounces) whole
   tomatoes, crushed in a bowl

1 cup water

1 teaspoon dried oregano

½ teaspoon crushed red
   pepper

Salt and black pepper, to taste

1 pound macaroni

1 cup freshly grated Parmesan

1. In a large, flameproof casserole, heat the oil. Cook the onion over medium heat, stirring often, for 10 minutes or until it softens. Stir in the garlic and cook for 1 minute. **2.** Add the ground beef and cook over medium-high heat, stirring often, until the meat loses its pink color. Tip the pan and spoon off any fat. **3.** Add the tomatoes and their juices to the meat mixture. Stir in the water, oregano, red pepper, salt, and black pepper. Bring the mixture to a boil. Cover the pan and simmer the sauce for 30 minutes. **4.** Meanwhile, bring a large pot of salted water to a boil. Add the macaroni and let the water return to a boil. Cook, stirring often, for 10 minutes or until the pasta is tender but still has some bite. Drain the pasta into a colander. **5.** Stir the macaroni into the meat sauce. Serve sprinkled with Parmesan.

Sheryl Julian & Julie Riven

Pad Thai

Almost everything here—except tamarind pulp and dried shrimp—comes from the supermarket. Do all the chopping and assemble the ingredients on a tray, so the cooking is streamlined. You'll also need a deep wok or skillet.

SERVES 4

2 tablespoons tamarind pulp

3 tablespoons warm water

2 tablespoons Thai fish sauce

1 teaspoon brown sugar

4 tablespoons peanut oil

1 shallot, thinly sliced

3 cloves garlic, finely chopped

3 ounces firm tofu, cut into
    narrow 2-inch-long strips

1 tablespoon dried shrimp,
    finely chopped

3 eggs, lightly beaten

1/2 pound dried rice stick
    noodles (about the thickness
    of linguine), soaked in warm
    water for 20 minutes and
    drained

3 cups fresh bean sprouts

2 scallions, trimmed and cut
    into 1-inch lengths

2 cups dry-roasted peanuts,
    coarsely chopped

1 cup fresh cilantro leaves

2 limes, cut into small wedges

1. In a bowl, combine the tamarind pulp and water. Set aside for 10 minutes. Press the mixture through a sieve. **2.** In a small bowl, mix together the tamarind pulp, fish sauce, and brown sugar. **3.** Heat a large wok or skillet over high heat until smoking. Add 2 tablespoons of the oil and swirl the pan to coat it. Add the shallot and stir-fry for 20 seconds or until it begins to change color. Add the garlic and stir-fry 10 seconds more. **4.** Add the tofu and dried shrimp and press them gently against the hot sides of the wok for 20 seconds to sear them. **5.** Pour in the eggs and stir-fry for 30 seconds. Transfer the mixture to a plate and set aside. **6.** Return the wok or skillet to high heat. Add the remaining 2 tablespoons of oil and swirl the pan to coat it. Add noodles and stir-fry for 30 seconds, pressing the noodles against the hot wok to sear them. **7.** Add the tamarind mixture and stir-fry for 30 seconds more. Add 2 cups of the bean sprouts and the scallions. Toss for 30 seconds. Return the egg mixture to the pan; toss thoroughly. **8.** Gently transfer the pad Thai to a platter, folding in the remaining bean sprouts. Garnish with the chopped peanuts, cilantro leaves, and limes.

Jonathan Levitt

Sesame-Peanut Noodles

Sesame-Peanut Noodles

The ultimate kid dish: peanut butter, spaghetti, and a little hot chili oil. You can't beat the combination.

SERVES 6

1 cup smooth or chunky peanut
  butter

1¼ cup brewed black tea (lap-
  song souchong if possible)

½ cup soy sauce

¼ cup dark sesame oil, plus
  more for sprinkling

¼ cup red wine vinegar

¼ cup granulated sugar

2 tablespoons garlic, finely
  chopped

2 teaspoons hot chili oil, or to
  taste

1 pound spaghetti

1. In a bowl with a large fork, blend the peanut butter with the tea until smooth. Stir in the soy sauce, sesame oil, and red wine vinegar until the mixture is well blended. **2.** In a small bowl, combine the sugar with a few spoonfuls of the peanut butter mixture. Stir until the sugar dissolves, then stir the sugar mixture into the remaining peanut butter mixture. Blend well. **3.** Stir in the garlic and hot chili oil; set aside. **4.** Bring a large pot of salted water to a boil. Add the spaghetti, stir well, and let the water return to a boil. Cook for 10 minutes or until the pasta is tender but still has some bite. Drain the spaghetti and rinse briefly with cold water. **5.** Add the noodles to the peanut butter mixture and toss well. The sauce will thicken on standing. Serve warm or at room temperature, sprinkled with additional sesame oil, if you like.

Jane Dornbusch

Instant Mac and Cheese

Some nights the kids are cranky and hungry and you're tired too and there's nothing in the house. We keep a mixture of grated cheeses around for pasta and egg dishes. Add some to a pan of macaroni or shells and you've got dinner in minutes.

SERVES 4

Salt and pepper, to taste

1 pound macaroni or small
    pasta shells

4 tablespoons butter, cut up

3 tablespoons each grated
    fresh Parmesan, mozzarella,
    and Monterey Jack

1. Bring a large saucepan of salted water to a boil. Add the macaroni or shells and cook, stirring often, for 10 minutes or until they are tender. **2.** Drain the pasta into a colander, shake it, and return the pasta to the pan. **3.** Add the butter with pepper and shake the pan well. **4.** Add the cheeses and toss the pasta.

Sheryl Julian

Quick-Soaking Beans

You can soak dried beans overnight, or let them sit in boiling water for 1 hour. This quick-soak method is just as effective as the overnight method.

Use 1 cup of beans to 1 quart of water. In a large pot, bring the beans and water to a boil. Simmer for 2 minutes. Remove from the heat and let the pot stand, covered, for 1 hour.

Drain the beans into a colander and rinse with cold water. Simmer as directed.

Maple Baked Beans

Maple Baked Beans

Traditional baked beans are made with salt pork, which is becoming increasingly difficult to find. We like the taste of beans made with bacon. In this recipe, the beans are simmered first, then baked, a method designed so they come out saucy. If you prefer a drier pot of baked beans with a crusty top, continue baking, uncovered, for 30 minutes more. Allow enough time for the beans to soak overnight, or use the quick-soak method (see page 65).

SERVES 6

4 cups dried yellow eye,
    Jacob's cattle, white, or pinto
    beans, picked over

½ pound bacon, cut into bite-
    size pieces

½ cup maple syrup

1 teaspoon dry mustard

1½ teaspoons salt

1 teaspoon black pepper

1. In a bowl, combine the beans and water to cover them by 1 inch. Set aside to soak overnight. **2.** Drain the beans and transfer to a large pot. Add enough water to cover them by 1 inch. Bring to a boil, lower the heat, and simmer for 30 minutes or until the skins start to split and peel back. Drain the beans, reserving the cooking liquid. **3.** Set the oven at 250°F. Put the beans in a 4-quart bean pot or heavy casserole. Stir in the bacon pieces, maple syrup, mustard powder, salt, and pepper. Add the reserved cooking liquid. The beans should be covered with water; add more water if necessary. Cover the pot and transfer to the oven. **4.** Bake the beans for 4 to 6 hours, tasting occasionally, or until the beans are soft enough to mash against the side of the pan. When they are ready, remove the cover, and return the beans to the oven. Continue cooking for 30 minutes more to thicken the liquid. Serve with brown bread and coleslaw.

Jonathan Levitt

30-Minute Baked Beans

If you need a quick supper or potluck dish, begin with canned beans. This recipe uses pinto beans, since canned white beans tend to turn mushy.

SERVES 6

7 strips of bacon, cut into
 ¼-inch strips

1 onion, chopped

⅔ cup ketchup

3 tablespoons dark or light
 brown sugar

⅔ cup maple syrup

⅛ teaspoon cayenne pepper

Salt and black pepper, to taste

3 cans (15 ounces each) pinto
 beans, drained and rinsed
 well

1. Set the oven at 350°F. Have on hand a 2-quart baking dish. **2.** In a deep skillet over medium heat, render the bacon until browned and almost crisp. Remove it from the pan and set on paper towels to drain. **3.** Pour off all but 1 tablespoon of fat from the pan. Add the onion and cook, stirring often, for 8 minutes or until it softens. **4.** Add the ketchup, brown sugar, maple syrup, cayenne pepper, salt, and black pepper. Bring to a boil. Remove from the heat and stir in the beans and bacon. **5.** Transfer the mixture to the baking dish and bake uncovered for 25 minutes or until the beans are bubbling at the edges.

Christine Merlo

30-Minute Baked Beans

Warm Lentils in Vinaigrette

French lentils are smaller and firmer than flat American lentils. Toss them with a mustard vinaigrette, plenty of red onion and scallions, and they make a nice warm salad to serve with leg of lamb or roast chicken.

SERVES 4

1 quart water

1 cup French Le Puy lentils

1/2 teaspoon salt, or to taste

1/4 teaspoon pepper, or to taste

2 tablespoons white wine
   vinegar

1 teaspoon Dijon mustard

1/3 cup olive oil

1/4 red onion, finely chopped

4 scallions, finely chopped

1/2 cup chopped fresh parsley

1. In a saucepan, bring the water to a boil. Stir in the lentils, turn down the heat, and cook for 20 to 25 minutes or until the lentils are tender but still have some bite. **2.** Meanwhile, in a bowl, whisk together the salt, pepper, and vinegar until the salt dissolves. **3.** Whisk in the mustard. Add the oil in a thin steady stream, whisking until the dressing emulsifies. **4.** When the lentils are cooked, drain them into a colander. Transfer the lentils to a bowl. Spoon half of the dressing over the lentils while they are hot. Stir gently. Let them sit until they are just warm. **5.** Add the onion, scallions, and parsley. Stir and add enough of the remaining dressing to coat the lentils.

Sheryl Julian

Long-Grain White Rice

Use this method for any long-grain white rice. Aromatic rices, such as basmati or jasmine, need nothing but salt. More common rices might benefit from adding a lemon half to the water while simmering.

SERVES 6

1 1/2 cups long-grain white rice

8 cups water

Pinch of salt

1. Rinse the rice in a strainer. **2.** In a large saucepan, bring the water and salt to a boil. While the water is bubbling, add the rice a spoonful at a time. Let the water return to a boil, stirring once or twice to prevent the rice from sticking to the bottom. Cook, uncovered, at a rolling boil, for 12 minutes exactly. The rice should be tender but not mushy. **3.** Drain the rice into a colander and use the handle of a wooden spoon to poke half a dozen holes in the rice so it can drain. Set the colander on the saucepan and cover the top with a clean paper towel or dish towel. Let the rice sit for 2 minutes. **4.** Transfer the rice to a bowl.

Sheryl Julian

Red and Black Bean Salad with Lime Vinaigrette

Because beans are a plain-tasting and simple-looking food, they need something flavorful to bring them to life. Here red kidney beans are mixed with black beans and served with a vinaigrette of lime juice, cayenne pepper, Dijon mustard, and ground cumin. You can use any mixture of beans—black and white, red and white, or black, red, and white. Serve with grilled chicken, broiled salmon, or swordfish steaks.

SERVES 6

2 cans (15 ounces each) red
  kidney beans, rinsed and
  drained

1 can (15 ounces) black beans,
  rinsed and drained

Salt and black pepper, to taste

¼ cup lime juice

Pinch cayenne pepper

1 teaspoon Dijon mustard

¼ teaspoon ground cumin

¼ cup olive oil

½ red onion, very thinly sliced

1 red pepper, cored, seeded,
  and cut into fine matchsticks

1 stalk celery, very thinly sliced

3 tablespoons chopped fresh
  parsley sprigs

1. In a bowl, combine the red and black beans. Add salt and black pepper; set aside. **2.** In another bowl, whisk together the lime juice, cayenne pepper, mustard, cumin, salt, and black pepper. Gradually whisk in the oil a spoonful at a time until the dressing emulsifies. **3.** Pour the dressing over the beans. Toss gently. **4.** Add the onion, red pepper, celery, and parsley. Toss again. Taste the beans for seasoning and add more salt, black pepper, or cayenne, if you like. **5.** Cover the salad loosely; set aside for 30 minutes for the flavors to mellow.

Sheryl Julian

Couscous Salad with Vegetables

Instant couscous is the busy host's friend. It can be mixed with all kinds of vegetables. Here the grains are tossed with grilled red onion and red bell pepper.

SERVES 6

1 small red onion, cut into
　¼-inch rounds
1 red bell pepper, cored,
　seeded, and cut in 4 pieces
2 zucchini, halved lengthwise
3 tablespoons olive oil
Salt and black pepper, to taste
2 teaspoons ground cumin
1½ cups chicken stock
1½ cups couscous
¼ cup chopped fresh mint

1. Turn on the broiler. Set the onion, bell pepper, and zucchini, cut sides up, on a rimmed baking sheet. Using 1½ tablespoons of the olive oil, brush the vegetables with oil and sprinkle them with salt and black pepper. Broil the vegetables about 10 inches from the element, turning often, and watching them carefully, for 10 minutes or until they are cooked through. Set them aside. When the vegetables are cool enough to handle, chop them coarsely. **2.** In a saucepan off the heat, combine the onion, bell pepper, zucchini, and cumin. Stir well. Add the stock and remaining 1½ tablespoons oil. Bring to a boil. Stir in the couscous and cover the pan. Remove from the heat and let the mixture sit for 5 minutes so the couscous absorbs the liquid. **3.** Add the mint and fluff with a fork. Taste for seasoning and add more salt and black pepper, if you like.

Tony Rosenfeld

Vietnamese Pot-Fried Rice

In this dish, fried rice is made by browning raw rice in oil, adding ginger and garlic, and finishing the cooking in water.

SERVES 6

1 tablespoon vegetable oil
2 cups uncooked long-grain
　white rice
2 cloves of garlic, finely
　chopped
1-inch piece fresh ginger,
　peeled and finely chopped
Generous pinch of salt
1 bunch scallions (white part
　only), finely chopped
4 cups water
¼ cup chopped fresh cilantro
1 hot red chili pepper, cut into
　very thin slices

1. In a flameproof casserole with a tight-fitting lid, heat the oil and cook the rice, stirring often, for 5 minutes. **2.** Add the garlic and ginger and cook for 1 minute. Add salt, scallions, and water. Bring the rice to a boil and let the water bubble vigorously, stirring constantly. **3.** Cover the pot and set it over very low heat. Cook the rice for 12 to 15 minutes or until it is tender and all the water is absorbed. **4.** Sprinkle with cilantro, and chili pepper.

Sheryl Julian

Fried Rice

This colorful dish begins with leftover rice, to which you add vegetables, eggs, and meat.

SERVES 4

3 tablespoons plus 1 teaspoon
  canola oil

1 onion, chopped

2 carrots, chopped

2 celery stalks, chopped

½ red bell pepper, cored,
  seeded, and chopped

Salt and black pepper, to taste

1 thick slice baked or smoked
  ham, cut into ¼-inch dice

4 cups cooked rice, cold or
  room temperature

2 teaspoons dark sesame oil

1 tablespoon soy sauce

2 eggs, beaten to mix

2 scallions, trimmed and
  chopped

1. In a large nonstick skillet over medium heat, heat 2 tablespoons of the canola oil. Add the onion, carrots, celery, red pepper, salt, and black pepper. Stir-fry for 5 minutes. Transfer to a serving dish. **2.** Add 1 tablespoon more canola oil to the skillet. Stir-fry the ham for 2 minutes. **3.** Add the rice and stir-fry for 3 minutes until the rice is hot and the grains are separate. **4.** Add the vegetables and sprinkle with 1 teaspoon of the sesame oil. Stir-fry for 1 minute. **5.** Add the soy sauce and mix well. Push the rice and vegetables to one side of the pan, leaving half the pan empty. **6.** Add the remaining 1 teaspoon of sesame oil to the beaten eggs. Add the remaining 1 teaspoon of canola oil to the empty part of the skillet. Pour in the eggs and cook until they just begin to set. **7.** With a spatula, gradually mix the egg, little by little, with the rice, until it is all incorporated. Taste for seasoning and add more salt and black pepper, if you like. **8.** Transfer the mixture to the serving dish. Sprinkle with scallions.

Debra Samuels

Brown Rice

Learn to love brown rice and you'll always feel satisfied at the end of a meal.

SERVES 6

2 cups long-grain brown rice

4½ cups water

½ teaspoon salt

1. Rinse the rice in a strainer. **2.** In a heavy-based saucepan, combine the rice with the water and salt. Bring it to a vigorous boil and boil for 1 minute. Skim any scum on the surface. **3.** Lower the heat, cover the pan, and simmer the rice over very low heat, without stirring, for 45 to 50 minutes or until the kernels are a little firm on the outside but tender inside. **4.** Remove the pot from the heat and let it stand for 15 minutes before stirring the rice gently.

Sheryl Julian

Curried Brown Rice Salad with Cashews

Nourishing and filling, this bowl of brown rice is tossed with curry, carrots, cashews, plenty of ginger, scallions, red bell pepper, and raisins. It has crunch, sweetness, and a little heat from the onion and scallions.

SERVES 6

1½ cups long-grain brown rice, fully cooked (see page 74)

2 tablespoons peanut oil

1 tablespoon curry powder

Salt and freshly ground black pepper, to taste

2 tablespoons chopped fresh ginger

3 carrots, grated

½ cup roasted unsalted cashews

1 bunch scallions, trimmed and finely chopped

½ red onion, finely chopped

1 red bell pepper, cored, seeded, and cut into matchsticks

¼ cup chopped fresh parsley

3 tablespoons rice wine vinegar

½ cup golden raisins

¼ cup dark raisins

1. Transfer the rice to a large bowl and let it cool completely. **2.** In a skillet, heat the oil, add the curry powder, and cook for 30 seconds or until the curry is aromatic. Pour the curry mixture over the rice and toss thoroughly. **3.** Add plenty of salt and pepper, and the ginger, carrots, cashews, scallions, red onion, bell pepper, and parsley. Toss well. **4.** In a bowl, combine the vinegar with the golden and dark raisins. Let them sit for 5 minutes. **5.** Add the raisins to the brown rice and toss again. Taste for seasoning, add more salt and pepper if necessary, and cover tightly. Refrigerate for 30 minutes so the flavors can mellow.

Sheryl Julian

Coarse Bulgur

Middle Eastern markets have a system for numbering bulgur according to the milling process. The coarsest is usually marked No. 4. Other markets call this rough bulgur "coarse."

SERVES 4

1 teaspoon canola oil

1 cup No. 4 or coarse bulgur

1¼ cups chicken or vegetable broth

½ teaspoon salt

1. In a saucepan, heat the oil over medium heat. Add the bulgur and cook, stirring constantly, for 3 minutes or until the grains are lightly toasted. **2.** Pour in the broth (watch out for sputtering oil) and the salt. Bring to a boil, stirring. **3.** Lower the heat, cover the pan, and simmer the bulgur for 20 minutes, without stirring, or until the liquid is completely absorbed and the grain is tender but chewy. Fluff with a fork before serving.

Quinoa

Quinoa is a highly nutritious ancient grain that is increasing in popularity. It cooks relatively quickly.

SERVES 4

1 teaspoon canola oil

1½ cups quinoa

3 cups chicken or vegetable stock

¾ teaspoon salt

1. In a saucepan, heat the oil over medium heat. Add the quinoa and cook, stirring constantly, for 3 minutes or until the grains are lightly toasted. **2.** Pour in the stock (watch out for sputtering oil) and the salt. Bring to a boil, stirring. **3.** Lower the heat, cover the pan, and simmer the quinoa for 15 minutes, without stirring, or until the liquid is completely absorbed and the grain is tender but chewy. Fluff with a fork.

Andrea Pyenson

Vegetables and Side Dishes

Where once a woefully overcooked vegetable took up a tiny corner of the plate each night, today's modern cooks celebrate vegetables. They start their kids early on steamed broccoli "trees" and make sure carrot sticks are tucked into the lunch box. Vegetable stir-fries are common now on family tables, and often a main course is accompanied by both a vegetable and a salad.

Vegetables also play a starring role on special occasions. A roast pork loin is an elegant entree, but it needs something equally spectacular beside it. That might be a casserole bursting with cubes of butternut squash, shiitakes, green beans, and sweet onions or creamed spinach with a hint of nutmeg.

And while leafy greens and glazed roots please some guests, others just want potatoes. The universal favorite is creamy mashed potatoes, and instead of a smooth puree, you can also smash the spuds with garlic and sour cream. Classic scalloped potatoes with cheese turn golden brown and delightfully crusty on top and go well with roast lamb or beef.

Sweet potatoes, which are becoming increasingly popular, can be candied the traditional way for the holiday table, pureed with maple syrup and cinnamon, or roasted individually and filled with lots of grated ginger and soy sauce.

Whatever vegetables you're making, prepare much more than you need. On weekdays, the leftovers can top your salad at lunch. At parties, the vegetarian guest who forgot to inform you that grilled steaks and ribs are off limits has something substantial to eat.

At the end of the week, you can combine all the vegetable odds and ends in one pot, add a little chicken stock, some leftover tomato sauce, bits and pieces of main course meats, and pasta if you've got it, along with the sauce. Bring it all to a boil and let it simmer for 20 minutes. This nourishing bowl—often quite good, depending upon what's on hand—defines potluck.

Roasted Vegetable Casserole

Colorful vegetables, packed into a casserole and roasted until they're tender, release all their juices into the dish, so the only necessary accompaniment is white rice (see page 68) or brown rice (see page 74). You can also spoon these vegetables beside slices of roast chicken or turkey breast.

SERVES 4

Olive oil (for the pan and for sprinkling)

4 large carrots, thickly sliced

8 small red potatoes, halved

1 pound ready-peeled and seeded butternut squash, cut into 2-inch pieces

½ pound white mushrooms or shiitakes, stemmed and halved or quartered

1 bunch radishes, root ends trimmed

½ pound green beans, stem ends trimmed

1 large sweet onion, cut into 8 wedges

Salt and pepper, to taste

½ cup chicken stock or water

2 tablespoons chopped fresh parsley

1. Set the oven at 400°F. Lightly oil a heavy-based casserole (about 2½-quart capacity) with a tight-fitting lid. **2.** In the casserole, layer the carrots, potatoes, squash, mushrooms, radishes, green beans, and onion, sprinkling each layer with oil, salt, and pepper. Pour the stock or water into the pan at the sides. **3.** Cover the pan and roast the vegetables for 1½ hours, basting them several times with the juices in the pan, or until all the vegetables are tender. **4.** Sprinkle with parsley.

Sheryl Julian

Roasted Vegetable Casserole

Vegetable Lasagna

If you slice zucchini, yellow or patty pan squash, and tomatoes thinly enough, when you layer them in a baking dish, they hold together and you can cut the "lasagna" into squares. Use a long chef's knife or handheld slicing machine, such as a mandoline, to make very thin slices of zucchini and yellow squash, and a serrated knife for the tomatoes. After the vegetables have cooked together, sprinkle the top with cheese, and return the dish to the oven to melt the cheese. To add more protein to this dish, slice two large balls of fresh mozzarella and layer them with the vegetables. The next day, reheat pieces of the lasagna in a microwave and top each serving with a poached or soft-cooked egg.

SERVES 6

Olive oil (for drizzling)

5 medium zucchini

2 medium yellow squash

6 medium tomatoes

Salt and pepper, to taste

¼ cup chopped fresh thyme, marjoram, or oregano

1 cup grated Gruyere, sharp cheddar, or other firm cheese

1. Set the oven at 400°F. Lightly oil a 9 x 13-inch baking dish. **2.** Using a long chef's knife or a handheld slicing machine, cut the zucchini and squash on a slight diagonal into ⅛-inch slices. Use a serrated knife to cut the tomatoes into thin slices. **3.** Arrange half the zucchini in the dish, then half the squash, followed by half the tomatoes. You can overlap the slices if the squashes are thinly cut. Drizzle with a little oil and sprinkle with salt, pepper, and thyme, marjoram, or oregano. Make another layer just like the first, ending with tomatoes, oil, salt, pepper, and fresh herbs. **4.** Cook the vegetables for 35 minutes or until they are almost tender when pierced with a skewer. **5.** Sprinkle the cheese all over the tomatoes. Continue cooking the vegetables for 10 minutes more or until the cheese melts. **6.** Turn on the broiler. Slide the dish under the broiler for 2 minutes or until the cheese browns.

Sheryl Julian

Stir-Fried Chinese Vegetables

Stir-fries take minutes to cook. Have everything ready and beside the burner before you begin, and time the rice so it's done when you take the vegetables from the pan. Serve with white rice (see page 68) or brown rice (see page 74).

SERVES 4

2 tablespoons canola oil

2 cloves garlic, finely chopped

1 piece (1 inch) fresh ginger
   root, chopped

4 scallions, chopped

¼ head Chinese cabbage,
   cored and sliced

8 shiitake mushrooms,
   stemmed and quartered

2 stalks celery, thickly sliced on
   a diagonal

1 red bell pepper, seeded and
   cut into strips

1 large carrot, thickly sliced on
   a diagonal

½ head of broccoli, tops cut
   into florets and stems peeled
   and thickly sliced

¼ cup chicken stock

2 tablespoons soy sauce

1 teaspoon sugar

½ teaspoon salt

2 tablespoons Chinese rice
   wine

1 cup bean sprouts

2 teaspoons sesame oil

1. Heat a wok or large frying pan over high heat for 30 seconds. Add the oil and swirl it around pan. Add the garlic, ginger, and scallions. Stir-fry for 30 seconds. **2.** Add the cabbage, shiitake mushrooms, celery, red pepper, carrot, and broccoli florets and stems. Stir-fry for 2 minutes. **3.** Add the stock, soy sauce, sugar, salt, and rice wine. Cover with a lid and cook the vegetables on medium-high heat for 2 minutes more. **4.** Uncover the pan. Add the bean sprouts. Cook 1 minute more. Turn off the heat. Sprinkle with sesame oil. Stir gently.

Debra Samuels

Baked Stuffed Zucchini

Stuffing vegetables with meat is an easy way to stretch a pound of ground dark-meat turkey or beef. It turns into a kind of meat loaf mixture when mixed with bread crumbs, Parmesan, and herbs. Lay thin slices of fresh tomatoes over the ground meat to flavor the filling and keep it moist.

SERVES 4

1 overgrown zucchini or 4
    medium zucchini

2 tablespoons olive oil

1 medium onion, chopped

1 pound ground dark-meat
    turkey or beef

1 cup plain white bread crumbs,
    or more if necessary

1/4 cup freshly grated Parmesan

Salt and pepper, to taste

1 tablespoon each chopped
    fresh thyme and oregano

Juice of 1/2 lemon

4 medium tomatoes, cored and
    thinly sliced

Extra Parmesan (for sprinkling)

1. Set the oven at 350°F. Have on hand a large roasting pan. **2.** Halve the large or medium zucchini lengthwise. If using the large one, cut into 8 pieces. **3.** With a spoon, remove the seeds from the zucchini and discard them. Use a small knife to remove as much of the flesh as possible from the shells, taking care not to puncture the shells. Transfer the flesh to a bowl. **4.** Place the outer shells in the roasting pan with 1/4 inch of water. Bake them for 15 minutes or until they are softened but not fully cooked. Leave the oven on. **5.** Chop the zucchini flesh coarsely. **6.** In large skillet, heat the oil and cook the onion, stirring often, for 8 minutes or until softened. Add the turkey or beef and continue cooking, stirring, until it breaks up. Remove the skillet from the heat. **7.** Add the bread crumbs, Parmesan, salt, pepper, thyme, oregano, and lemon juice. Stir in the chopped zucchini flesh. **8.** Divide the filling among the zucchini shells. Cover with tomatoes. Bake for 20 minutes. **9.** Sprinkle the filling with more Parmesan and continue cooking for 20 minutes or until the cheese melts and the squash is tender when pierced with a skewer. (Total cooking time is 40 minutes.)

Janet McLeod

Baked Stuffed Zucchini

Glazed Carrots

Instead of simmering carrots in water and removing them from their cooking liquid, these rounds are left in the water until it bubbles up and eventually evaporates from the pan. A little sugar in the water glazes them.

SERVES 4

1 pound slender carrots

2 cups water

½ teaspoon salt

¼ teaspoon pepper

1 teaspoon sugar

2 tablespoons chopped fresh
   parsley (for garnish)

1. Peel the carrots and slice them thickly on the diagonal. **2.** In a large saucepan, combine the carrots, water, salt, pepper, and sugar. Add enough additional water to cover the carrots. Bring to a boil, lower the heat, cover the pan, and simmer for 10 minutes or until the carrots are tender. **3.** Remove the lid and turn up the heat. Let the water bubble steadily, shaking the pan occasionally, for 10 minutes or until all the water has evaporated from the pan and the carrots are shiny and glazed. Sprinkle with parsley.

Sheryl Julian

Creamed Spinach

What may seem like a lot of spinach when it's raw collapses into a small amount when cooked. To make the instant white sauce, whisk a paste of butter and flour into simmering milk.

SERVES 4

2 cups water

2 pounds spinach, stems
   removed and well rinsed

½ cup whole milk

1 tablespoon butter, at room
   temperature

1 tablespoon flour

Salt and pepper, to taste

⅛ teaspoon freshly grated
   nutmeg

1. In a large soup pot, bring the water to a boil. Add the spinach, cover the pot, and let the spinach cook for 3 minutes or until it wilts completely. **2.** Drain the spinach into a colander and rinse it with cold water until it is no longer warm. Set it aside to cool until you can handle it. With your hands, squeeze the spinach a handful at a time to remove the excess water. Continue until all of the spinach has released its moisture. **3.** Chop the spinach finely and set it aside. **4.** In a large saucepan, heat the milk. On a plate, combine the butter and flour. Mash the butter and flour together until they are smooth. When the milk is bubbling at the edges, whisk the butter mixture into the hot milk a little at a time. The milk will thicken slightly. Continue whisking in the butter mixture until it is all added. Simmer the milk over very low heat for 2 minutes. **5.** Add the spinach, salt, pepper, and nutmeg. Continue cooking over low heat for 2 minutes or until the spinach is hot.

Julie Riven

Grilled Summer Vegetable Salad

SERVES 6

DRESSING

2 tablespoons red wine vinegar

1 clove garlic, chopped

1 tablespoon lemon juice

$1/2$ teaspoon salt

$1/4$ teaspoon pepper

$1/2$ teaspoon Dijon mustard

4 tablespoons olive oil

SALAD

2 medium eggplants, sliced

2 green or red bell peppers, seeded and cut into wide strips

2 medium summer squash, sliced

Olive oil (for brushing)

Salt and pepper, to taste

1 cup cherry tomatoes, cut in half

4 scallions, chopped

1 medium cucumber, chopped

$1/2$ cup chopped fresh herbs (basil, parsley, thyme, and chives)

$3/4$ cup pitted kalamata olives

4 ounces crumbled feta

DRESSING

In a bowl, combine the vinegar, garlic, lemon juice, salt, pepper, and mustard. Whisk well. Whisk in the oil a little at a time until it is all added; set aside.

SALAD

1. Light a charcoal grill or turn a gas grill to medium-hot. **2.** In a roasting pan, brush the eggplants, bell peppers, and squash with olive oil, salt, and pepper. **3.** Grill the eggplants, peppers, and squash for 5 to 8 minutes, turning, or until tender; set aside to cool slightly. **4.** Cut the vegetables into 2-inch pieces. Transfer to a serving bowl. Whisk the dressing and add enough dressing to moisten the vegetables. **5.** Add the tomatoes, scallions, cucumber, fresh herbs, salt, and pepper. Toss gently. Top with olives and feta.

Danielle Andrews

Romano Beans

Roasted Garlicky Romano Beans

Romano beans are meatier than green beans, and a favorite among Italian cooks. They're also known as Italian green beans, Italian string beans, Italian flat beans, and pole beans. They're flat and broad (about 1 inch wide), tender, and sweet.

SERVES 4

1 pound Romano beans, stem
   ends trimmed

¼ cup olive oil

3 cloves garlic, smashed

3 sprigs of fresh thyme, broken
   in half

Salt and pepper, to taste

1. Set the oven at 450°F. **2.** On a large rimmed baking sheet, toss the whole beans with the oil, garlic, thyme, salt, and pepper. Spread the beans into a single layer. **3.** Roast for 15 to 20 minutes, turning once, or until the beans are tender and browned. Serve warm or at room temperature.

Rachel Travers

Caramelized Cauliflower with Raisins and Almonds

Sliced cauliflower florets caramelized in olive oil taste buttery sweet. Add golden raisins, crushed red pepper, and sliced almonds. To turn it into a main course, mash one-third of the cooked mixture into a coarse puree, toss it with ½ pound of cooked penne, and add a little pasta cooking water to loosen the mixture.

SERVES 4

½ cup golden raisins

⅓ cup brandy

1 large cauliflower (2½ pounds)

⅓ cup sliced almonds

6 tablespoons olive oil

Salt, to taste

1 small onion, finely chopped

¼ teaspoon crushed red
  pepper, and more to taste

2 cloves garlic, finely chopped

4 anchovy fillets, finely
  chopped

1 tablespoon lemon juice

1. In a small bowl, soak the raisins in the brandy. **2.** Remove the outside leaves from the cauliflower, core the head, and cut it into florets. Slice them into ½-inch thick pieces. Submerge them in a bowl of cold water, then drain and set aside. **3.** In a large skillet, place the almonds over medium heat and toast them, shaking the pan, for 3 minutes or until golden. Transfer to a bowl. **4.** In the same skillet, warm 4 tablespoons of the olive oil over medium heat. Toss the cauliflower well in the oil, season generously with salt, and cover the pan. Cook for 7 minutes, shaking the pan occasionally. **5.** Uncover the pan, turn the heat to high, and cook the cauliflower, tossing occasionally, for 5 to 8 minutes or until browned. Transfer to a bowl. **6.** Return the skillet to medium heat. Add the remaining 2 tablespoons of olive oil. Add the onion and red pepper. Cook, stirring often, for 3 minutes or until the onion is translucent. **7.** Add the garlic and anchovies and cook, stirring often, for 2 minutes or until the anchovies dissolve. Pour in the brandy and raisins and let the mixture bubble until most of the liquid evaporates. **8.** Add the lemon juice. Taste for seasoning and add more salt or red pepper, if you like. Fold the onion mixture into the cauliflower. Sprinkle with almonds.

Jill Santopietro

Brussels Sprouts with Potatoes and Cauliflower

At Verrill Farm in Concord, Massachusetts, this dish was added to the Thanksgiving repertoire recently to offer patrons a healthy side.

SERVES 10

1 pound small red potatoes, cut
    in eighths

1 pound small Yukon Gold or
    Yellow Finn potatoes, cut in
    eighths

1 small head cauliflower, broken
    into florets

1 pound Brussels sprouts, split
    lengthwise

3 tablespoons olive oil

½ teaspoon dried thyme

½ teaspoon salt

½ teaspoon pepper

1. Set the oven at 425°F. **2.** In a bowl, toss the red and yellow potatoes, cauliflower, and Brussels sprouts with olive oil, thyme, salt, and pepper. Spread the vegetables on a rimmed baking sheet in one layer. **3.** Roast for 35 to 45 minutes, turning once, or until the vegetables are tender.

Verrill Farm,
Concord, Massachusetts

Brussel Sprouts with Potatoes and Cauliflower

Vegetarian Stuffed Winter Squash

Vegetarian Stuffed Winter Squash

Ideal for vegetarians who are visiting in the fall, this pudgy squash is filled with a mushroom-chestnut stuffing. Choose a round squash with a flat bottom, such as Jarrahdale, kabocha, or buttercup. Ready-made unseasoned bread cubes or homemade croutons form the foundation. Toast fresh cubes in a 350°F oven for 10 minutes. Add mushrooms, plenty of onions and celery, chestnuts, lots of herbs, eggs, and vegetable stock.

SERVES 6 AS A MAIN COURSE

1 squash (5 to 7 pounds)

Olive oil (for brushing)

Salt and pepper, to taste

½ cup (1 stick) butter

2 stalks celery, chopped

1 medium onion, chopped

8 ounces mixed mushrooms, sliced

1 can (14 ounces) chestnuts, chopped

2 tablespoons chopped fresh sage

½ bunch fresh parsley, stemmed and chopped

2 tablespoons chopped fresh thyme

5 cups cubed bread

2 eggs

2 cups vegetable stock

1. Set the oven at 350°F. **2.** Score a circle 1½ inches around the stem end of the squash. Cut and remove the top; set it aside. Scoop seeds and stringy pulp from the base, brush it inside and out with olive oil, and sprinkle with salt and pepper. Set squash bottom and top on a rimmed baking sheet. Bake for 30 minutes. **3.** In a large skillet over medium heat, melt the butter. Cook the celery and onion with salt and pepper, stirring often, for 5 minutes. Add the mushrooms and cook, stirring, for 5 minutes more. Add the chestnuts, sage, parsley, thyme, and bread cubes; set aside. **4.** In a bowl, whisk the eggs and stock; stir the liquids into the bread mixture. **5.** Press the stuffing into the squash, making a small mound on top. Bake the squash for 1 hour and 15 minutes or until it is tender and a knife inserted into the center is hot to the touch when withdrawn.

Karoline Boehm Goodnick

Salt-Roasted Beets

Beets that roast inside foil are especially sweet. You can use both red and yellow beets (keep them separate while roasting so the red ones don't stain the lighter rounds), then slice them and sprinkle with ricotta salata—a firm slicing cheese—or feta.

SERVES 4

4 medium beets

2 tablespoons olive oil, or to taste

Kosher salt and pepper, to taste

2 ounces ricotta salata or feta cheese

1. Set the oven at 350°F. **2.** Cut off any greens on the beets and trim both ends. Wash the beets well. Tear off a long sheet of foil. Set the beets in the center of the foil and sprinkle with 1 tablespoon of the olive oil, salt, and pepper. Wrap up the foil to enclose the beets. Set them in a baking dish. **3.** Roast the beets for 1 to 1½ hours or until they are tender when pierced with a skewer. **4.** Let the beets cool slightly, then open the foil. Leave the skins on or peel them. To peel, place the beets on paper towels; use the towels to rub the skins off. **5.** Slice the beets and sprinkle with oil. Lay them on a serving plate. **6.** Thinly slice the ricotta salata or crumble the feta. Add to the beets.

Vox Populi, Boston, Massachusetts

Danish Braised Red Cabbage

For the best flavor, make the cabbage up to the point where it is fully cooked and the jelly has been stirred in. Refrigerate for a day or two. Then reheat and serve.

SERVES 6

1 large head (3 pounds) red cabbage

6 tablespoons unsalted butter, cut into pieces

½ cup distilled white vinegar

¼ cup water

1½ teaspoons salt

2½ tablespoons sugar

½ cup red currant jelly

1. Set the oven at 325°F. **2.** Quarter the cabbage. With a long chef's knife or a handheld slicing machine, cut the cabbage into the thinnest possible slices. **3.** In a large flameproof casserole, combine the butter, vinegar, water, salt, and sugar. Cook the mixture over medium heat for 2 minutes or until butter melts. **4.** Turn up the heat and bring the mixture to a boil. Add the cabbage and turn it in the liquid. **5.** Press a piece of foil on top of the casserole, then cover with the lid. Transfer to the oven and cook the cabbage for 2 hours, stirring once after 1 hour. **6.** Stir in the jelly and cook for 20 minutes more. **7.** If the cooked cabbage has a lot of excess liquid, set a large strainer over another saucepan. Tip the cabbage into the strainer. Return the cabbage to its cooking pan. **8.** Bring the cooking liquid to a boil over high heat, and let it bubble steadily for 5 minutes or until it reduces to a syrupy glaze. Pour it over the cabbage.

Ingrid Lysgaard

Unstuffed Cabbage

Sweet and sour stuffed cabbage is a traditional recipe of Jewish families with Eastern European roots. This dish came about when Boston Globe contributor Rachel Travers set out to make her mother's stuffed cabbage—filled with a seasoned meat and rice mixture—but didn't want all the work. Instead Rachel simmered chopped cabbage in one pot and in another made a ground beef sauce with tomatoes and the classic sweet and sour seasonings—lemon juice, golden and dark raisins, brown sugar, and red wine vinegar. Then she put them together with rice and kept simmering.

SERVES 6

1 large head green cabbage

2 cups chicken stock

1 tablespoon olive oil

1 large onion, chopped

1 clove garlic, chopped

$1/2$ teaspoon salt, or to taste

$1/2$ teaspoon pepper, or to taste

2 pounds lean ground beef

Juice of 1 lemon

$1/4$ cup golden raisins

$1/4$ cup dark raisins

3 tablespoons dark brown
   sugar

1 tablespoon red wine vinegar

1 can (16 ounces) tomato sauce

1 can (28 ounces) whole
   tomatoes, crushed in a bowl

$1/2$ teaspoon ground allspice

$1/2$ teaspoon ground cinnamon

$1/4$ teaspoon fresh ground
   nutmeg

$1/2$ cup uncooked white rice

1. Core the cabbage, quarter it, and chop it coarsely. **2.** In a large flame-proof casserole, bring the chicken stock to a boil. Add the cabbage, lower the heat, and partially cover the pan. Simmer for 30 minutes or until cabbage is tender when pierced with a fork. **3.** Meanwhile, in a large deep skillet, heat the olive oil. Add the onion, garlic, salt, and pepper. Cook, stirring often, for 5 minutes. Add the beef to the pan, breaking it up as you stir it in. Cook, stirring often, until the meat is browned. **4.** Add the lemon juice, golden and dark raisins, sugar, vinegar, tomato sauce, tomatoes, allspice, cinnamon, and nutmeg. Bring to a boil, lower the heat, and simmer for 20 minutes. **5.** Stir the meat mixture and rice into the cabbage. Return to a boil, lower the heat, and cover the pan. Simmer for 30 minutes, stirring once or twice, or until the rice is cooked through. (Total simmering time is 50 minutes.) Taste for seasoning and add more salt and pepper, if you like.

Rachel Travers

Gingery Baby Bok Choy

Baby bok choy are the new darlings in the produce department. They're fist-sized and, because they're a little deli-cate, often come packaged together or tied with rubber bands. Here, the little heads are halved lengthwise, stir-fried in a hot pan with garlic and ginger, then finished by steaming in the same pan.

SERVES 4

8 heads baby bok choy

1 tablespoon peanut or canola oil

2 slices fresh ginger, cut into thin matchsticks

2 cloves garlic, thinly sliced

Salt and pepper, to taste

1/2 cup water, or more if necessary

1 tablespoon soy sauce

1. Halve the heads of bok choy lengthwise. **2.** In a wok or medium skil-let, heat the oil over medium-high heat until very hot. Add the ginger and garlic, and stir-fry for 20 seconds. **3.** Add the bok choy and salt. Stir-fry for 1 minute. **4.** Pour in the water, bring to a boil, and cover the pan with a lid. Let the vegetables steam for 2 minutes. Remove the lid and continue to cook for 1 minute or until the water evaporates. **5.** Add the soy sauce and cook for 30 seconds more. Sprinkle with pepper.

Debra Samuels

Broiled Onion Wedges

Onions are a pantry staple but are overlooked as a vegetable dish (except at Thanksgiving, when many cooks prepare creamed baby onions). Here, large wedges of onion are broiled until the edges char, then roasted until the onions release their liquid and turn deliciously sweet.

SERVES 4

3 Spanish onions, each cut into 8 wedges

Olive oil (for sprinkling)

Salt and pepper, to taste

1. Turn on the broiler. Adjust a rack so it's 10 inches from the broil-ing element. Have on hand a 9-inch baking dish. **2.** Pack the onion wedges into the dish—it's okay if they're very tight—so all the cut sides are up. Sprinkle sparingly with olive oil, salt, and pepper. **3.** Slide the dish under the broiler and cook the onions, turning the dish several times, for 5 minutes or until the edges are lightly charred. **4.** Loosely cover the dish with foil. Turn the oven temperature down to 400°F. **5.** Continue cooking the onions for 25 minutes or until they are ten-der when pierced with a skewer.

Sheryl Julian

Sauteed Swiss Chard

Leafy greens are cheap, filling, and good for you. Is there a better reason to eat them? They're unwieldy because the leaves are large, so cut them several times to make them smaller, then saute with garlic and sprinkle with crushed red pepper. To rid the leaves of their sand, soak them in several changes of cold water.

SERVES 4

1 bunch green or rainbow Swiss chard
2 tablespoons olive oil
1 clove garlic, crushed
Salt and black pepper, to taste
Generous pinch crushed red pepper

1. Discard the stems from the Swiss chard. Rinse the leaves in several changes of cold water. Shake them dry. **2.** With a large chef's knife, cut the leaves two or three times to make the pieces more manageable. They should still be quite large. **3.** In a large deep skillet, heat the olive oil. When it is hot, add the garlic and cook, stirring constantly, for 2 minutes. Add the Swiss chard, salt, and black pepper. Cook, stirring constantly, for 2 minutes or until they are coated all over with oil. **4.** Cover with the lid and cook for 2 minutes more. The leaves are done when they're tender when pierced with the tip of a knife. Sprinkle with red pepper.

Sheryl Julian

Open-Faced Fiddlehead Sandwiches

The locals in Maine who pick fiddleheads in the spring eat them with plenty of butter on toast.

SERVES 4

1 pound fresh fiddleheads
Salt and pepper, to taste
½ cup (1 stick) butter
1 tablespoon water
4 thick slices white bread, toasted

1. Submerge the fiddleheads in a bowl of cold water. Use your fingers to rub off the papery brown skins. Cut off the stalk just below the coiled tip. **2.** Bring a large saucepan of salted water to a boil. Drop in the fiddleheads and cook for 5 minutes. Drain into a colander and transfer to paper towels to dry. **3.** Set the saucepan over medium heat. Melt the butter. Add the water and cook for 1 minute more. Add the fiddleheads with plenty of salt and pepper. Stir well. **4.** Spoon the fiddleheads over the toast.

Jonathan Levitt

Tomatoes Provençal

When tomatoes are plentiful, this is a fine summer vegetable dish, but you can also make it with large hothouse tomatoes any other time of year. Roasting intensifies their flavor.

SERVES 6

6 large tomatoes, cored and
   halved horizontally

Olive oil (for sprinkling)

Salt and pepper, to taste

2 tablespoons chopped
   mixed herbs (basil, oregano,
   parsley)

1. Set the oven at 400°F. **2.** On a large rimmed baking sheet, arrange the tomatoes cut sides up. Sprinkle with oil, salt, and pepper. **3.** Roast the tomatoes for 30 minutes or until they are very tender but not collapsed. **4.** Sprinkle with the herbs and serve at once.

Sheryl Julian

Succotash

Native Americans introduced colonists to New World crops like corn and beans. These complimentary crops were combined and called succotash (from the Narragansett word for whole boiled corn). In the summer, succotash was made from fresh sweet corn and shell beans (particularly cranberry beans) or tender string beans. In the winter the same dish was cooked with dried corn and dried beans. These days New Englanders make succotash with frozen corn and frozen lima beans, whatever the season. Nothing wrong with that, but the corn and green bean version is a winning combination.

SERVES 4

4 ears fresh corn, kernels
   removed (save cobs)

4 tablespoons butter

Salt and pepper, to taste

$1/2$ pound small green beans,
   trimmed and cut into thirds

1. With the back of a knife, scrape the corn milk off the cobs into a bowl. **2.** In a large skillet, melt the butter over medium heat. Add the corn kernels, corn milk, salt, and pepper. Stir well. Cook, stirring often, for 5 minutes. **3.** Add the green beans and cook, stirring often, for 5 minutes or until the beans turn bright green. Taste for seasoning and add more salt and pepper, if you like.

Jonathan Levitt

Succotash

Creamy Mashed Potatoes

Old-fashioned buttery, creamy mashed potatoes are as much a part of the American table as the roast chickens, pork chops, and turkeys the dish accompanies.

SERVES 4

2 pounds Yukon Gold, Yellow Finn, or other yellow-fleshed potatoes, unpeeled, quartered, and scrubbed

Salt and pepper, to taste

1/2 cup (1 stick) unsalted butter

1/2 cup heavy cream

1. In a large pot, combine the potatoes with water to cover them by a couple of inches and plenty of salt. Bring the water to a boil over high heat. Lower the heat and simmer the potatoes for 15 to 20 minutes or until tender. **2.** In a medium saucepan, combine butter and cream. Heat gently until the butter melts; keep warm. **3.** Drain the potatoes into a colander. Set a food mill or ricer over the cooking pot off the heat. If your ricer does not discard the skins, use tongs to pull off the potato skins. While the potatoes are still hot, work them through the mill or ricer. **4.** Stirring with a wooden spoon over low heat, slowly work in the cream mixture. When it has been absorbed by the potatoes, add more salt and some pepper.

Jonathan Levitt

Garlic-Smashed Potatoes

Not quite mashed, these potatoes are chunky and garlicky, ideal as a side dish for roast leg of lamb or pork loin.

SERVES 4

1 3/4 pounds small red potatoes, cut in half (or large red potatoes cut into 1-inch pieces)

2 cloves garlic, smashed with the side of a knife

1 teaspoon kosher salt, and more to taste

1/2 cup sour cream

1/2 cup freshly grated Parmesan

2 tablespoons unsalted butter, cut up

1/2 teaspoon pepper, and more to taste

1. In a medium saucepan, combine the potatoes, garlic, salt, and water to cover by a couple of inches. Bring to a boil, lower the heat, cover, and simmer for 10 minutes or until the potatoes are tender when pierced with a fork. **2.** Drain the potatoes into a colander. Return them to the saucepan. Add the sour cream, Parmesan, butter, and pepper. **3.** Using a potato masher or whisk, smash the potatoes. Taste for seasoning and add more salt and pepper, if you like.

Tony Rosenfeld

Make-Ahead Mashed Potatoes

You won't know what you did on Thanksgiving before you tried this recipe. The potatoes are simmered in a combination of milk and water, drained, mashed, and set aside with a thin layer of hot milk on top. They're fine for several hours. Before serving, reheat the potatoes over low heat, and they come back to life.

SERVES 10

8 medium potatoes (a mixture of Idaho or russet and Yellow Finn or Yukon Gold), peeled

Salt and pepper, to taste

2 cups milk (1 or 2 percent)

1 quart whole milk, heated to scalding

4 tablespoons butter, or to taste

1. Cut the potatoes into 2-inch pieces. In a large flameproof casserole, combine the potatoes with water to cover them by 1-inch. Add plenty of salt and the 2 cups of 1 or 2 percent milk. Bring to a boil, lower the heat, cover the pan, and simmer the potatoes for 15 minutes or until they are tender. Drain them into a colander. **2.** Return the potatoes to the pan and add 1 cup of the whole milk with 2 tablespoons of the butter, and plenty of pepper. With a potato masher, mash the potatoes until they are smooth. **3.** Add ½ cup more milk and the remaining butter. Continue mashing until the potatoes are fluffy. (You can add even more butter, if you like.) Add ½ cup more milk, if necessary. The potatoes should be the consistency you like. Taste for seasoning and add more salt and pepper if necessary. **4.** Use a plastic spatula to scrape down the sides of the pan. Smooth the top. Pour enough of the remaining milk on top of the potatoes to make a thin layer that covers them completely. **5.** Cover the pan with the lid and set the potatoes aside for several hours. **6.** Just before serving, set the pan over medium heat and reheat the potatoes, stirring constantly, until they are hot and fluffy. Transfer to a warm bowl.

Sheryl Julian

Roasted Potato Wedges

Crisp on the outside, tender inside, these chubby potato wedges are simmered in water first, then roasted until golden brown.

SERVES 4

8 medium Yukon Gold or
  Yellow Finn potatoes,
  scrubbed and cut into
  quarters

Salt and pepper, to taste

2 tablespoons olive oil

8 sprigs of fresh thyme, leaves
  removed from stems

1. In a large pot, combine the potatoes with water to cover them by a couple of inches and plenty of salt. Bring the water to a boil over high heat. Lower the heat and simmer the potatoes for 15 to 20 minutes or until tender. **2.** Set the oven at 400°F. **3.** Pour the olive oil into a large, heavy roasting pan. Transfer to the oven and heat the oil for 5 minutes or until it is hot. **4.** Using tongs, carefully set the potatoes in the hot oil. Roll them around so that they are completely coated in oil. **5.** Roast the potatoes for 1 hour or until crisp and golden brown. Shake the potatoes every 20 minutes to keep them from sticking. After 30 minutes in the oven, toss the potatoes with the thyme, and more salt and some pepper.

Jonathan Levitt

Scalloped Potatoes

Irresistibly creamy and cheesy, this golden dish of potatoes can accompany a Sunday roast beef or classic leg of lamb on the bone.

SERVES 6

Butter (for dish)

3 cups whole milk

2 cups water

Salt and pepper, to taste

4 large russet potatoes (such
  as Idaho), peeled and left in
  bowl of cold water

¼ pound cheddar, grated

1. Set the oven at 375°F. Generously butter a 12-inch baking dish. **2.** In a large saucepan that will hold all the potatoes, combine 2 cups of the milk with the water and a pinch of salt. **3.** Using a chef's knife or a handheld slicing machine, cut the potatoes thinly and transfer them to the milk-water mixture. Bring to a boil, then lower the heat and cook the potatoes for 5 minutes or until they are no longer raw but not yet cooked through. (Take care that the potatoes don't overcook and break up.) **4.** With a slotted spoon, transfer half the potatoes to the baking dish. (Save 1 cup of the potato cooking water.) Sprinkle with the cheese, ½ cup of the remaining milk, salt, and pepper. **5.** Make another layer of potatoes. Add the reserved potato cooking water, the remaining ½ cup milk, salt, and pepper. **6.** Bake the potatoes for 1 hour or until the top is golden brown and the potatoes are tender when pierced with a skewer.

Sheryl Julian

Roasted Potato Latke

Latke is the traditional Jewish potato pancake served at Hanukkah. Instead of cooking potato pancakes individually, this method makes one large latke in the oven. Oven roasting, of course, means no stovetop mess. Don't skimp on the oil or the potatoes will stick to the pan. You'll need a professional-grade, aluminized-steel sheet pan that measures 12 x 17 inches, with 1-inch-high sides (www.chefscatalog.com or www.williams-sonoma.com).

MAKES 32 PIECES OR ENOUGH TO SERVE 10

4 large (about 2½ pounds) baking or russet potatoes

1 medium onion, halved

4 eggs, lightly beaten

2½ teaspoons kosher salt

½ teaspoon black pepper

¼ cup canola or vegetable oil

1. Set the oven at 475°F. **2.** Peel the potatoes and slice them in half lengthwise. In a food processor fitted with the grating disk, grate the potatoes and onions through the feed tube. Transfer the mixture to a colander. With your hands, squeeze the mixture to rid it of excess water. **3.** In a large bowl, combine the potato mixture, eggs, salt, and pepper. Mix well. **4.** Pour the oil into the pan and set it in the oven. Heat for 2 to 3 minutes or until the oil is very hot, but not smoking. **5.** With a potholder in each hand, remove the pan carefully from the oven and set it on a heatproof surface. Gently swirl the oil around the pan to fully coat the bottom and halfway up the sides. Set the pan down again. Quickly transfer the potato mixture to the pan—it will sizzle—spreading it with the back of a spoon to form an even layer. Immediately return the pan to the oven. **6.** Bake the latke for 25 to 30 minutes or until the bottom is golden brown. **7.** Turn on the broiler. Slide the pan so it is about 6 inches from the broiling element. Broil the cake for 5 to 8 minutes, watching it carefully, or until it is browned and crisp on top. If not serving immediately, turn the oven off and let the pancake sit for up to 10 minutes. Make 7 lengthwise cuts and 3 crosswise cuts to form 32 pieces. Use an off-set spatula to lift them out of the pan.

Lisa Zwirn

Baked Sweet Potatoes with Ginger

Save these—tender baked sweet potatoes with gingery soy sauce poured into the flesh—for a day when everyone's tired and in need of something nourishing and comforting.

SERVES 4

Sea salt, to taste

4 sweet potatoes

1 piece (4 inches) fresh ginger grated (with the juices)

2 tablespoons soy sauce

1 tablespoon olive oil

1. Set the oven at 350°F. Have on hand a cast-iron skillet or 10-inch baking dish. Sprinkle the bottom with a layer of sea salt. **2.** Prick the potatoes well all over. Set them on the sea salt. Roast the potatoes for 1 hour or until they are tender when pierced with a fork. **3.** Meanwhile, in a bowl, stir together the ginger, soy sauce, and olive oil. **4.** Cut a deep slit in the top of each potato. Set each one on a plate. Divide the ginger mixture among the potatoes.

Jane Levy Reed

Candied Sweet Potatoes

A classic Thanksgiving side dish, these candied sweet potatoes are glazed with orange juice, corn syrup, crushed pineapple, brown sugar, marmalade, and candied ginger. No marshmallows—but add them if you like and slip the finished dish, covered with marshmallows, under the broiler.

SERVES 12

6 large sweet potatoes, peeled

Salt, to taste

1 cup orange juice

½ cup dark corn syrup

1 can (8 ounces) crushed pineapple, drained

½ cup dark brown sugar

3 tablespoons ginger or orange marmalade

3 pieces candied ginger, finely chopped

1 tablespoon vegetable oil

1. Set the oven at 350°F. Have on hand a 14-inch baking dish. Peel the potatoes and cut them into eighths. **2.** In a large pot, combine the potatoes, water to cover them by 1 inch, and a generous pinch of salt. Bring to a boil and simmer for 15 minutes or until the potatoes are almost tender (they will not be cooked through). **3.** With a slotted spoon, transfer the potatoes to the baking dish. **4.** In a bowl combine the orange juice, corn syrup, pineapple, brown sugar, marmalade, candied ginger, oil, and salt. Pour the mixture over the sweet potatoes. **5.** Cover with foil and bake for 30 minutes. Remove the foil, baste the potatoes with the cooking juices, and return the potatoes to the oven without foil. **6.** Continue baking for 1 hour, basting occasionally, or until the potatoes are tender and caramelized at the edges. (Total cooking time is 1½ hours.)

Gertrude Cherenson

Mashed Sweet Potatoes

Roast these potatoes first, then mash them with butter, aromatic spices, and maple syrup.

SERVES 6

3 large sweet potatoes, peeled
    and cut into 3-inch pieces
4 tablespoons butter, cut up
1 teaspoon ground nutmeg
½ teaspoon ground cinnamon
2 tablespoons maple syrup
Salt and pepper, to taste

1. Set the oven at 350°F. **2.** In a roasting pan, place the sweet potatoes in one layer. Sprinkle them with the butter, nutmeg, cinnamon, maple syrup, salt, and pepper. **3.** Cover with foil and bake the sweet potatoes for 30 to 40 minutes or until they are tender. **4.** In a large bowl with a potato masher, mash the sweet potatoes until they are pureed but not overworked. Taste for seasoning and add more salt and pepper if you like.

Dorset Inn, Dorset, Vermont

Cranberry Chutney

Sweet, vinegary, gingery cranberries are simmered here until they form a savory chutney to accompany all kinds of poultry. It's also ideal for Thanksgiving.

SERVES 8

3¾ cups (12 ounces) fresh
    cranberries, picked over
1 cup dried cranberries
1 cup golden raisins
1 navel orange, peeled, coarsely
    chopped, and seeded
1 medium onion, coarsely
    chopped
8 ounces dried apricots,
    coarsely chopped
⅓ cup crystallized ginger,
    coarsely chopped
1½ cups light brown sugar
1 cup orange juice
½ cup cider vinegar
2 tablespoons fresh thyme
1 teaspoon salt

1. In a large saucepan, combine the fresh and dried cranberries, raisins, orange, onion, apricots, ginger, sugar, orange juice, vinegar, thyme, and salt. Cook over medium-low heat, stirring, for 3 to 4 minutes or until sugar dissolves. **2.** Turn the heat to medium-high. Let the mixture come to a boil. Cook until the fresh cranberries pop. Turn the heat to low. Continue cooking, stirring occasionally, for 30 to 40 minutes or until the chutney thickens. **3.** Remove the saucepan from the heat and let the chutney cool, stirring several times. Refrigerate in covered containers for up to 4 weeks.

Carol Wasik

Cranberry-Orange Chutney

Deborah Taylor of Deborah's Kitchen, a Massachusetts company that makes spreadable fruits and chutneys, prepares this chunky orangey cranberry chutney. Substitute dates for raisins, if you like, or add ½ cup chopped walnuts to the finished mixture.

SERVES 8

1 medium navel orange

½ red onion, chopped

1 tablespoon finely chopped
   fresh ginger

3¾ cups (12 ounces) fresh
   cranberries, picked over

½ cup apple cider vinegar

½ cup packed light brown
   sugar

½ cup raisins

¼ teaspoon cumin

¼ teaspoon salt

⅛ teaspoon crushed red
   pepper

1. Scrub the orange. Cut it into 8 wedges and place the wedges in a food processor. Work the machine in on-off motions until the orange flesh and rind are chopped. **2.** Add the onion and ginger and pulse again a few times until the mixture is finely chopped. **3.** In a large saucepan, combine the orange mixture, cranberries, vinegar, sugar, and raisins. Stir in the cumin, salt, and red pepper. Bring the mixture to a boil, lower the heat to medium, and simmer gently, stirring occasionally, for 25 minutes or until the chutney is thick and dark. **4.** Let the mixture cool to room temperature. Refrigerate in a covered container for up to 10 days or freeze for 1 month.

Deborah Taylor

Breakfast and Brunch:
Eggs, Muffins, Pancakes, and Quick Breads

Even as busy as families are, everyone seems to take time once in a while to enjoy a big weekend breakfast or brunch together. It's an ideal way to entertain informally, and it suits ski or beach weekends, visits from grandparents, holiday guests, or groups of old friends who meet up at someone's house every year.

If you're eating later than usual, breakfast or brunch options multiply. A noon meal is usually more substantial than an early morning meal. To consider all the possibilities, we offer many familiar egg dishes here, several pies (some with crust and some without), a Spanish tortilla, an Italian frittata, granola, blueberry muffins, doughnut muffins (the cinnamon-sugar coating is just like doughnuts), banana-walnut bread, tangy lemon curd for toast, and other satisfying dishes.

While most of these recipes seem like daytime fare, they shouldn't be limited to that. Blueberry pancakes are great when the sun is shining, but they're also welcome as a weeknight supper (just add a bowl of fruit and some yogurt to make a nutritious meal). Scrambled egg and potato burritos, another good breakfast or brunch choice, can also be served as an end-of-day dish.

For some people, comfort food means curling up in a chair with a big bowl of mac and cheese. For others, it means a long, lazy morning with fresh eggs, a sweet treat, and a big pot of coffee. If you're in the second category, the choices are endless. Consider yourself comforted.

Soft-Cooked Eggs

The only perfect eggs—tender whites and soft yolks—are made at home.

SERVES 4

4 eggs

Salt and pepper, to taste

1. Bring a large saucepan of water to a boil. **2.** With a slotted spoon, lower the eggs into the water. Use the handle of the spoon to stir the eggs in the water in a circular motion until the water returns to a boil. **3.** Let the water bubble gently for 3 minutes exactly. Transfer the eggs to egg cups and serve with salt and pepper.

Sheryl Julian

Hard-Cooked Eggs

Stir the water as the eggs come to a boil, so the yolks set in the center of the whites (this helps when you're making deviled eggs). The important part is to get the eggs quickly from the boiling water to very cold water. Immediately remove a wide band of shell from each one. The whites shrink a little to make peeling easier and prevent a green line from forming around the yolks.

SERVES 4

4 eggs

Salt and pepper, to taste

1. Bring a large saucepan of water to a boil. **2.** With a slotted spoon, lower the eggs into the water. Use the handle of the spoon to stir the eggs in the water in a circular motion until the water returns to a boil. **3.** Let the water bubble gently for 9 minutes exactly. Have on hand a large bowl of cold water. Transfer the eggs to the water. Use the back of a spoon to tap the shell to crack it. Remove a strip of shell and return the egg to the cold water. Do the same with the remaining eggs. When they are cold, remove the remaining shell. **4.** Serve with salt and pepper.

Sheryl Julian

Whole Soft-Cooked Eggs

Similar to poached eggs, but slightly more cooked (both whites and yolks are firmer), these whole soft-cooked eggs are called oeufs mollets *in French. They're simpler than poached eggs, so we use them whenever a poached egg is called for. Use this technique to make a nourishing supper if you're not feeling well: Set one of these peeled eggs in a bowl of hot chicken broth, sprinkle it with cheese and parsley, then break into the egg. The yolk will flow into the soup and thicken it.*

SERVES 4

4 eggs

Salt and pepper, to taste

1. Bring a large saucepan of water to a boil. **2.** With a slotted spoon, lower the eggs into the water. Use the handle of the spoon to stir the eggs in the water in a circular motion until the water returns to a boil. **3.** Let the water bubble gently for 5 minutes exactly. Have on hand a large bowl of cold water. Transfer the eggs to the water. Use the back of a spoon to tap the shell to crack it. Do this very carefully since the whites are delicate. Do the same with the remaining eggs. Then remove the remaining shell. Serve with salt and pepper.

Sheryl Julian

Breakfast Pie

You don't have to make a crust for this pie. Layer cubes of potato, onions, ham, cheese, and eggs in a deep pie pan, bake it until just set, and cut into wedges.

SERVES 6

Butter (for the dish)

2 Yukon Gold potatoes, peeled and cut into 1/2-inch cubes

Salt and pepper, to taste

2 tablespoons butter

1 Spanish onion, coarsely chopped

2 thick slices (1/2 pound) Black Forest or other flavorful ham, cut into 1/2-inch cubes

4 eggs

1 cup whole milk

1/4 teaspoon ground nutmeg

1 cup grated Gruyère cheese

1. Set the oven at 350°F. Lightly butter a deep 9-inch glass or ceramic pie pan. **2.** In a saucepan, combine the potatoes with salted water to cover them. Bring to a boil, lower the heat, and simmer the potatoes for 10 minutes or until they are tender. Drain them, shaking them to remove the excess moisture; set them aside. **3.** In a skillet, melt the butter. Add the onion, salt, and pepper. Cook over medium heat, stirring often, for 10 minutes or until the onion softens. Transfer the onion to the pie pan. Add the potatoes and ham. **4.** In a bowl, beat the eggs, milk, nutmeg, salt, and pepper. Pour the egg mixture into the pie pan. Sprinkle with Gruyère. **5.** Set the pie pan on a rimmed baking sheet. Bake the pie for 30 to 35 minutes or until it is just set and browning at the edges. Remove from the oven and set aside for 10 minutes to cool slightly. Cut into wedges to serve.

Sheryl Julian

Potato Tortilla

A simple pie of potatoes and eggs, called tortilla *in Spain, is served in most tapas bars. Recipes usually call for cooking the potatoes in oil before combining them with eggs. This healthier version uses steamed yellow potatoes; peel them or leave the skins on.*

SERVES 4

1 tablespoon olive oil

3 large Yukon Gold or Yellow
   Finn potatoes

Salt and pepper, to taste

6 eggs, lightly beaten

1. Set the oven at 375°F. Pour the oil into a deep 9-inch pie pan. Swirl it around so it covers the bottom and sides. **2.** Fit a large saucepan with a steamer insert and enough water to come up to the level of the steamer. Bring the water to a boil. **3.** Slice the potatoes ¼ inch thick. Set them in the steamer, cover the pan, and steam over high heat for 10 minutes or until the potatoes are tender when pierced with the tip of a knife. **4.** Arrange the potatoes in the pie pan, sprinkling the layers with salt and pepper. Let them cool for 5 minutes. **5.** Stir some salt and pepper into the egg mixture. Pour the eggs over the potatoes. Use the back of a spoon to press the potatoes into the eggs. **6.** Bake the tortilla for 35 minutes or until the eggs are set in the middle and the top is brown. If the eggs set before the top browns, slip the dish under the broiler for 30 seconds (watch it carefully) just until the top browns. Let the tortilla sit for 5 minutes.

Sheryl Julian

Ricotta Frittata

Begin by sauteing onion, zucchini, and summer squash in oil, then adding ricotta cheese, lots of fresh herbs, and eggs. The mixture bakes into a firm egg pie.

SERVES 6

2 tablespoons olive oil

1 tablespoon butter

1 onion, thinly sliced

1 zucchini, thickly sliced

1 summer squash, thickly sliced

Several sprigs each fresh
 parsley, sage, rosemary,
 and thyme (2 tablespoons
 chopped)

1½ cups fresh ricotta cheese

½ cup freshly grated Parmesan

1 teaspoon salt

½ teaspoon pepper

4 eggs

½ cup shredded cheddar

1. Set the oven at 350°F. Have on hand a deep 9-inch pie pan. **2.** In a large skillet over medium heat, heat the oil. When it is hot, add the butter. Add the onion and cook for 8 minutes or until softened. Add the zucchini and squash and cook for 5 minutes more or until the vegetables are just tender. Sprinkle with 1 tablespoon of the herbs; toss gently. Transfer to the pie pan. **3.** In a bowl with a fork, beat the ricotta, Parmesan, salt, and pepper until smooth. Add the eggs one by one, the remaining 1 tablespoon herbs, and the cheddar. Pour the mixture onto the vegetables. **4.** Bake the frittata for 40 minutes or until the mixture is set in the middle.

Debra Samuels

Quiche Lorraine

France's classic quiche Lorraine, made with Gruyère cheese and bacon, has been popular on brunch and lunch tables for decades. Make your own pastry shell (see page 299) or use a ready-made crust. Prebake it before you fill it.

SERVES 6

3 thick slices bacon

2 tablespoons butter

1 medium onion, chopped

1 pastry shell (8½ to 9 inches), baked blind for 12 to 15 minutes (see below)

1 cup grated Gruyère cheese

3 eggs

1 cup whole milk

Salt and pepper, to taste

1. Set the oven at 375°F. **2.** In a skillet, render the bacon, turning often, for 5 minutes or until it is golden brown. Transfer to paper towels to drain. When it is cool, crumble the bacon. **3.** Spoon off the fat from the skillet. Add the butter and cook the onion, stirring often, for 8 minutes or until softened. Transfer to the pastry shell. Scatter the bacon and cheese on top. **4.** In a bowl, beat the eggs, milk, salt, and pepper. Pour the egg mixture into the shell. Set the pie pan on a rimmed baking sheet. Bake the quiche for 30 minutes or until it is just set and browning at the edges.

Sheryl Julian

Baking pastry without a filling

In general, if you're adding a liquid filling to a pie shell, it's a good idea to bake it partially first, a technique called "baking blind." Prick the dough well all over, line it with a piece of foil, pressing it down firmly onto the crust, then fill it with dried beans. Bake the shell at 375 degrees for 15 minutes. Lift out the foil and beans and continue baking for 5 minutes. The shell is now ready to be baked again with the filling. If you want a fully cooked crust, after removing the beans, continue baking for 15 minutes or until the bottom of the crust is lightly golden all over.

Leek and Goat Cheese Quiche

If you buy a pastry shell, follow the manufacturer's instructions for baking it "blind," that is, without a filling (see page 113).

SERVES 6

2 tablespoons butter

2 leeks (white and light green parts) thinly sliced and well rinsed

Salt and pepper, to taste

1 pastry shell (8½ to 9 inches), prebaked

½ round or log (2½ to 3 ounces) fresh creamy goat cheese

3 eggs

½ cup light cream

1. Set the oven at 375°F. **2.** In a large skillet over medium heat, melt the butter. Add the leeks, salt, and pepper. Cook, stirring often, for 8 minutes, until they soften. **3.** Spoon them into the prebaked pie shell. Dot with the goat cheese. **4.** In a small bowl, whisk together the eggs, cream, salt, and pepper. Pour the mixture into the shell. **5.** Set the pie pan on a rimmed baking sheet. Bake the quiche for 30 minutes or until it is just set and browning at the edges.

Jennifer Wolcott

Western Omelet

A diner favorite for breakfast or lunch, a Western omelet is traditionally made with onions, bell pepper, and ham, but you can use any other leftover bits such as steak.

SERVES 4

4 tablespoons butter

1 onion, chopped

½ green bell pepper, seeded and chopped

8 eggs

3 tablespoons milk

½ teaspoon salt

Pepper, to taste

½ pound thickly sliced ham, coarsely chopped

1. Heat a 12-inch nonstick skillet. Add 1 tablespoon of the butter. Cook the onion and green pepper over medium heat, stirring often, for 8 minutes or until tender. Transfer the mixture to a bowl. **2.** In another bowl, beat the eggs, milk, salt, and pepper. **3.** Add the remaining 3 tablespoons butter to the skillet. Pour in the egg mixture. Add the onion mixture and ham. With a heatproof rubber spatula, pull the cooked edges of the egg into the center, then tip the skillet so the runny egg fills the spots along the edges, until the egg is cooked all over. **4.** Holding onto the skillet by the handle, tip the handle up, and use the spatula to fold the edge closest to the handle over to make a half-moon shape. **5.** Cut the omelet in the pan into four pieces.

Leek and Goat Cheese Quiche

Luchen Kugel

Many Jewish families make this traditional Eastern European noodle pudding for the holiday table. There are many versions. This one contains cottage cheese, sour cream, apricot preserves, and golden raisins, and is ideal for brunch.

SERVES 14

Butter (for the dish)

Salt, to taste

1/2 pound wide noodles

4 eggs

1 container (8 ounces) cottage cheese

1 container (8 ounces) sour cream

1/4 cup (1/2 stick) butter, melted and cooled slightly

1 1/4 cups whole milk

1/4 cup granulated sugar

1/2 teaspoon vanilla extract

1/2 teaspoon salt

3/4 cup apricot preserves

3/4 cup golden raisins

1/4 teaspoon ground cinnamon mixed with 1 1/2 tablespoons granulated sugar

1. Set the oven at 350°F. Lightly butter a 9 x 13-inch baking dish. **2.** Bring a large pot of salted water to a boil. Add the noodles and cook for 8 minutes or until the noodles are tender but still have some bite. Drain them into a colander. **3.** In a large bowl, whisk 2 of the eggs. Whisk in the cottage cheese, sour cream, butter, 1/4 cup of the milk, sugar, vanilla, and a generous pinch of salt. **4.** Gently stir in the apricot preserves, raisins, and noodles. Transfer the mixture to the baking dish. **5.** In a medium bowl, whisk together the remaining 2 eggs and 1 cup of milk. Pour this evenly over the noodle mixture. Sprinkle the cinnamon-sugar mixture on top. **6.** Bake for 45 to 50 minutes or until a thin knife inserted into the center comes out clean. Leave to settle for 5 minutes, then cut into squares.

Sandy Bass

Luchen Kugel

Scrambled Egg and Potato Burritos

Wrapped with scrambled eggs, Monterey Jack, avocado, homemade salsa, and a dash of hot sauce, these breakfast burritos are a satisfying, vaguely Southwestern take on egg sandwiches. Use last night's leftover roasted potatoes (if you need to cook some, simmer them in boiling salted water for 15 minutes or until tender) and pile them on the rounds. Then roll up.

SERVES 4

SALSA

4 serrano chilies, stemmed,
   seeded, and very finely
   chopped

6 tablespoons lime juice

¼ cup chopped fresh cilantro

2 tablespoons vegetable oil

½ teaspoon ground cumin

2 tomatoes, cored and finely
   chopped

Salt, to taste

BURRITOS AND FILLING

8 eggs, lightly beaten

Salt and pepper, to taste

3 tablespoons butter

4 (10-inch) flour tortillas

1 cup grated Monterey Jack

8 medium cooked potatoes,
   coarsely chopped

2 avocados, pitted, peeled, and
   chopped

Hot sauce, to taste

SALSA

In a medium bowl combine the chilies, lime juice, cilantro, oil, cumin, and tomatoes. Season with salt.

BURRITOS AND FILLING

1. Set the oven at 350°F. Have a rimmed baking sheet on hand. **2.** Beat the eggs with salt and pepper. In a skillet, melt the butter and scramble the eggs into soft curds. **3.** Lay 1 tortilla on the counter. In a mound from the top to the bottom of the tortilla, layer ¼ of the cheese, ¼ of the salsa, ¼ of the eggs, ¼ of the potatoes, and ¼ of the avocados. Add a couple of shots of hot sauce. **4.** Fold the top and bottom edges of the tortilla over the filling. Roll up the tortilla, completely encasing the filling. Wrap in foil and set on the baking sheet. Repeat the layering and folding with the remaining tortillas and filling. **5.** Heat the burritos for 20 minutes or until they are warm.

Jonathan Levitt

Brazilian Breakfast

When Sandra Silva, a native of São Paulo, Brazil, has a crowd for brunch at her home near Boston, Massachusetts, she serves a dish she calls Cafe Brasil. Instead of making eggs individually, she has perfected this dish, which can be prepared for four people at once. It begins with cheese-topped toasts, which she covers with meringue, then slips an egg yolk into each mound of white, and bakes it just until firm.

SERVES 4

Butter (for toast)

4 thick slices French bread, toasted

4 slices cheddar cheese

4 eggs, separated

8 slices of bacon

Salt and pepper, to taste

1. Set the oven at 350°F. Butter each piece of toast. Set them on a rimmed baking sheet. Add a slice of cheese to each one. **2.** In an electric mixer, beat the egg whites until they hold stiff peaks. **3.** With a spoon, divide the whites among the toasts. Spread the meringue so it covers the cheese, keeping it mounded slightly higher in the center. Use the spoon to make an indentation in each meringue just deep enough to hold a yolk. Slip a yolk into each one. **4.** Bake the eggs for 12 minutes or until the meringue is lightly browned and the eggs set. Meanwhile, in a skillet, fry the bacon for 5 minutes or until crisp. Drain on paper towels and cut into small squares. **5.** Divide the bacon among 4 plates. Set an egg toast on each one. Sprinkle with salt and pepper.

Sandra Silva

Huevos Rancheros

Even though you have to fry the eggs at the last minute, huevos rancheros are worth the trouble. The combination of a smoky tomato sauce, black beans, Monterey Jack cheese, and eggs makes it a terrific and popular brunch dish. You can prepare the tomato sauce and beans in advance and reheat before serving.

SERVES 6

1 tablespoon olive oil

1 small onion, chopped

2 cloves garlic, finely chopped

1 can (28 ounces) crushed
   tomatoes

2 teaspoons chopped canned
   chipotle peppers in adobo
   sauce

4 tablespoons chopped fresh
   cilantro

Salt and black pepper, to taste

4 tablespoons canola oil, or
   more to taste

12 corn tortillas (5½ inches)

1 can (15 ounces) black beans,
   rinsed and drained

¼ teaspoon ground cumin

4 tablespoons water, or more
   to taste

2 tablespoons unsalted butter

12 eggs

⅔ cup shredded Monterey Jack

1. In a large nonstick skillet over medium heat, heat the olive oil. Add the onion and cook, stirring often, for about 8 minutes or until softened. Add the garlic and cook for 1 minute more. **2.** Stir in the tomatoes and chipotle. Simmer, stirring occasionally, for 10 minutes or until the sauce thickens slightly. Stir in 2 tablespoons of the cilantro with salt and black pepper. **3.** Set the oven at 300°F. Have on hand a rimmed baking sheet. **4.** In a large, heavy nonstick skillet, heat 2 teaspoons of the canola oil over medium-high heat. Add 2 tortillas and cook for 30 seconds or until they just start to brown. Turn and cook the other side. Transfer the tortillas to the baking sheet. Cover loosely with foil. Repeat with the remaining tortillas, adding a little oil to each batch. Set the tortillas in the oven. **5.** In a small skillet, heat the remaining 1 tablespoon of canola oil over medium heat. Add the beans and cumin. With a potato masher, coarsely mash the beans. Stir in enough water to moisten the mashed beans. Add salt and pepper. Keep warm over low heat, stirring occasionally. **6.** In the same skillet used for the tortillas, melt 1 tablespoon of butter over medium heat. Break 6 eggs into the skillet and fry until the whites are almost set. Using the edge of a spatula, separate the eggs and flip them, if you like, cooking the other side for about 1 minute more. Transfer the eggs to a large plate and cover loosely with foil to keep warm. Cook the remaining eggs in the remaining 1 tablespoon of butter. **7.** Serve each person 2 warm tortillas, 2 eggs, some tomato sauce on the eggs, a sprinkle of cheese, and cilantro. Garnish with the beans.

Lisa Zwirn

Egg Biscuits

Substitute ham or sausage patties for the bacon, if you like; cook them in 1 tablespoon of butter and also use 1 tablespoon of butter for the eggs.

SERVES 4

BISCUITS

2 cups flour

2 teaspoons baking powder

1 teaspoon salt

8 tablespoons chilled butter, cut in 8 pieces

³/₄ cup whole milk, or more if necessary

Flour (for sprinkling)

Extra milk (for brushing)

SANDWICHES

4 slices of bacon

8 eggs

¹/₄ cup milk

Salt and pepper, to taste

BISCUITS

1. Set oven at 425°F. Line a baking sheet with parchment paper. **2.** In a large bowl, combine the flour, baking powder, and salt. Add the butter and, with a pastry blender or two blunt forks, blend the butter into the flour mixture until it resembles coarse meal. **3.** Add the milk and stir with a knife or a fork until just combined. Add another tablespoon of milk, if necessary, so the dough comes together. **4.** Turn the dough out onto a floured surface and press the dough together to form a ball. Flatten it into a square about 1 inch thick. Cut into 4 equal pieces. Brush with the remaining milk. **5.** Bake for 15 to 20 minutes or until firm and golden brown.

SANDWICHES

1. In a large skillet over medium heat, render the bacon for about 5 minutes, turning often, or until crisp. Transfer to a plate lined with paper towels. **2.** In a bowl, whisk together the eggs, milk, salt, and pepper. **3.** Pour off all but 1 tablespoon of the fat from the skillet. Add the egg mixture and cook, stirring often, for 3 to 5 minutes, or until it is set. With the tip of a rubber spatula, roll the omelet up onto itself to form a thick oval. Cut it into 4 even pieces. **4.** Split each biscuit. Cut the bacon in half. Add 2 pieces of bacon and some egg to each one and close the tops.

Keri Fisher

Blueberry Muffins

Anyone who grew up in the Boston, Massachusetts, area in the 1950s remembers the famous—and delicious— Jordan Marsh blueberry muffins. They were offered in the old department store's bakery and you had to wait in line to buy them. Of course, we wonder if memory has improved their taste (were they really that good?) and if they would pass muster by today's standards. These berry-loaded muffins with their sugary tops will.

MAKES 12

Butter (for the pan)

2 cups flour

$\frac{1}{2}$ teaspoon salt

2 teaspoons baking powder

$\frac{1}{2}$ cup (1 stick) unsalted butter, at room temperature

$\frac{3}{4}$ cup granulated sugar

2 eggs

1 teaspoon vanilla extract

Grated rind of $\frac{1}{2}$ lemon

Juice of 1 lemon

$\frac{1}{2}$ cup milk

1 pint fresh blueberries, picked over for stems and leaves

Extra granulated sugar (for sprinkling)

1. Set the oven at 375°F. Grease a 12-cup muffin pan, including top surface. Have on hand a rimmed baking sheet. **2.** In a bowl, sift the flour, salt, and baking powder; set aside. **3.** In an electric mixer, cream the butter and sugar. Gradually add the eggs and mix until blended. Beat in the vanilla, lemon rind, and lemon juice. **4.** With the mixer set on its lowest speed, beat the flour mixture into the batter alternately with the milk. **5.** Remove the bowl from the mixer stand, and use a rubber spatula to fold in the berries. Divide the batter among the muffin cups and sprinkle the tops with sugar. **6.** Set the muffins on the baking sheet. Bake for 20 to 25 minutes or until they are golden, turning the pan halfway through baking. Leave to cool in the pan for a few minutes, then turn out onto a wire rack to cool completely.

Rebecca Dalzell

Blueberry Muffins

Banana-Walnut Breads

Moms who keep overripe bananas on the counter for days are always making banana bread to use them up. It's a simple solution, and kids who won't touch a ripe banana are never shy when the bread emerges from the oven. This is a good choice for weekday breakfast because the moist loaves keep well.

MAKES 2
Butter (for pans)
Flour (for pans)
1 cup light brown sugar
1 cup granulated sugar
3 cups flour
1½ teaspoons baking soda
1 teaspoon salt
1 teaspoon ground cinnamon
¼ teaspoon ground nutmeg
4 ripe bananas
3 eggs, lightly beaten
1 teaspoon vanilla extract
¼ cup buttermilk
Grated rind of 1 orange
½ cup (1 stick) butter, melted
½ cup canola oil
1 cup walnuts, toasted and
  coarsely chopped

1. Set the oven at 350°F. Have on hand two 8½ x 4½-inch loaf pans. Butter the pans and dust them with flour, tapping out the excess. **2.** In a large mixing bowl, break up the clumps of brown sugar with a wooden spoon. With a whisk, stir in the granulated sugar, flour, baking soda, salt, cinnamon, and nutmeg. **3.** In a medium mixing bowl, mash the bananas. With a wooden spoon, stir in the eggs, vanilla, buttermilk, orange rind, butter, and oil. **4.** Add the flour mixture to the egg mixture, stirring until just combined. Stir in the walnuts. **5.** Divide batter between the pans. Bake the cakes for 1 hour or until the tops are firm to the touch and a skewer inserted into the cakes comes out clean. **6.** Set the cakes on a wire rack to cool for 15 minutes. Then turn the cakes out of the pans and set them right side up to cool completely.

Emily Schwab

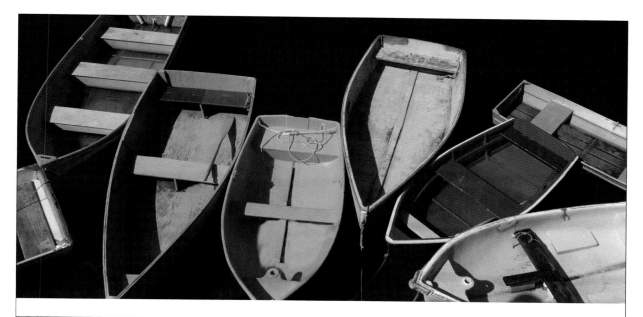

Doughnut Muffins

These are muffins, but their buttery cinnamon-sugar topping resembles doughnuts. At the Rockport, Maine, shop where they're made, they're wildly popular.

MAKES 12

BATTER

Butter (for the muffin tin)

2 cups flour

¹/₂ cup granulated sugar

1 tablespoon baking powder

¹/₂ teaspoon salt

1 egg

³/₄ cup vegetable oil

³/₄ cup buttermilk

¹/₄ cup sour cream

COATING

2 tablespoons butter

¹/₄ cup granulated sugar

¹/₂ teaspoon ground cinnamon

BATTER

1. Set the oven at 375°F. Butter a 12-cup muffin tin; set it aside. **2.** In a large bowl whisk the flour, sugar, baking powder, and salt just to blend them. **3.** In another bowl, whisk together the egg, oil, buttermilk, and sour cream. Add the buttermilk mixture to the flour mixture. With a wooden spoon, stir until the mixture is combined. **4.** Divide the batter among the muffin cups. **5.** Bake the muffins for 20 minutes or until they are firm and golden. Let the muffins cool in the tin for 5 minutes.

COATING

1. In a small saucepan, melt the butter. **2.** In a large shallow bowl, combine the sugar and cinnamon. Stir well. **3.** While the muffins are still hot, turn them out of the tin and set them on a large rimmed baking sheet. **4.** Brush each muffin with butter. Dip the muffins upside-down in the sugar mixture, then set them right side up on the baking sheet. Let them sit for 30 minutes.

The Market Basket, Rockport, Maine

Boston Brown Bread

The old-fashioned technique of making brown breads in coffee cans is no longer possible because the rims are fashioned so it's difficult to pull the breads out. But you need something that can withstand 2 hours in a kettle of boiling water. We like using a classic souffle dish because the sides are high.

MAKES ONE 8-INCH ROUND

Butter (for the dish and foil)

½ cup rye flour

½ cup yellow cornmeal

½ cup whole-wheat flour

1 teaspoon baking soda

½ teaspoon salt

¼ cup maple syrup

2 tablespoons molasses

1 cup buttermilk

½ cup currants

1. Butter a 6-cup souffle dish or other high-sided baking dish. Butter a sheet of foil slightly larger than the dish. **2.** Bring a large kettle of water to a boil. **3.** In a mixing bowl, stir together the rye flour, cornmeal, whole-wheat flour, baking soda, and salt. **4.** In another bowl, mix together the maple syrup, molasses, and buttermilk. Stir the maple mixture into the flour mixture until smooth. Fold in the currants. **5.** Transfer the batter to the baking dish. Cover with foil, buttered side down. **6.** Set the dish in the bottom of a soup pot. Pour the boiling water around it until the water comes about halfway up the sides of the dish. **7.** Bring the water back to a simmer over high heat. Lower the heat, cover the pot, and steam the bread for 2 hours or until a skewer inserted into the middle of the bread comes out clean. During simmering, check the water level and add more boiling water if necessary. **8.** Remove the lid and let the bread sit until the dish is cool enough to handle. Wipe the bottom of the dish, turn the bread out onto a board, and set it right side up. Cut into slices.

Jonathan Levitt

Dutch Babies

A cross between pancakes and popovers, Dutch babies are breakfast fare. The recipe came originally from Mary Lindeblad of Spokane, Washington, who serves them with fresh berries.

SERVES 4

2 tablespoons butter

4 eggs

1 cup whole milk

1 cup flour

½ teaspoon salt

Squeeze of lemon juice

Confectioners' sugar (for
    sprinkling)

1. Set the oven at 475°F. Have on hand four ramekins or custard cups (3½ inches by 1½ inches) or a 10-inch skillet with a heatproof handle. Divide the butter among the cups or put it all in the skillet. Set the ramekins on a baking sheet. Slide the sheet or skillet into the oven to melt the butter. **2.** In a blender, combine the eggs, milk, flour, and salt. Blend thoroughly. **3.** Carefully remove the ramekins or skillet from the oven. With a brush, butter the top edges of the ramekins or skillet. **4.** Pour the batter into the ramekins or skillet. Bake the ramekins for 8 to 10 minutes and the skillet for 10 to 12 minutes or until the batter is puffed and brown. **5.** Sprinkle with lemon juice and sugar.

Debra Samuels

Irish Pancakes

Brian Dixon, former pastor of the First Baptist Church in Lexington, Massachusetts, got this recipe for pancake mix from his Irish mother. This mix makes 5 cups. Use it in two batches (3 cups makes 23 pancakes; 2 cups makes 15 pancakes). Store the mix in a jar in the pantry.

MIX

3³/₄ cups flour

1 cup granulated sugar

2 tablespoons cream of tartar

1 tablespoon baking soda

1 tablespoon salt

PANCAKES

3 cups mix

3 eggs

1½ cups whole milk

About 2 tablespoons butter
(for frying)

MIX

In a large bowl, combine the flour, sugar, cream of tartar, baking soda, and salt. Blend well with a whisk.

PANCAKES

1. In a bowl, stir the mix with a whisk. **2.** In another bowl, combine the eggs and milk. Add the egg mixture to the dry mix, stirring until all the liquid is incorporated. **3.** Set the bowl aside for 30 minutes. **4.** Heat a griddle or nonstick skillet. Add about 2 teaspoons of butter. When it foams, use a ¼-cup measure to ladle batter into the pan. **5.** Let the pancakes cook until the undersides are golden and bubbles appear on the surface. Turn and brown the other side. Add more butter to the pan, if necessary. Serve with maple syrup or fresh fruit.

Note: To use 2 cups of mix to make pancakes, add 2 eggs and 1 cup milk to the dry mix. Follow the instructions above.

Amy Dixon

Cinnamon Buns

These are made with biscuit dough, which is rolled out, spread with a cinnamon-sugar mixture, rolled up, sliced, baked, and glazed.

MAKES 12

DOUGH

Butter (for the pan)

3 cups flour

1 teaspoon baking powder

1 teaspoon baking soda

1/4 teaspoon salt

2 tablespoons granulated sugar

6 tablespoons butter

1 cup buttermilk

FILLING

1/3 cup granulated sugar

1/3 cup brown sugar

2 teaspoons ground cinnamon

1/4 teaspoon ground cloves

4 tablespoons butter, melted

GLAZE

3/4 cup confectioners' sugar

2 tablespoons buttermilk

DOUGH

1. Set the oven at 400°F. Butter an 8- or 9-inch square pan. **2.** In a large bowl, whisk 2¾ cups of the flour, baking powder, baking soda, salt, and sugar. **3.** In a small saucepan, melt the butter. Add the buttermilk. With a fork, stir the liquids into the flour mixture until it forms a dough. **4.** Sprinkle counter with remaining ¼ cup flour. Turn dough out onto the counter and knead lightly until smooth. Roll the dough into a 7 x 12-inch rectangle, with the long side facing you.

FILLING

1. In a bowl, combine the granulated and brown sugars with the cinnamon and cloves. Mix well. **2.** Brush the dough with some of the butter. Spread the filling evenly over the dough, leaving a 1-inch plain border on one long side (the side farthest from you). Begin rolling up from the side closest to you, like a jelly roll. Cut the log in half. Cut each half in half again. Cut the pieces into thirds to make 12 coils. **3.** Transfer them to the baking pan, cut sides up, setting them in 4 even rows (3 in each). Brush with the remaining butter. **4.** Bake the rolls for 30 to 35 minutes or until they are golden and firm at the edges. Set the pan on a wire rack to cool slightly.

GLAZE

While rolls are baking, sift the confectioners' sugar into a bowl. Add the buttermilk and stir until the mixture forms a pourable glaze. Spoon the glaze onto the warm rolls and set them aside to cool completely.

From Far Land Provisions,
Provincetown, Massachusetts

Lemon Curd

Lemon Curd

Use unwaxed lemons for this bright yellow mixture since so much rind goes into the curd. Lemon curd is a rich spread for toast, though it can also fill a tart shell (in which case it needs softly whipped cream as well). To make a smooth curd, stir some of the hot lemon juice into the eggs to make the temperatures even. Otherwise you risk scrambling the eggs. It's also a good idea to start with the eggs at room temperature.

MAKES ABOUT 1¹/₂ CUPS

¹/₂ cup (1 stick) unsalted butter, cut up

Grated rind and juice of 3 large lemons (1 scant cup)

1 egg

3 egg yolks

Pinch of salt

Scant 1 cup sugar

1. Add enough water to the bottom of a double boiler to half fill it. Set it over low heat. In the top pot, let the butter melt very slowly. **2.** In a small bowl, combine the lemon rind and juice. Discard any seeds. **3.** In a medium bowl, whisk the egg and yolks. **4.** When the butter melts, add the rind and juice, salt, and sugar. Stir constantly over low heat for 3 minutes or until the sugar dissolves. Remove the pan from the heat. **5.** Remove about ¼ cup of the lemon mixture and whisk it quickly into the beaten eggs. **6.** Start whisking the remaining lemon mixture in the top of the double boiler. Whisk in the egg mixture in a thin, steady stream. Return the pan to medium heat. **7.** Cook the mixture, whisking constantly, for 10 minutes or until the curd thickens and turns glossy. Do not let the curd boil or it will curdle. It should be about the texture of honey and will thicken more as it cools. **8.** Remove the pan from the heat. Scrape the curd into a bowl, cover with plastic wrap, and leave to cool for 1 hour. **9.** Transfer to a jar, cover tightly, and refrigerate for up to 1 week.

Robin Shepard

Baked French Toast with Apple Compote

Made in layers in a baking dish, this French toast is served with an apple compote. Instead of apples, you can use Bartlett or Anjou pears. Prepare them the same way as the apples. The dish improves if made a day in advance and baked just before serving.

SERVES 6
FRENCH TOAST

Butter (for the dish)

3 cups whole milk

6 eggs, beaten to mix

4 tablespoons butter, melted
    and cooled

1/2 teaspoon vanilla extract

1 teaspoon salt

1/4 cup granulated sugar

1/4 cup brown sugar

1 teaspoon ground cinnamon

1/8 teaspoon ground nutmeg

12 slices white sandwich bread

COMPOTE

2 tablespoons butter

2 tablespoons brown sugar

1/2 teaspoon ground cinnamon

2 tablespoons maple syrup

4 baking apples (Baldwin,
    Golden Delicious, Ida
    Red, Northern Spy, Rome,
    Gravenstein), peeled, halved,
    cored, and coarsely chopped

FRENCH TOAST

1. Butter a 9 x 13-inch baking dish. **2.** In a bowl, whisk together the milk, eggs, butter, vanilla, and salt. **3.** In another small bowl, combine the granulated and brown sugars, cinnamon, and nutmeg. **4.** Using 6 slices of the bread, dip both sides into the egg mixture and arrange in a layer on the bottom of the baking dish (you will need to overlap them slightly to fit them in). Sprinkle with half of the sugar mixture. Dip the remaining 6 slices into the egg mixture and set them on the first layer. Pour any egg mixture in the bowl over the bread. With a wide metal spatula, press down firmly so the bread soaks up all of the liquid. **5.** Sprinkle with the remaining sugar mixture. Cover the dish with plastic wrap and refrigerate for at least 30 minutes or for up to overnight. **6.** Let the dish sit at room temperature for 30 minutes. **7.** Set the oven at 400°F. Bake the French toast for 20 to 25 minutes until it is golden brown and a knife inserted into the center comes out clean.

COMPOTE

1. In a skillet over medium heat, melt the butter. Add the brown sugar, cinnamon, and maple syrup. Stir well to combine them. Add the apples and cover the pan. Turn the heat to medium-high. When the mixture begins to bubble, remove the lid, stir, and turn the heat to low. **2.** Continue cooking, stirring occasionally, for 5 minutes or until the apples are soft. Set the compote beside servings of French toast.

Christine Merlo

Salads

Some families live on salads. Others turn to them when it's time to lose weight—or when they want to feel healthy. Nutritionists often point out that many salad-bar salads are high in fat, as are bottled salad dressings. But since you need the vitamins and minerals that come from these vegetables, you'll also hear the same experts advising you to order a salad when you call up for a pizza.

If you want to eat well and watch calories, the best salads are made at home. Today's supermarkets make it easy, offering a variety of greens and crisp vegetables—often already cut up—so it's no longer difficult to add a salad to every meal. The newest lettuce spinners do a wonderful job of drying lettuces, and many are designed so you can refrigerate rinsed greens right in the spinner basket. The nightly task becomes almost effortless. In addition, all homemade dressings keep well for weeks in the refrigerator. Although olive oil may solidify when chilled, it will pour again if you leave the dressing container in a bowl of warm water for a few minutes.

Salads can be main course meals, especially if you get into the practice on the weekends of roasting a couple extra chicken breasts or grilling more steak than you plan on using. The next day, cut up your cooked poultry or beef and lay some strips over your favorite noodle dish or salad greens. Even in the winter, lively potato salads are nice accompaniments to roast meats, and slaws are welcome on a plate with meat loaf, pork chops, or broiled fish.

Though locally grown lettuces, tomatoes, and the other salad essentials are best in the summer months, salads aren't just warm-weather fare. A good chicken salad is terrific inside crusty bread for a weekend lunch in the chilliest weather, and a Caesar, accompanied by a bowl of soup, is a satisfying supper year-round.

If you're feeding finicky children who don't seem to like salad, try this: Lay all the salad ingredients without the lettuce on a plate in clusters, but don't toss it. Put the dressing into a small bowl, and turn the nightly salad into a crudité platter. You'll be surprised that the identical vegetables, tossed in a salad and refused at another meal, will now be met with smiles.

Salads, like many things, come in all shapes and sizes.

Thousand Island Dressing

There are three American salad dressings that were once quite different but have, over the years, merged to become the same: Russian dressing, Louis dressing, and Thousand Island dressing. Louis originally appeared on the West Coast and accompanied crab meat in crab Louis. Russian dressings are pink because the French chefs in the Czarist court mixed their classic mayonnaise with the plentiful Russian beets, then tossed in eggs and a little sour pickle for flavor. This Thousand Island is practically identical.

MAKES ABOUT 1¹/₂ CUPS

1 cup mayonnaise

¹/₄ cup spicy salsa

¹/₄ cup ketchup

3 tablespoons sweet pickle relish

³/₄ cup finely chopped scallions (white part only)

Salt and pepper, to taste

1–2 teaspoons water

1. In a bowl, whisk together the mayonnaise, salsa, and ketchup. When the mixture is smooth, stir in the relish, scallions, salt, and pepper. Taste for seasoning and add more salsa or pickles if you like. Transfer the dressing to a plastic container and refrigerate for at least 1 hour or for up to 5 days. **2.** Just before using, stir the dressing and add the water, a few drops at a time, until the mixture is a pouring consistency.

French Dressing

Real French dressing is a vinaigrette. This version of French dressing, made red by paprika and ketchup, was wildly popular in the 1950s and bottled by many commercial companies. To capture the old taste, pour it over iceberg lettuce.

MAKES ²/₃ CUP

¹/₃ cup cider vinegar

Salt and pepper, to taste

2 teaspoons granulated sugar

1 teaspoon paprika, or to taste

2 tablespoons ketchup

1 teaspoon dry mustard

1 clove garlic, crushed

¹/₃ cup canola oil

1. In a bowl, whisk the vinegar, salt, pepper, sugar, paprika, ketchup, mustard, and garlic. **2.** Whisk in the oil a little at a time until it is all added. Taste for seasoning and add more salt, pepper, or paprika, if you like.

Blue Cheese Dressing

Everyone has strong feelings about blue cheese—either you adore it or you avoid it. For those who can't get enough, this version is especially satisfying. Use it as a dressing for wedges of iceberg or as a dip for crudités. Karoline Boehm Goodnick, a writer and food stylist for The Boston Globe, *who was a pastry chef at Flour Bakery and Cafe in Boston, Massachusetts, got the recipe from her husband's sister. She makes it the day before a party because it tastes even better once the flavors mellow.*

MAKES ABOUT 2 CUPS OR ENOUGH TO SERVE 8

2 large shallots, finely chopped

8 ounces blue cheese, crumbled

1 pint sour cream

Juice of 1 lemon

½ bunch parsley, stems removed, leaves finely chopped

Salt and pepper, to taste

2 tablespoons whole milk (optional)

1. In a large bowl, combine the shallots with half the blue cheese and half the sour cream. With a fork, blend the mixture until it is almost smooth. **2.** Stir in remaining sour cream with the lemon juice and parsley. **3.** Gently stir in remaining blue cheese crumbles, taking care not to break up the larger pieces. Add salt and pepper. If the mixture is too thick, add the milk, 1 teaspoon at a time.

Karoline Boehm Goodnick

Caesar Salad

Alice Berlow of Martha's Vineyard, an island off the coast of Massachusetts, serves this salad with good crusty bread. Boiling the egg for 1 minute thickens the dressing. Berlow is the voice behind National Public Radio's "A Cook's Notebook."

SERVES 4

1 egg

2 cloves garlic, mashed with a pinch of salt to form a paste

Juice of ½ lemon

2 anchovy fillets, mashed to form a paste

1 teaspoon Dijon mustard

½ cup olive oil

1 cup grated Parmesan

Salt and pepper, to taste

1 head romaine lettuce, coarsely chopped

2 cups toasted croutons

1. Bring a small saucepan of water to a boil. Lower in the egg and let it cook for 1 minute. Transfer it to cold water and, when it is cold enough to handle, crack the shell all over. Return it to the cold water until cold. Remove the egg from the shell, break it into a bowl, and with a fork cut it up. **2.** In another bowl, combine the garlic, lemon juice, and anchovies. Beat in the egg and mustard. Slowly whisk in oil until the dressing emulsifies. Stir in ¾ of the Parmesan with salt and pepper. **3.** In a large bowl, toss the lettuce with enough dressing to coat it all over. Add the remaining ¼ cup cheese and croutons. Sprinkle with more pepper.

Alice Berlow

Turkey Salad with Red Grapes and Green Apple

Red grapes and tart apples are in the market year-round, so you can make this salad when you have leftover meat from roasting a turkey.

SERVES 4

4 thick slices turkey breast

2 teaspoons Dijon mustard

1 tablespoon cider vinegar

Salt and pepper, to taste

½ cup mayonnaise

2 cups seedless red grapes, halved

¼ small red onion, coarsely chopped

1 Granny Smith or another tart apple, peeled, cored, and coarsely chopped

1. Cut the turkey into 1-inch pieces. Transfer to a bowl. **2.** In a bowl, whisk together the mustard, vinegar, salt, pepper, and a large spoonful of the mayonnaise. When the mixture is smooth, whisk in the remaining mayonnaise. **3.** Add the mayonnaise dressing to the turkey with the grapes, onion, and apple. Refrigerate until chilled.

Sheryl Julian

Grilled Chicken and Orzo Salad

In this simple dish, cucumber, tomato, and red onion, mixed with grilled chicken and orzo pasta, make a substantial salad. It's tossed with a lemon-mustard vinaigrette to brighten the flavors.

SERVES 6

CHICKEN AND ORZO

¼ cup olive oil

3 tablespoons red or white wine vinegar, plus a splash for the orzo

2 cloves garlic, chopped

Pinch of crushed red pepper

¼ teaspoon salt, and more to taste

¼ teaspoon black pepper, and more to taste

3 chicken breast halves (on the bone)

1 pound orzo pasta

1 pint cherry tomatoes, halved

½ English cucumber, unpeeled and thinly sliced

1 bunch scallions, thinly sliced

2 tablespoons chopped fresh basil

VINAIGRETTE

2 teaspoons lemon rind

1 tablespoon Dijon mustard

2 tablespoons red wine vinegar

Salt and pepper, to taste

¼ cup olive oil

CHICKEN AND ORZO

1. In a small bowl, combine the olive oil, vinegar, garlic, red pepper, salt, and black pepper. Pour the marinade into a resealable plastic bag and add the chicken. Cover and refrigerate for 1 hour. **2.** Heat a grill or broiler. Grill or broil the chicken for 8 minutes on a side or until an instant-read meat thermometer registers 165°F in the thickest part of the breast. Remove them from the heat and set aside to cool. **3.** In a large pot of boiling salted water, cook the orzo for 8 minutes or until it is tender but still has some bite. Drain it into a colander. **4.** Tip the orzo into a serving bowl. Add salt, pepper, and a generous splash of vinegar. Stir well. **5.** Remove the chicken from the bone, and slice it thinly into 2-inch pieces. Add it to the salad with the tomatoes, cucumber, scallions, and basil.

VINAIGRETTE

1. In a small bowl, whisk together the lemon rind, mustard, vinegar, salt, and pepper. Slowly whisk in the olive oil until it is all combined. The vinaigrette is lemony but will balance out when combined with the salad ingredients. **2.** Sprinkle the salad with the dressing and toss gently.

Christine Merlo

Grilled Chicken and Orzo Salad

Chicken Salad with Walnuts

Begin by poaching chicken breasts on the bone, which makes moist, flavorful poultry. Use the broth to make soup on another day. Add lots of scallions, celery, and parsley to the chicken to make a crunchy salad to spread on crusty bread.

SERVES 4

2½ pounds chicken breast
   halves (on the bone)

2 quarts water

Salt and pepper, to taste

1 bay leaf

1 carrot, halved

1 onion, halved

1 clove garlic, halved

3 whole peppercorns

1 cup walnuts, toasted

2 teaspoons Dijon mustard

1 tablespoon cider vinegar

½ cup mayonnaise

1 bunch scallions, finely
   chopped

4 stalks celery, thinly sliced

¼ cup Italian parsley leaves,
   chopped

1. In a large flameproof casserole, combine the chicken, water, and salt. Bring to a boil, skim the surface thoroughly, and turn down the heat. **2.** Add the bay leaf, carrot, onion, garlic, and peppercorns. Cover the pan, lower the heat, and cook the chicken for 25 minutes or until it is cooked through. **3.** Let the chicken cool in the broth. **4.** Remove the chicken from the broth. Strain the broth into a bowl and refrigerate it for several hours. Skim off and discard the fat; use the broth to make soup on another day. **5.** In a cast-iron or another heavy skillet, toast the walnuts in a dry pan for 4 minutes, tossing constantly, until they are fragrant. **6.** In a bowl, whisk together the mustard, vinegar, salt, pepper, and a large spoonful of the mayonnaise. When the mixture is smooth, whisk in the remaining mayonnaise. **7.** Remove and discard the chicken skin and bones. Cut the meat into bite-size pieces. **8.** In a bowl, combine the chicken, mayonnaise mixture, walnuts, scallions, celery, and parsley. Add salt and pepper. Toss gently.

Sheryl Julian

Cobb Salad

Invented at the Brown Derby restaurant in Los Angeles, apparently by accident (the owner cobbled together dinner from what he could find in the fridge), Cobb salad has become a lunch favorite. The greens are heaped with chicken, avocado, hard-cooked eggs, and bacon. Make your own variation; it's hard to go wrong.

SERVES 6

DRESSING

1/4 cup red wine vinegar

1 teaspoon Worcestershire sauce

1/2 teaspoon Dijon mustard

1 small clove garlic, crushed

Salt and pepper, to taste

1/2 cup canola oil

1/4 cup olive oil

SALAD

2 ripe avocados

Juice of 1/2 lemon

1/2 head romaine, leaves cored
   and torn

1/2 head red leaf lettuce, leaves
   cored and torn

1/2 bunch watercress, stems
   removed

4 grilled chicken breast halves,
   thickly sliced

1 pint cherry tomatoes, quartered

Salt and pepper, to taste

8 strips bacon, cooked until
   golden and broken into small
   pieces

1/4 pound blue cheese, crumbled

3 hard-cooked eggs (see page
   108), peeled and quartered
   lengthwise

2 tablespoons chopped fresh
   parsley

DRESSING

1. In a bowl, whisk together the vinegar, Worcestershire sauce, mustard, garlic, salt, and pepper. **2.** Slowly whisk in the canola and olive oils until the dressing emulsifies.

SALAD

1. Halve, pit, and slice the avocados, discarding the skin. On a plate, sprinkle the slices with lemon juice. **2.** In a large bowl, combine the romaine, red leaf lettuce, and watercress. Toss with enough of the dressing to barely moisten the greens. Divide among 6 dinner plates. **3.** Arrange the chicken, avocado, and tomatoes on the greens. Sprinkle lightly with dressing, salt, and pepper. **4.** Add the bacon, blue cheese, and more pepper. Set the eggs around the edges of the greens, sprinkle with parsley. Pass the remaining dressing separately.

Tuna, Green Beans, and Chickpea Salad

Large flakes of Italian tuna in olive oil make this simple salad, with green beans, cherry tomatoes, and the tiny French cornichon pickles, a memorable dish. Canned Italian tuna is available at specialty markets. Our favorite imported brand is Flott.

SERVES 4

1 pound green beans, trimmed

1 pint cherry tomatoes, halved

1 poblano pepper, cored, seeded, and thinly sliced

½ cup chopped black olives

1 can (1 pound) chickpeas, drained and rinsed

1 jar or can (7½ ounces) Italian tuna in olive oil

½ cup thinly sliced cornichons

¼ cup chopped fresh parsley

Salt and black pepper, to taste

1 heaping teaspoon whole grain mustard

3 tablespoons white wine vinegar

¼ cup olive oil

1. Bring a saucepan of water to a boil. Add the beans and cook them for 2 minutes. Drain into a colander and rinse with cold water until the beans are no longer warm. Shake the colander to remove excess moisture. **2.** Cut the beans in half and transfer them to a mixing bowl. Add the tomatoes, poblano pepper, olives, and chickpeas. **3.** In a small bowl with a fork, flake the tuna into large pieces. Add the tuna, cornichons, and parsley to the salad; set aside. **4.** In a small bowl, whisk together the salt, black pepper, mustard, and vinegar. Gradually whisk in the oil until the dressing emulsifies. **5.** Add half the dressing to the salad and toss gently. Add just enough of the remaining dressing to moisten the vegetables and tuna. Pass the remaining dressing separately.

Sheryl Julian

Creamy Deli-Style Tuna Salad

Made in a food processor, this tuna salad contains finely chopped carrots and celery, which add crunch; bread-and-butter pickles give it a sweet finish. Add any or all of these: 2 tablespoons chopped dill, 2 tablespoons capers, ¼ cup pitted olives, or 2 chopped scallions.

MAKES 3½ CUPS

2 carrots, cut into thirds

2 celery stalks, strings removed, stalks cut into thirds

3 cans (6 ounces each) white albacore tuna in water, drained

½ cup mayonnaise

2 tablespoons lemon juice

½ cup bread-and-butter pickles

1 tablespoon pickle juice

Salt and pepper, to taste

1. In a food processor, combine the carrots and celery and pulse several times until they're coarsely chopped. **2.** Add the tuna, mayonnaise, and lemon juice. Pulse 3 or 4 times or until the mixture is smooth but not pastelike. Transfer to a bowl. **3.** Place the pickles in the food processor and pulse until finely diced. Fold into the tuna salad. Add pickle juice and salt and pepper.

Debra Samuels

Garden Salad with Kidney Beans

This is a farmers' market specialty—or better yet, supper from your own backyard garden. It begins with canned kidney beans, which offer substance (you can also use pasta). Cherry or regular tomatoes are essential for juiciness; cucumber, celery, and sugar snap peas for something crisp; blanched green beans because they're so meaty at the height of their season; olives for saltiness; fresh herbs for aromatics; and cooked chicken or salmon or canned tuna for protein. Improvise and make it your own.

SERVES 4

2 cans (1 pound each) red
    kidney beans

2 tablespoons olive oil

Salt and pepper, to taste

2 tablespoons white wine
    vinegar, or to taste

1/2 pound green beans

1 pint cherry tomatoes,
    quartered, or 2 medium
    tomatoes, cut into thin
    wedges

2 small cucumbers, thinly
    sliced

2 stalks celery, thinly sliced

1/4 pound sugar snap peas,
    trimmed and halved on the
    diagonal

1/2 cup pitted black or green
    olives

2 grilled chicken breasts or
    whole legs, or 1-pound piece
    grilled salmon, or 1 can
    (7 ounces) tuna in oil

2 tablespoons chopped fresh
    thyme, basil, or parsley

1. Drain the kidney beans into a colander, rinse well, and shake to remove excess moisture. Tip the beans into a bowl. Add olive oil, salt, pepper, and vinegar. **2.** Bring a large saucepan of salted water to a boil. Add the green beans and cook for 3 minutes or until just tender but still crisp. Drain and rinse with cold water. **3.** Add the green beans to the kidney beans with the tomatoes, cucumbers, celery, sugar snaps, and olives. Cut the chicken or salmon into 1½-inch strips. Drain and flake the tuna. Add the chicken, salmon, or tuna to the salad with thyme, basil, or parsley. **4.** With a large spoon, stir the salad gently. Taste for seasoning and add more salt and pepper, if you like.

Sheryl Julian

Garden Salad with Kidney Beans

Russian Beet and Potato Salad

The beets stain the potatoes a little, which only makes this salad more charming. A chopped pudgy sour or half-sour pickle, vinegar, and dill cut the richness.

SERVES 4

4 large beets

2 russet potatoes, peeled and
    quartered

2 large carrots, cut into 3-inch
    pieces

1 sour or half-sour pickle, cut
    into ½-inch pieces

1 bunch scallions (white part
    only), thinly sliced

2 tablespoons cider vinegar

2 tablespoons mayonnaise

Salt and pepper, to taste

½ teaspoon sugar

¼ cup vegetable oil

¼ cup chopped fresh parsley

2 tablespoons chopped fresh
    dill

8 leaves Boston or leaf lettuce
    (for serving)

1. Set the oven at 450°F. Wrap the beets in foil, shiny side inside. Set the beets in a baking dish and roast them in the hot oven for 1 hour or until they are tender. Remove the beets from the oven and set them aside to cool. **2.** Meanwhile, in a saucepan fitted with a steamer insert, combine the potatoes and carrots. Fill the pan with water up to the level of the steamer. Cover the pot and steam the vegetables over medium-high heat for 15 minutes or until they are tender. If the potatoes are done before the carrots, remove them from the pan. **3.** When all the vegetables are cool enough to handle, cut them into ½-inch pieces. (Cut the beets in a large shallow bowl, because the juices can stain your counter.) **4.** Transfer all the vegetables to the bowl. Add the pickle and scallions. **5.** In a separate bowl, whisk together the vinegar, mayonnaise, salt, pepper, and sugar. Whisk in the oil a teaspoon at a time. **6.** Pour the dressing over the vegetables and toss them gently to coat them all over. **7.** Stir in the parsley and dill. Taste for seasoning and add more salt and pepper if you like. Cover the salad and refrigerate it for several hours for the flavors to mellow. Serve on lettuce leaves.

Sheryl Julian

Three-Pepper Salad

In this version of the classic Italian salad of bell peppers, the peppers aren't cooked over a wood fire or roasted until charred. Instead they're sauteed in olive oil, then mixed with deep purple Gaeta olives, which grow on the hillsides outside Rome, and a handful of briny capers.

SERVES 6

2 tablespoons olive oil

4 cloves of garlic, 3 whole and
  1 chopped

6 large bell peppers (2 red,
  2 yellow, 2 orange), cored,
  seeded, and cut into thick
  strips

Salt and black pepper, to taste

¼ pound pitted Gaeta olives,
  chopped

3 tablespoons capers

2 tablespoons chopped Italian
  parsley

1. In a large skillet, heat the olive oil over medium-high heat. Add the whole garlic cloves and all the bell peppers. Cook, tossing the peppers occasionally, for 15 minutes or until they just begin to soften and the skins start to wrinkle. Remove and discard the whole garlic cloves. **2.** Add the chopped garlic, salt, and pepper to the pepper mixture. Cook for 1 minute. Stir in the olives and capers and cook for 1 minute more. **3.** Transfer to a platter and sprinkle with parsley. Let the mixture cool to room temperature. Cover loosely and refrigerate for at least several hours or for up to 1 day.

Michelle Conway

Quinoa Salad

To make a salad, treat the ancient grain quinoa like rice. In this dish, cucumbers, red bell pepper, scallions, and feta are tossed with the cooked grain.

SERVES 6

QUINOA

1 cup quinoa

2 cups water

¼ teaspoon salt

SALAD

2 garlic cloves, chopped

Juice of 1 lemon

1 teaspoon Dijon mustard

Salt and pepper, to taste

⅓ cup olive oil

½ seedless cucumber, peeled, seeded, and cut into ½-inch cubes

½ cup pitted kalamata olives, halved

½ large red bell pepper, seeded and cut into ½-inch dice

2 scallions, thinly sliced

1 cup crumbled feta cheese

QUINOA

1. In a dry nonstick pan over medium heat, toast the quinoa, stirring often, for 4 minutes or until the kernels begin to brown and are fragrant. Tip the quinoa into a strainer and rinse it under cold running water until the water runs clear. **2.** In a saucepan, combine the quinoa, water, and salt. Bring to boil, lower the heat, and simmer for 10 to 15 minutes or until the grain absorbs the water; set aside to cool.

SALAD

1. In a bowl, whisk the garlic, lemon juice, mustard, salt, and pepper. Whisk in the oil a little at a time. **2.** Transfer the quinoa to a serving bowl. Add the cucumbers, olives, bell pepper, scallions, and feta. Pour the dressing over the salad and toss gently. **3.** Cover and refrigerate the salad for 2 hours. Taste for seasoning and add more salt or pepper, if you like.

Gillian O'Callaghan

Classic Creamy Potato Salad

If you like your potatoes to have lots of crunch, plenty of onions, and taste like your childhood picnic salads, this is for you.

SERVES 6

4 russet (baking) potatoes, peeled and quartered

2 tablespoons cider vinegar

Salt and pepper, to taste

4 stalks celery, halved lengthwise and thinly sliced

½ small red onion, finely chopped

1 bunch scallions, finely chopped

¼ cup chopped fresh parsley

¾ cup mayonnaise

2 tablespoons sour cream

2 tablespoons warm water, or more if needed

1. In a saucepan fitted with a steamer insert and several inches of water, steam the potatoes in a covered pan over medium-high heat for 15 to 20 minutes or until the potatoes are tender. Transfer them to a large shallow bowl. **2.** While the potatoes are still quite hot, slice them into ¼-inch-thick rounds. Transfer to a large bowl. Sprinkle them with vinegar, salt, and pepper. Set aside to cool. **3.** Add the celery, onion, scallions, and parsley. **4.** In a small bowl, whisk together the mayonnaise, sour cream, 1 tablespoon of the water, salt, and pepper. The dressing should pour easily. Add the remaining water, 1 teaspoon at a time, if necessary. **5.** Pour the dressing over the potatoes and toss gently. Taste for seasoning and add more vinegar, salt, and pepper if you like. **6.** Serve at once or cover tightly with plastic wrap and refrigerate for several hours or overnight. If the salad seems too thick the following day, add 1 to 2 teaspoons of vinegar and stir gently.

Sheryl Julian

Warm Yellow Potato Salad

To give these potatoes a good texture and great flavor, first boil the potatoes halved in their skins in generously salted water. Then slice them, sprinkle the hot slices with vinegar, and let them sit for a few minutes before dressing. In this elegant presentation, the golden potatoes are arranged on a platter and a vinaigrette dressing is sprinkled on top. The salad tosses as you serve it.

SERVES 6

8 medium Yellow Finn or Yukon
   Gold potatoes (about 4
   pounds), halved

Salt and pepper, to taste

4 tablespoons cider vinegar

1 tablespoon Dijon mustard

¼ cup canola oil

3 green scallions, very thinly
   sliced

2 tablespoons chopped fresh
   parsley

1. Fill a large saucepan with the whole unpeeled potatoes, water to cover them by 2 inches, and a generous pinch of salt; bring the water to a boil. Cover with the lid and boil the potatoes for 20 minutes, or until the potatoes are tender when pierced with a skewer. **2.** With tongs, remove the potatoes from the pot and set them on a board. Let them sit for 5 minutes. Cut them into ¼-inch slices. Arrange half the potatoes on a shallow platter. Sprinkle with 1 tablespoon of the vinegar, salt, and pepper. Layer the remaining slices, 1 tablespoon vinegar, salt, and pepper. Set the potatoes aside for 5 minutes. **3.** In a bowl, whisk the remaining 2 tablespoons of vinegar, another pinch each of salt and pepper, and mustard. Whisk in the oil a teaspoon at a time until the dressing emulsifies. Pour the dressing over the potatoes and sprinkle with scallions and parsley. Serve warm.

Sheryl Julian

Three-Bean Salad

Canned red kidney beans, chickpeas, and green beans go into this quick dish, great for potluck suppers or summer cookouts.

SERVES 8

Salt and black pepper, to taste

2 garlic cloves, peeled

1 pound green beans, stem ends snipped, beans halved diagonally

1 can (1 pound) red kidney beans, drained

1 can (1 pound) chickpeas, drained

½ medium red onion, finely chopped

½ red bell pepper, seeded and finely chopped

3 tablespoons red wine vinegar

1 teaspoon lemon juice

⅓ cup olive oil

2 tablespoons chopped fresh parsley

1. Bring a large pan of salted water to a boil. Add the garlic and cook for 2 minutes. Use a slotted spoon to remove the garlic from the water, set aside. **2.** To the same water, add the green beans and simmer for 4 to 5 minutes until they are tender but still have some bite. Drain into a colander and rinse with cold water until cool. Shake the colander to remove excess liquid. **3.** In a bowl, combine the green beans, kidney beans, chickpeas, onion, and bell pepper. **4.** Finely chop the garlic. In a bowl, whisk the garlic, vinegar, lemon juice, salt, and black pepper. Slowly whisk in the oil until the dressing emulsifies. **5.** Pour the dressing over the beans and stir gently. Cover and refrigerate for 1 hour for the flavors to mellow. Sprinkle with parsley. Taste for seasoning and add more salt and pepper, if you like.

Lisa Zwirn

Red and Green Slaw

Adding some shredded red cabbage to a head of green cabbage gives the slaw a more interesting texture and appearance. The dressing is sweetened mayonnaise with a little pucker from white vinegar.

SERVES 6

1 medium head green cabbage,
    quartered and cored

1/2 head red cabbage, cored

1 tablespoon coarse salt

2 carrots, grated

1 green bell pepper, cored,
    seeded, and cut into fine
    strips

1 bunch scallions, finely
    chopped

1/4 cup mayonnaise

1/3 cup granulated sugar

1/2 cup distilled white vinegar

1. With a sharp knife or a handheld slicer, cut the cabbages into thin shreds. Set a colander over a large bowl. Layer the cabbage and salt in the colander. Set aside for 30 minutes. **2.** Use your hands to squeeze excess moisture from the cabbage. Transfer it to a large bowl. Add the carrots, green pepper, and scallions. Toss thoroughly. **3.** In a small bowl, whisk the mayonnaise until smooth. Whisk in the sugar and vinegar. Add the dressing to the cabbage mixture and toss well. Taste for seasoning and add more salt, vinegar, or mayonnaise, if you like. Cover with plastic wrap and refrigerate for at least 2 hours or for as long as overnight. Toss again just before serving.

Sheryl Julian

Corn Salad

Many farm stands let you shuck corn at the stand, which makes this step easy when you get home. To remove kernels from ears of corn, lay the cobs on the table and pull a knife across several rows of corn at a time. Keep turning the cob until all the kernels have been removed. Blanch the kernels briefly, then toss them with chili peppers, red onion, fresh herbs, and a light vinaigrette.

SERVES 6

8 ears fresh corn, kernels cut from the cobs

1/2 teaspoon salt, or to taste

1/4 teaspoon black pepper, or to taste

3 tablespoons white wine vinegar

1/4 cup canola oil

1/2 small red onion, halved and thinly sliced

4 scallions, very thinly sliced

1 red bell pepper, cored, seeded, and cut into thin strips

1 poblano chili pepper, cored, seeded, and cut into thin strips

Handful of fresh flat-leaf parsley, coarsely chopped

Handful of fresh basil leaves, torn into pieces

1. Bring a large saucepan of water to a boil. Add the corn and cook it for 1 minute. Drain the corn into a colander, shake the colander to remove the excess moisture, and transfer the corn to a large bowl. **2.** In a small bowl, whisk the salt, black pepper, and vinegar just until the salt dissolves. Gradually whisk in the oil until all of it has been added. **3.** Spoon the dressing over the warm corn. Add the onion, scallions, bell pepper, poblano, parsley, and basil. Stir gently and taste for seasoning. Add more salt and pepper if you like. Cover tightly and refrigerate for up to 4 hours before serving.

Sheryl Julian

Raita (*Indian yogurt and cucumber salad*)

The classic Indian raita, a mixture of cooling yogurt, shredded cucumbers, and strips of tomato, offsets hot curries. All Indian restaurants offer it as a side dish, and it's simple to put together at home. It goes well with summer grills.

SERVES 4

2 cucumbers

Salt and black pepper, to taste

2 medium tomatoes, peeled, seeded, and cut into strips

2 tablespoons chopped fresh cilantro

½ red onion, very finely chopped

1 green chili pepper, cored, seeded, and finely chopped

1 clove garlic, crushed

¼ teaspoon cayenne pepper

2 cups plain low-fat yogurt

1. Peel the cucumbers, halve them lengthwise, and use a spoon to scoop out the seeds. Use a coarse grater to grate the cucumbers. Transfer them to a colander and place it in a bowl. Sprinkle the cucumbers with salt and set the bowl aside for 20 minutes. **2.** Discard the liquid in the bowl and wipe it out. Squeeze the cucumbers in your hands to remove as much liquid as possible. Transfer them to the bowl. **3.** Add the tomatoes, cilantro, onion, chili pepper, garlic, cayenne pepper, and black pepper. Stir well. Add the yogurt several spoonfuls at a time, stirring until the vegetables are coated all over.

Sheryl Julian

Cold Soft Tofu

High in protein and mild, tofu goes well with strong seasonings—here grated fresh ginger, soy sauce, and cilantro. This is an instant dish, ideal for vegetarians. Serve it with gingery baby bok choy (see page 95) and brown rice (see page 74).

SERVES 4

1 package (1 pound) silken or soft tofu

1 piece fresh ginger, peeled and grated

¼ cup soy sauce

Juice of ½ lemon

2 tablespoons chopped fresh cilantro

1. Cut the tofu into 1-inch cubes. Transfer to a shallow bowl. Sprinkle with ginger, soy sauce, lemon juice, and cilantro. **2.** Cover and refrigerate for 1 hour.

Jane Levy Reed

Seafood

A few hundred years ago in New England, there was so much fish that people near the sea lived on it. Lobsters were so abundant that they were fed to the servants. All that has changed, of course, but not the public's appetite for seafood.

Fish is so much a part of the New England table that you can go way inland—to the part of Vermont that borders New York State, or the western region of Massachusetts in the Berkshire Hills—and still find very fresh seafood on restaurant menus.

The fishing industry is international, so no one depends exclusively on what North Atlantic fishermen are bringing in. Still, Boston, Massachusetts—the Home of the Bean and the Cod—Providence, Rhode Island, and Portland, Maine, seem to be seafood central. Tourists expect all kinds of fish on restaurant menus (and chefs comply), supermarkets and specialty fish markets do a thriving retail business in fresh seafood, and caterers are asked to offer a choice of meat or fish at nearly every event.

Even home cooks who have not mastered much in the kitchen pride themselves on being able to grill thick tuna steaks or pieces of boneless salmon successfully. And seafood is so well liked that hosts rarely ask their guests if they eat fish. It's just expected that everyone does.

As fishing stocks go down, and regulations are put in place to help the fisheries thrive, fish has become more and more expensive. Aquaculture farms keep the supply up (though practices in some, like salmon, have been controversial). In the past few years, families who might have dined on seafood at least once a week now eat it only on special occasions.

So it's especially important to cook fish correctly, get comfortable with a few recipes that become your specialties, and be able to set forth delicious, juicy seafood bursting with good flavor. You'll find fish recipes are in the chapters on chowders, pasta, and salads, too. You get the fish. We've found the best ways to cook it.

Court Bouillon

Court bouillon is the liquid you use to poach salmon or other fish. It means that you're not adding any fat to the dish, and it's a good way to cook if you're watching your waistline or your cholesterol. This mixture makes enough for several nights or for a seafood stew. To use it, strain the liquid, set the fish you're about to cook in a skillet, and add enough court bouillon to barely cover it. Simmer on top of the stove for 10 minutes per inch of fish (a ¾-inch salmon or halibut steak will take about 7 minutes). Cool slightly in the broth, then serve with plenty of lemon.

MAKES ABOUT 6 CUPS

7 cups water

½ cup apple cider vinegar

4 sprigs fresh thyme

½ leek, cut in half

1 small carrot, halved

1 small stalk celery, halved

1 bulb fresh fennel, trimmed
   and cut in half

3 cloves garlic

3 bay leaves

1 star anise

½ teaspoon crushed red
   pepper

1 teaspoon salt

1 teaspoon black peppercorns

1. In a large soup pot, combine the water, vinegar, thyme, leek, carrot, celery, fennel, garlic, bay leaves, star anise, red pepper, salt, and peppercorns. Bring to a boil over high heat. **2.** Simmer uncovered for 20 minutes. **3.** Strain and use as directed.

Jonathan Levitt

Court Bouillon

Boiled Lobsters with Butter

Go to a dependable market for your lobster, haul out the big pots and nutcrackers, and strap a bib around each guest.

SERVES 6

Salt, to taste

6 live lobsters (1½ to 2 pounds each)

1 cup (2 sticks) butter, melted

1. Bring two soup pots of salted water to a boil. Add the lobsters and return the water to a boil. Adjust the heat so the water boils gently, and cook the lobsters for 15 to 20 minutes (about 10 minutes per pound) or until they are bright red and cooked through. **2.** Using tongs, lift the lobsters from the pots and transfer them to a clean sink. Use nutcrackers to crack the claws. Use strong kitchen shears to cut through the shell on the underside of each lobster. Drain any excess water into the sink. **3.** Set the lobsters on each of six large plates. Serve with butter for dipping.

Baked Stuffed Lobster

Multiply this recipe to serve four or six. After that, the dish gets cumbersome. Ask the fish market to split and clean the lobsters. You don't want the stomach, but you do want the liver (which is grayish green) for the stuffing.

SERVES 2

2 lobsters (1½ to 2 pounds each), split and cleaned

30 round crackers, finely crushed (1 cup cracker crumbs)

½ cup (1 stick) unsalted butter, melted

1 tablespoon Worcestershire sauce

Generous dash hot sauce

Lobster liver, chopped

1 lemon, halved

1. Set the oven at 400°F. Have on hand a rimmed baking sheet. **2.** Place the lobsters cut sides up on the baking sheet. **3.** In a bowl, combine the crackers, butter, Worcestershire, hot sauce, and lobster liver. Blend well. **4.** Mound the stuffing on the lobsters, dividing it evenly. **5.** Bake the lobsters for 25 minutes or until the meat is cooked and the topping is hot. Serve with lemon.

Lobster Rolls

One of New England's quirkiest and most popular dishes, lobster rolls are traditionally made with pan-grilled hot dog rolls and lobster salad. There are many theories about the origins of the dish. The tradition probably came about because lobsters at one time were cheap, so it didn't matter that the meat was going inside ordinary bread.

SERVES 4

ROLLS

4 hot dog rolls

2 tablespoons unsalted butter, at room temperature

LOBSTER

1 pound cooked lobster meat, cut into 1/2-inch pieces

2 stalks celery, finely chopped

4 scallions, finely chopped

1/4 cup chopped fresh parsley

1/2 cup mayonnaise

1/4 cup plain whole-milk yogurt

2 tablespoons lemon juice

1 teaspoon cayenne pepper

Salt and black pepper, to taste

ROLLS

1. Spread both sides of the rolls with a faint coating of soft butter.
2. Heat a cast-iron pan over medium heat for 1 minute. Place the rolls buttered side down in the hot pan. Cook the rolls until the undersides are golden brown. Turn and toast the other side.

LOBSTER

1. In a bowl, combine the lobster, celery, scallions, and parsley.
2. In a small bowl, mix together the mayonnaise, yogurt, lemon juice, cayenne pepper, salt, and black pepper. Stir well. **3.** Spoon the dressing over the lobster and mix thoroughly. Taste for seasoning and add more salt and pepper if you like. **4.** Fill the rolls with lobster salad.

Sheryl Julian & Julie Riven

Clams with Spicy Turkey Sausages

Portuguese fishermen taught us the remarkably good combination of clams and spicy sausage. Don't let the clams overcook. They're ready when they open.

SERVES 4

1 tablespoon olive oil

1 pound spicy Italian or
  andouille sausage, halved
  lengthwise and sliced into
  1-inch chunks

3 pounds littleneck clams, well
  rinsed

1 clove garlic, chopped

¾ cup dry white wine

2 tablespoons unsalted butter

¼ cup chopped fresh parsley

1. In a flameproof casserole over medium-high heat, heat the oil until hot. Cook the sausages, turning often, for 5 minutes or until they are browned all over. **2.** Stir in the clams and garlic. Cook for 1 minute. **3.** Pour in the wine, cover the pan, and cook over high heat for 3 minutes, shaking the pan occasionally, or until all the clams open. Discard any clams that do not open. **4.** Remove the pan from the heat and dot the clams with the butter. Shake the pan until the butter melts. Sprinkle with parsley and serve in deep bowls with crusty bread.

Jonathan Levitt

Clams with Garlic and Ginger

These Asian-style clams are aromatic from an accent of fresh basil.

SERVES 4

1 tablespoon canola oil

1 clove garlic, chopped

1 Thai or other hot chili pepper

1 piece (2 inches) fresh ginger,
  chopped

3 pounds littleneck clams, well
  rinsed

½ cup water

3 tablespoons chopped fresh
  basil

1. In a large flameproof casserole, heat the oil. Add the garlic, hot pepper, and ginger. Cook, stirring constantly, for 1 minute. **2.** Add the clams and cook, stirring constantly, for 30 seconds. **3.** Pour in the water, cover the pan, and cook over high heat, shaking the pan often, for 3 minutes or until all the clams open. Discard any clams that do not open. **4.** Sprinkle with basil and serve in deep bowls with crusty bread.

Larry Reed

Seared Scallops with Cider Cream

Some markets sell skinned hazelnuts, but if you need to skin them, toast them on a rimmed baking sheet in a 375°F oven for 8 minutes or until they smell fragrant. Then rub them in an old towel (this makes a mess), until the skins fall off.

SERVES 4

1½ cups hard apple cider

½ cup crème fraiche

Salt and pepper, to taste

1¼ pounds fresh sea scallops

1 tablespoon vegetable oil

1 cup skinned hazelnuts,
  roughly chopped

1. In a saucepan bring the cider to a boil. Lower the heat and simmer until it reduces by half. It should have the consistency of a syrupy glaze. **2.** Stir in the crème fraiche, salt, and pepper. **3.** Pat the scallops dry with paper towels. Sprinkle with salt. **4.** In a medium skillet over high heat, heat the oil. When it is hot, add the scallops. Sear for 2 minutes on each side or until they have a rich golden crust. Remove the scallops from the pan and arrange on four dinner plates. **5.** Spoon some of the apple-cider sauce over each one and sprinkle with hazelnuts.

From Rialto restaurant,
Cambridge, Massachusetts

Shrimp Scampi Limoncello

Shrimp Scampi Limoncello

To make this popular dish, the Boston, Massachusetts, restaurant Trattoria Il Panino uses a splash of the Italian import crema di limoncello, *which is both sweet and citrusy. You can substitute white wine.*

SERVES 8

STOCK

1½ cups dry white wine

1 head fresh fennel, chopped

3 stalks celery, chopped

3 medium onions, chopped

8 whole peppercorns

3 bay leaves

3 pounds shrimp shells

SHRIMP

¼ cup olive oil

3 tablespoons unsalted butter

4 dozen large shrimp, deveined
   and shelled, tails intact

Salt and pepper, to taste

6 cloves garlic, finely chopped

1 cup limoncello

1½ cups shrimp stock (see
   above, or use fish stock)

½ cup lemon juice

¼ cup fresh parsley leaves,
   torn

STOCK

In a stock pan, combine the wine, fennel, celery, onions, peppercorns, bay leaves, and shrimp shells. Bring to a boil. Turn down the heat, cover the pan, and simmer the stock for 1 hour. Strain.

SHRIMP

1. In a large skillet over high heat, heat the olive oil and butter. When the butter melts, add the shrimp, salt, and pepper. Cook them, turning once, for 2 minutes, or until they turn pink on both sides. **2.** Add the garlic and cook for 1 more minute. Remove the shrimp from the skillet. **3.** Add the limoncello and stock, bring to a boil, and let the mixture simmer for 5 minutes or until reduced slightly. **4.** Stir in the lemon juice and parsley. Return the shrimp to the pan, turn them in the sauce, and taste for seasoning. Add more salt and pepper, if you like. Serve with crusty bread.

*From Trattoria Il Panino,
Boston, Massachusetts*

Curried Shrimp with Green Apple

Shrimp and green apple are sauteed in a mild coconut-milk curry, then garnished with cilantro, mint, and peanuts.
Serve with rice.

SERVES 4

2 tablespoons vegetable oil

1 piece (1 inch) fresh ginger,
    finely chopped

1 clove garlic, finely chopped

1 tablespoon curry powder

¼ teaspoon sugar

Salt and black pepper, to taste

1 small hot chili pepper, cored,
    seeded, and chopped

1½ pounds shrimp, peeled with
    tails intact

1 green apple, cored, peeled,
    and diced

¾ cup unsweetened coconut
    milk

1 teaspoon cornstarch mixed
    with 1 tablespoon cold water

1 tablespoon chopped fresh
    cilantro

1 tablespoon chopped fresh
    mint

¼ cup roasted unsalted
    peanuts, coarsely chopped

1. In a large nonstick skillet, heat the oil. Add the ginger and garlic. Cook, stirring constantly, for 1 minute. **2.** Add the curry powder, sugar, salt, and black pepper. Continue cooking, stirring, for 1 minute more. **3.** Add the chili pepper, shrimp, and apple. Continue cooking, stirring constantly, for 1 minute. Add the coconut milk and cook for 2 minutes more or until the shrimp are pink and firm. **4.** Stir the cornstarch mixture until it is smooth. Add it into the shrimp mixture and heat, stirring, for 1 minute. The sauce will thicken slightly. **5.** Sprinkle with cilantro, mint, and peanuts.

Spanish Shrimp with Salt

Shrimp in their shells take a little work for the diner (they're a mess to eat), but the shells add great flavor. And after the intense heat of the broiler, the shells are actually tender enough to eat. Use coarse sea salt, so some crystals adhere to the shells. These are served all over southern Spain in tapas bars.

SERVES 8

1 tablespoon olive oil

1 clove garlic, left whole and
    crushed

1 pound large shrimp,
    unpeeled, tails intact

1 teaspoon large sea-salt
    crystals, or to taste

1 lemon, cut into 6 wedges

1. Turn on the broiler. Heat a large cast-iron skillet (or use another heavy-based skillet with a heatproof handle). Add the oil and then swirl it around quickly. Add the garlic and cook, shaking the pan constantly, until it is browned enough to infuse the oil with flavor. Discard the garlic. **2.** Lay the shrimp in the skillet so they make one tight layer. Sprinkle with salt. Slide the skillet under the broiler and cook the shrimp for 3 minutes, turning once, or until they are pink and cooked through. **3.** Transfer the shrimp to individual plates, garnish with lemon, and serve at once.

Sheryl Julian

Scalloped Oysters

Oysters, their liquid (called liquor*), crackers, butter, and cream—if you love oysters you'll be in heaven. A version of this dish has been served in New England restaurants for decades.*

SERVES 4 AS AN APPETIZER

1 pint fresh oysters and their
    liquid

1/2 cup (1 stick) butter, melted

Salt and pepper, to taste

2 cups soft white bread
    crumbs

1/4 cup heavy cream

1. Set the oven at 400°F. Have on hand an 8-inch baking dish. **2.** Set a strainer over a bowl. Drain the oysters, saving the liquor. Set the oysters in the baking dish. **3.** In a bowl, combine the butter, salt, pepper, and bread crumbs. Sprinkle the mixture on the oysters. **4.** In the same bowl, combine the oyster liquor and cream. Pour the mixture over the bread crumbs. **5.** Bake the dish for 20 to 25 minutes or until the liquid is bubbling at the edges and the crumbs are brown.

Fish Cakes

Fish cakes have improved so much since they were first made, when dried salt cod would be soaked overnight. Bacon fat was always in the skillet, turning the cakes golden. Today, many seafood establishments feature fish cakes made with fresh cod (as well as scrod, haddock, hake, flounder, and pollock). These can be made with any plain white fish, along with a golden potato, scallions, parsley, and hot sauce. The patties have a crisp bacon topping.

SERVES 4

1 medium Yukon Gold or Yellow Finn potato

¾ pound skinless, boneless cod, cut into chunks

1 tablespoon butter, cut up

½ teaspoon salt, and more to taste

½ teaspoon pepper, and more to taste

3 scallions, finely chopped

2 tablespoons chopped parsley

¼ teaspoon liquid hot sauce

2 strips of bacon

½ cup panko or plain white bread crumbs

1. Wash and prick the potato with a fork. Cook it in the microwave for 7 to 9 minutes or until it is cooked through. Set aside to cool. **2.** In a food processor, pulse the fish five times. Add the butter and pulse again three times until the fish is shredded. **3.** Peel the potato. In a large bowl with a fork, mash the potato with the ½ teaspoon salt and pepper, leaving small chunks. **4.** Add the fish to the potatoes with the scallions, 1 tablespoon of the parsley, and the hot sauce. Work with your hands to combine it. Form four cakes and place them on a plate. Refrigerate for 15 minutes. **5.** Set the oven at 425°F. **6.** In a small skillet, render the bacon until golden. Transfer it to paper towels. When cool, crumble the bacon. **7.** Add the bacon, bread crumbs, remaining parsley, salt, and pepper to the fat in the pan. Mix well. **8.** Set the cakes on a rimmed baking sheet. Place enough topping on each of the cakes to cover the top. Bake them for 20 minutes or until they are golden brown.

Christine Merlo

Crab Cakes

Crab cakes are one of those unusual dishes that are easy to make at home, but have maintained their status on luxurious restaurant menus. Great cakes are long on crab and short on filler, as in this version. Those proportions make the cakes difficult to handle, so it's best to refrigerate them for a few hours before frying.

SERVES 4

1 pound fresh lump crabmeat

1 tablespoon mayonnaise

1 teaspoon Dijon mustard

2 teaspoons flour

Salt and pepper, to taste

Extra flour or fresh bread
  crumbs (for dredging)

3 tablespoons butter

½ cup tartar sauce

1 lemon, cut into 4 wedges

1. In a large bowl gently combine the crabmeat, mayonnaise, mustard, the 2 teaspoons of flour, salt, and pepper. Cover the mixture and refrigerate for 10 minutes. Form into 4 patties. Line a plate with plastic wrap and put the crab cakes on it. Cover with more plastic wrap and refrigerate for about 2 hours. **2.** Put the extra flour or bread crumbs in a shallow bowl for dredging. **3.** In a large skillet over medium heat, melt the butter. Meanwhile, quickly and gently, dredge the cakes in the flour or crumbs, tapping off the excess. Add the cakes to the skillet. **4.** Cook for 8 minutes, turning halfway through cooking, or until both sides are golden brown. Serve with tartar sauce and lemon wedges.

Jonathan Levitt

Mackerel with Lemon and Thyme

Dark-fleshed, muscular, and streamlined for constant swimming, the tiger-striped Atlantic mackerel is a treat best eaten freshly caught. Right out of the water mackerel are rich, clean, and mild, but two days later the high oil content can cause the fish to go off. If you've caught your own, have fish for breakfast, coated in oatmeal and pan-fried in bacon fat. Most of the time, simple is best: stuffed with sprigs of fresh thyme and roasted whole with lemons, a drizzle of olive oil, and some white wine.

SERVES 4

Olive oil (for sprinkling)

4 whole mackerel (1 to 2
  pounds each), cleaned with
  heads and tails intact

1 bunch fresh thyme or lemon
  thyme

2 lemons, very thinly sliced

½ cup white wine

Salt and pepper, to taste

1. Set the oven at 400°F. Have on hand a baking dish or roasting pan large enough to hold the four mackerel without overlapping. Oil it lightly. Stuff each mackerel cavity with a few sprigs of thyme. **2.** Lay the lemon slices in the dish or pan. Lay the remaining sprigs of thyme on top of the lemons. Set the fish on top. Pour the white wine over the fish and sprinkle with olive oil, salt, and pepper. **3.** Roast the fish for 15 minutes without turning them over, or until the flesh is opaque all the way to the bone. Serve with steamed potatoes.

Jonathan Levitt

Fish in a Dish

Cambridge, Massachusetts, caterer Ariadne Clifton says this is one of her favorite dishes, great for hosts who want to serve fish but are worried guests might not like it. To make it, haddock or cod is smothered in sliced potatoes and tomatoes, and baked with olive oil and lemon juice.

SERVES 4

Olive oil (for the dish)

4 Yukon Gold or Yellow Finn potatoes, thickly sliced

1 sweet onion, sliced into thin rounds

4 cloves garlic, smashed with the side of a knife

1 cup fresh parsley, basil, or oregano

3 large ripe tomatoes, thinly sliced

1 fresh hot chili pepper, seeded and finely chopped

Salt and black pepper, to taste

1 cup pitted black olives

½ cup olive oil

Juice of 1 lemon

1½ pounds haddock or cod or other firm white fish

1. Set the oven at 350°F. Lightly oil a 12-inch baking dish. **2.** In a saucepan fitted with a steamer insert and several inches of water, steam the potatoes in a covered pan over high heat for 8 minutes or until they are almost tender. **3.** Lay half the onions in the baking dish, then half the garlic, and half the parsley, basil, or oregano. Add a layer of potatoes, then a layer of tomatoes, chili pepper, salt, black pepper, and olives. Sprinkle with half the oil and half the lemon juice. **4.** Add the fish, then continue layering, beginning with onions and ending with olives, oil, and lemon. **5.** Cover with foil and bake the fish for 20 minutes. **6.** Remove the foil and continue baking for 15 minutes or until the fish is cooked through and flaky.

Ariadne Clifton

Country Salmon Pie

Salmon, peas, and corn get a mashed potato crust in this "pie," a favorite of Cambridge, Massachusetts, caterer Ariadne Clifton. Cook the salmon according to the recipe for oven-poached salmon (see page 182).

SERVES 6

5 large boiling potatoes, cut up

2 cloves garlic

Salt and black pepper, to taste

½ cup sour cream

8 tablespoons (1 stick) butter

2½ pounds skinless, boneless
  salmon, cooked

Butter (for the dish)

2 tablespoons flour

2 cups whole milk, or more if
  necessary

Juice of ½ lemon, or to taste

1 fresh chili pepper, finely
  chopped or 1 teaspoon
  crushed red pepper

1 cup frozen baby peas

1 cup frozen corn

3 scallions, chopped

¼ cup chopped fresh parsley

¼ cup chopped fresh dill

1 cup grated sharp cheddar

1. In a large saucepan, combine the potatoes, garlic, and a generous pinch of salt. Add water to cover by several inches. Bring to a boil, lower the heat, and simmer the potatoes for 15 minutes or until they are tender. Drain the potatoes into a colander. **2.** In a bowl, mash the potatoes with black pepper, sour cream, and 4 tablespoons of the butter. Taste for seasoning and add more salt and pepper if you like; set aside. **3.** When the salmon is cool enough to handle, flake it into a bowl. **4.** Set the oven at 350°F. Butter a deep 12-inch baking dish. **5.** In a large saucepan, melt 2 tablespoons of the butter. Whisk in the flour and cook, stirring constantly, for 2 minutes. Gradually whisk in the milk. Bring to a boil, stirring constantly, until the mixture thickens to make a white sauce. Whisk in the lemon, chili or red pepper, peas, corn, scallions, salt, parsley, and dill. Cook for 2 minutes more or until the vegetables are hot. **6.** Spoon half the white sauce into the baking dish. Add the fish and cover with the remaining white sauce. Spoon the mashed potatoes on top. Sprinkle with cheese and dot with the remaining 2 tablespoons butter. **7.** Bake the fish for 30 to 35 minutes or until the mixture is hot and golden brown.

Ariadne Clifton

Salmon Mousse with Sour Cream-Dill Sauce

A handsome mold of pink salmon, served with a sour cream–dill sauce, this mousse can be served on a spring buffet or as a first course for an elegant dinner.

SERVES 8

MOUSSE

1¼ pounds skinless, boneless salmon

6 tablespoons cold water

1 envelope unflavored gelatin

½ cup boiling water

1 tablespoon lemon juice

½ cup mayonnaise

1 teaspoon hot sauce

¼ teaspoon paprika

1 tablespoon grated onion

1 teaspoon salt

1 tablespoon capers

½ cup heavy cream, beaten until stiff

SAUCE AND GARNISH

1½ cups sour cream

1 tablespoon lemon juice

2 teaspoons sugar

1 teaspoon salt

2 tablespoons chopped fresh dill

½ pint cherry tomatoes, quartered

1 pickling cucumber, thinly sliced

Extra fresh dill leaves (for garnish)

MOUSSE

1. Have on hand one mold, loaf pan, or individual molds (total capacity 5 cups). **2.** In a microwave-safe dish, place the salmon and 4 tablespoons of the water. Cover with parchment paper and microwave on high for 8 minutes. If the salmon is not firm, microwave for 2 minutes more. With a slotted metal spatula, remove the salmon from the dish. **3.** In a bowl, sprinkle the gelatin over the remaining 2 tablespoons cold water. Set aside for 5 minutes. **4.** Pour the boiling water over the gelatin mixture and stir until it dissolves completely. **5.** In a food processor, combine the gelatin mixture, lemon juice, mayonnaise, hot sauce, paprika, onion, and salt. Pulse several times. **6.** Add half the salmon mixture and pulse until smooth. Add the remaining salmon with the capers. Pulse several times until completely blended. Transfer to a bowl. **7.** Stir 1 large spoonful of the whipped cream into the salmon mixture. Fold in the remaining cream. **8.** Moisten a paper towel and wring it out. Wipe the inside of your mold or molds. Add the salmon mixture to the mold, cover, and refrigerate for several hours or overnight.

SAUCE AND GARNISH

1. In a small bowl, whisk the sour cream and lemon juice until the mixture is smooth. **2.** Add the sugar, salt, and dill. Cover and refrigerate. **3.** To unmold the salmon mousse, run a thin-bladed knife carefully between the mousse and the mold. Invert a plate onto the mold. With your hand on top of the plate, flip the mold and plate over. **4.** Dampen a dish towel with hot water; wring it dry. Place the hot towel on the mold for several seconds to loosen the contents. Give the mold a gentle shake. You should hear the mousse release. Lift the mold from the mousse. **5.** Garnish with cherry tomatoes, cucumbers, and dill leaves. Serve with French bread and sour cream sauce.

Debra Samuels

Soy-Marinated Grilled Salmon

Use this simple gingery sauce to marinate fresh tuna and swordfish before grilling.

SERVES 8

½ cup soy sauce

1 piece (1½ inches) fresh ginger, peeled and grated

¼ cup chopped scallions

3 pounds skinless, boneless salmon

Black pepper, to taste

Canola oil (for the grill rack)

1. In a bowl, combine the soy sauce, ginger, and scallions. **2.** In a baking dish, set the salmon in the bottom and pour the marinade over it. Add pepper, cover, and refrigerate at least 1 hour. **3.** Light a charcoal grill or set a gas grill to medium-high. Scrape the rack to clean it, then brush it with oil. **4.** When the coals turn gray or the gas grill is hot, set the fish on the rack and cook for 10 to 12 minutes, turning once, or until it is cooked through, but still moist.

From Finely JPs,
Wellfleet, Massachusetts

Citrus-Marinated Swordfish Steaks

Like tuna and salmon, swordfish loves citrus and a little smoke from a hot grill. This swordfish is marinated in orange juice, olive oil, honey, balsamic vinegar, rosemary, and ginger, then set on charcoals.

SERVES 4

½ cup orange juice

2 tablespoons olive oil

2 tablespoons honey

2 tablespoons balsamic vinegar

2 cloves garlic, crushed

1 tablespoon chopped fresh rosemary

½ teaspoon chopped fresh ginger

2 teaspoons grated orange rind

Pinch of ground allspice

Salt and pepper, to taste

1½ pounds swordfish

Canola oil

1. In a large bowl, combine the orange juice, oil, honey, balsamic vinegar, garlic, rosemary, ginger, orange rind, allspice, salt, and pepper. **2.** Place the swordfish in a baking dish large enough to hold it in one layer. Pour the marinade over the fish, cover, and refrigerate for 2 to 3 hours. **3.** Light a charcoal grill or set a gas grill to medium-high. Scrape the rack to clean it, then brush it with oil. **4.** When the coals turn gray or the gas grill is hot, set the fish on the rack and cook for 8 to 10 minutes, turning once, or until it is cooked through, but still moist.

Debbie Barry

Grilled Swordfish Swimming in Thai Herbs

Swordfish grilled with a spicy aioli is served on a bed of salad greens and fresh herbs in this appealing dish.

SERVES 4

NUOC CHAM

¼ cup lime juice

¼ cup fish sauce

2 tablespoons sugar, or to taste

3 Thai bird chilies, cored and sliced

1 large clove garlic, grated

AIOLI

½ cup mayonnaise

2 teaspoons Dijon mustard

1 tablespoon lemon juice

¼ teaspoon kosher salt, or to taste

2 tablespoons sriracha (hot sauce)

Pinch of cayenne pepper

Dash of Worcestershire sauce

FISH

Salt, to taste

1 package (8 ounces) rice vermicelli noodles

4 swordfish steaks (6 ounces each)

Canola oil (for the grill rack)

1 head butter lettuce, cored and cleaned

½ bunch fresh cilantro (leaves only)

½ bunch fresh Thai basil (leaves only)

½ bunch fresh mint (leaves only)

NUOC CHAM

In a bowl, combine the lime juice, fish sauce, sugar, chilies, and garlic. Whisk thoroughly.

AIOLI

In a bowl, whisk the mayonnaise, mustard, lemon juice, salt, sriracha, cayenne pepper, and Worcestershire sauce. Taste for seasoning and add more salt, if you like.

FISH

1. Light a charcoal or gas grill. **2.** Bring a saucepan of salted water to a boil. Add the noodles. Cook, stirring occasionally, for 4 minutes. Drain into a colander. **3.** Rub the swordfish steaks all over with aioli. When the grill is ready, rub the grill rack with canola oil. **4.** Grill the swordfish for 4 minutes, turn it over, and cook on the other side for 4 minutes more. **5.** Divide the lettuce among four dinner plates. Scatter the cilantro, basil, and mint on top. Divide the vermicelli noodles among the plates. Place the grilled swordfish on top. Pour nuoc cham over the fish.

From Myers+Chang restaurant,
Boston, Massachusetts

Broiled Tuna Kebabs

A dark Asian marinade of soy sauce, rice vinegar, dark sesame oil, and wasabi goes onto pieces of tuna, which are threaded onto skewers and broiled. Use the same marinade and technique to cook swordfish or salmon.

SERVES 4

2 tablespoons soy sauce

1 tablespoon rice vinegar

1 teaspoon dark sesame oil

1 teaspoon powdered wasabi
   paste mixed with 1 teaspoon
   water

1 pound tuna steak, about 1
   inch thick, cut into 2-inch
   pieces

1. In a bowl, combine the soy sauce, rice vinegar, sesame oil, and wasabi. **2.** Add the tuna and toss well. Cover and refrigerate for 20 minutes. **3.** Turn on the broiler. **4.** Thread the tuna onto skewers. Set them in a baking dish. Broil them about 8-inches from the element for 4 minutes. Turn them and cook the other side for 4 minutes or until the tuna is opaque on the outside but still pink inside.

Lisa Zwirn

Mustard-Coated Mackerel

An oily dark-fleshed fish, mackerel needs smoke from an outdoor grill or lots of lemon juice and mustard. Any recipe that suits bluefish is also good for mackerel. Use leftover grilled mackerel to make smoked fish pâté (see page 13).

SERVES 2

Olive oil (for the sheet)

1 large mackerel (2 pounds)
   split and boned (or two
   1-pound mackerel)

1 tablespoon olive oil

1/2 teaspoon salt

Pepper, to taste

4 tablespoons lemon juice

1 tablespoon Dijon mustard

2 tablespoons butter, melted

2 tablespoons chopped fresh
   parsley

1. Set a rack about 4 inches from the broiling element. Turn on the broiler. Oil a rimmed baking sheet. **2.** Set the fish on the baking sheet skin side down. **3.** Sprinkle it with olive oil, salt, pepper, and 2 tablespoons of the lemon juice. **4.** Broil the fish for 5 minutes (it will not be cooked through). **5.** In a bowl, combine the remaining 2 tablespoons lemon juice, mustard, and butter. Spread on the fish. Continue broiling for 2 minutes or until the top is golden and the fish is cooked through. Sprinkle with parsley.

Oven-Poached Salmon with Cucumber "Scales"

Striking and elegant, this whole side of salmon, covered with thin slices of cucumber, can be served to a head of state. It's that beautiful—and delicious.

SERVES 6

1 skinless, boneless salmon
   fillet (2½ to 3 pounds)
Canola oil (for sprinkling)
Salt and pepper, to taste
2 seedless English cucumbers
   or 3 regular cucumbers
1 heaping teaspoon Dijon
   mustard
1 cup mayonnaise
1 tablespoon white wine
   vinegar
1 tablespoon warm water, or to
   taste
½ cup chopped mixed parsley,
   basil, and mint
1 tablespoon canola oil
1½ pounds sugar snap peas,
   trimmed with strings
   removed

1. Set the oven at 450°F. Line a jelly roll pan or another large rimmed baking pan with two sheets of parchment paper. Have on hand a platter slightly longer than the salmon. **2.** Set the salmon, skinned side up, on the parchment. Rub the fish with oil and sprinkle with salt and pepper. Cover the fish with another piece of parchment paper, tucking the sides down so it completely encases the fillet. Cover the pan with heavy-duty foil, shiny side down. **3.** Cook the salmon for 15 minutes or until it is cooked through. Loosen the foil at the edges of the pan and let the salmon cool completely. **4.** Trim the cucumbers at both ends. Remove the plastic on the English cucumbers, if necessary. On a mandoline or other handheld slicing machine, cut the cucumbers as thinly as possible. **5.** In a bowl whisk the mustard, mayonnaise, vinegar, and water. Add salt and pepper and enough additional water to make a mixture that holds its shape but pours easily. Stir in the parsley mixture. **6.** Use both sides of the parchment paper to lift the salmon from the baking pan and carefully transfer it to the platter. Tear the parchment and begin removing pieces of the paper until there is no more parchment under the fish. **7.** Starting at the widest part of the salmon, arrange rows of cucumbers so they overlap slightly. **8.** In a large skillet, heat the canola oil and add the sugar snap peas, salt, and pepper. Cook over high heat, stirring constantly, for 2 minutes or until the peas are tender. **9.** Garnish the salmon with the sugar snaps. Serve with the mayonnaise sauce.

Sheryl Julian

Halibut Roasted under Tomato Slices

Roasting suits dark-fleshed fish, but white fish can dry out. Cover it with sliced tomatoes, which protect the fish in a hot oven.

SERVES 4

Olive oil (for sprinkling)

1½ pounds boneless halibut, cut into 4 even-size pieces

Salt and pepper, to taste

3 tomatoes, cored and thinly sliced

15 pitted kalamata olives

Grated rind of ½ lemon

2 tablespoons chopped fresh parsley

1. Set the oven at 375°F. Lightly oil a 12-inch baking dish. **2.** Place the fish in the dish. Rub it with oil and sprinkle with salt and pepper. Cover the fish with overlapping slices of tomato. Sprinkle with more oil, salt, and pepper. Roast the fish for 15 minutes or until it is cooked through. **3.** Meanwhile, in a bowl combine the olives, lemon rind, and parsley. When the fish is cooked, sprinkle the mixture on the tomatoes.

Sheryl Julian

Vermicelli with White Clam Sauce

Because there were so many clams in the waters around their Cape Cod, Massachusetts, home, Gerri Sullivan's family collected and froze them for the winter, then made this white clam sauce for pasta. Sullivan's mother didn't like garlic, so there is none in this dish. Add it if you like.

SERVES 4

3 tablespoons olive oil

1 large onion, finely chopped

¼ cup chopped fresh Italian parsley

½ pound fresh clams, chopped

1 cup fresh or bottled clam broth

Salt and pepper, to taste

1 pound vermicelli, cooked until tender

1. In a large, heavy-based casserole, heat the oil and cook the onion over medium heat for 10 minutes, stirring often, or until the onion softens. **2.** Add the parsley, clams, and broth. Bring to a boil, lower the heat, and simmer for 5 minutes. **3.** Sprinkle with salt and pepper. **4.** In a large pasta bowl, spoon some of the clam sauce into the bottom. Place the pasta on top and then add the remaining clam sauce. Toss gently.

Gerri Sullivan

Spaghetti with Seafood in Tomato Sauce

Clams, shrimp, and mussels in a homemade tomato sauce are spooned over spaghetti. This is a popular Italian-American restaurant dish all over Boston, Massachusetts.

SERVES 4

1 can (28 ounces) whole peeled imported tomatoes

¼ cup olive oil

4 cloves garlic, smashed

2 teaspoons chopped fresh thyme

¼ teaspoon crushed red pepper, or to taste

1 cup dry white wine

Salt and black pepper, to taste

¾ pound spaghetti

1 pound littleneck clams, rinsed and scrubbed

½ pound large shrimp, peeled

¾ pound mussels, beards removed, rinsed and scrubbed

2 tablespoons chopped fresh parsley

1. In a food processor, puree the tomatoes with their juice. **2.** In a large flameproof casserole over medium heat, heat the oil and garlic. Cook, tossing the cloves occasionally, for 3 minutes or until they are brown. Add the thyme and red pepper and cook, stirring, for 30 seconds. Remove the garlic from the pan. **3.** Turn the heat to high; stir in the wine and tomato mixture. Bring to a boil, lower the heat, and set the cover on askewed. Simmer, stirring occasionally, for 15 minutes. **4.** Bring a large pot of salted water to a boil. Add the spaghetti and cook, stirring often, for 11 minutes or until it is tender but still has some bite. **5.** Meanwhile, add the clams to the tomato sauce. Turn the heat to medium-high, cover, and cook, shaking the pan occasionally, for 4 minutes or until most of the shells open. **6.** Add the shrimp, cover, and cook, stirring occasionally, for 3 minutes. Add the mussels, cover, and cook for 2 minutes or until they open. Discard any clams or mussels that do not open. Add salt and black pepper, to taste. **7.** Drain the pasta, return it to its pot, and add 1 cup of the tomato sauce. Cook over medium heat for 2 minutes, tossing until the pasta absorbs most of the sauce. **8.** Divide the pasta among four bowls, and top with sauce and shellfish. Sprinkle with parsley.

Tony Rosenfeld

Sicilian Fish Stew

Potatoes, green olives, lots of herbs, tomatoes, and red wine go into this cod stew. The potatoes simmer in a tomato-wine sauce, which gives them a great flavor.

SERVES 6

2 tablespoons olive oil

1 Spanish onion, sliced

1 clove garlic, finely chopped

1 can (28 ounces) whole peeled
   tomatoes and their juices,
   crushed in a bowl

1 cup tomato sauce

1 cup water

1 cup dry red wine

2 large russet potatoes, cut
   into ½-inch chunks

½ cup large green Sicilian
   olives, pitted and quartered

2 pounds skinless, boneless
   cod, cut into 2-inch chunks

1 teaspoon chopped fresh basil

1 teaspoon chopped oregano

1 teaspoon chopped parsley

Salt and pepper, to taste

1. In a large flameproof casserole over medium-high heat, heat the olive oil. Add the onion and cook, stirring often, for 3 minutes. Add the garlic and cook for 1 minute more. **2.** Add the tomatoes, tomato sauce, water, wine, potatoes, and olives. Bring to a boil, cover the pan, and simmer for 25 minutes or until the potatoes are tender. **3.** Add the fish, re-cover the pan, and simmer for 8 to 10 minutes or until the fish is opaque. Stir in the basil, oregano, parsley, salt, and pepper. Taste for seasoning, add more salt and pepper, if you like.

Christine Merlo

Oven-Fried Fish

Almost like deep-fat fried, this oven version is quick and healthy.

SERVES 4

1½ pounds firm-fleshed
    skinless white fish fillets
    (haddock, cusk, or pollock),
    cut into 4 pieces

Olive oil (for sprinkling)

Salt and pepper, to taste

¾ cup panko or other dry
    white bread crumbs

1. Set the oven at 450°F. Lightly oil a rimmed baking sheet. **2.** Rub the fish all over with oil. Sprinkle it with salt and pepper. Place the bread crumbs in a large shallow bowl. Press the fish into the crumbs and turn the fillets to coat both sides. Transfer the fish to the baking sheet. **3.** Bake the fish for 15 to 18 minutes or until it is golden and firm to the touch.

Sheryl Julian & Julie Riven

Oven-Fried Fish Sandwich

Begin with cooked fish, add a spicy Russian dressing and some lettuce, and tuck it all into a soft hamburger bun. You can use any simply prepared fish, including something off the grill.

SERVES 4

1 recipe Oven-Fried Fish (see
    above)

4 hamburger buns

⅓ cup mayonnaise

1 tablespoon spicy cocktail
    sauce or ketchup, or to taste

1 tablespoon prepared white
    horseradish, or to taste

2 teaspoons grated raw onion

1 tablespoon sweet pickle relish

Salt and pepper, to taste

4 iceberg or Boston lettuce
    leaves

1. Set the oven at 450°F. **2.** Wrap the buns in foil. Five minutes before the fish is ready, set the buns in the hot oven to warm them. **3.** In a small bowl, combine the mayonnaise, cocktail sauce or ketchup, horseradish, onion, relish, salt, and pepper. Taste for seasoning and add more cocktail sauce or ketchup or horseradish, if you like. **4.** Split the buns and spread dressing on both cut sides. Add a fish fillet and lettuce leaf.

Sheryl Julian & Julie Riven

Bluefish Wrapped in Grape Leaves

Grape leaves, preserved in brine, are bottled or canned. To make this dish, carefully remove a bunch of leaves, unroll them, and rinse them in one or two changes of cold water. Wrap the bluefish in them with lots of herbs. The fish for this recipe should be ¾ to 1 inch thick.

SERVES 4

¼ cup coarsely chopped basil
   leaves

¼ cup chopped parsley

2 tablespoons chopped fresh
   chives

1 tablespoon chopped fresh
   marjoram

3 tablespoons olive oil

4 thick pieces boneless
   bluefish, skin intact (6 to 8
   ounces each)

Salt and pepper, to taste

About 12 to 16 grape leaves,
   stems removed

1 lemon, cut into wedges

1. Light a charcoal grill or turn a gas grill to medium-high heat. **2.** In a bowl, combine the basil, parsley, chives, marjoram, and olive oil. Sprinkle the fish with salt and pepper. **3.** On a work surface, place 3 or 4 grape leaves, slightly overlapping, so the surface area is 2 to 3 inches larger than the piece of fish. Spoon some of the herb mixture onto the flesh side of the fish and place the fish flesh side down (skin side up) on the leaves. Spoon a little of the herb mixture onto the skin side. Fold the grape leaves over the fish to create a little bundle. (Don't make it too tight; the leaves will stick together during cooking.) Repeat with the remaining fish. **4.** Place the bundles seams up on the grill. Grill 5 to 6 minutes. With tongs, turn the fish and grill 5 to 6 minutes more. To determine if the fish is cooked through, stick the point of a small, sharp knife through the grape leaves into the fish, then touch the knife to the inside of your lower lip. If the knife is hot (not just warm), the fish is done. Serve with lemon wedges.

Adapted from Rocca restaurant,
Boston, Massachusetts

Tartar Sauce

Homemade tartar sauce is so different from store-bought, you'll think you've made another sauce. Begin with commercial mayonnaise and add gherkins, capers, and parsley. Serve this with plain grilled or broiled fish, or use it to spread on buns or toast for fish sandwiches.

SERVES 4

1 cup mayonnaise

2 tablespoons lemon juice, or
  to taste

1 clove garlic, crushed

¼ cup finely chopped gherkins,
  or to taste

2 tablespoons capers

¼ cup chopped fresh parsley

Salt and pepper, to taste

1. In a bowl, stir the mayonnaise and lemon juice until smooth. **2.** Stir in the garlic, gherkins, capers, parsley, salt, and pepper. Taste the tartar sauce for seasoning and add more salt, gherkins, or lemon juice if you like. Cover the bowl with plastic wrap and refrigerate until ready to use.

Sheryl Julian

Beef, Lamb, Pork, Chicken, and Other Meats

Meat and poultry are the center of the plate in most households in America, though many people claim to have cut down on meat because of high cholesterol. Even restaurants are trying to make portions smaller (it's better for the customers and for the establishment's bottom line).

But the fact remains that aside from vegetarians and heart-healthy diners, most people aren't satisfied unless they savor something beefy, a little taste of caramelized chicken, or a morsel of tender pork.

Today's supermarket meat case offers many cuts that do the prep work for consumers: Steaks are marinated, chicken is threaded onto kebabs, chops and poultry pieces are boned, and stew meat is packaged with vegetables already cut up. In fact, markets are so busy playing to harried cooks, that it's sometimes hard to find chicken breasts still on the bone and other old-fashioned bone-in cuts.

For people who love to cook, simmering a chuck roast isn't time-consuming because after the meat is in the oven, your work is done. Roasting a turkey once in a while means lots of leftovers for delicious sandwiches or dishes such as turkey pie with biscuit crust. And a simmering pot of corned beef and vegetables will produce New England boiled dinner and the famous breakfast dish red flannel hash the following morning.

If you're watching your wallet or your waistline, stretch ground meat the way our grandmothers did: Mix it into a meat loaf, simmer it with tomatoes for sloppy Joes, or roll it inside cabbage leaves.

People's appetite for meat may be changing, but consumers still demand it. Just pop into any steak house on a Saturday night to see the crowds. Avoid the wait and the bill by buying your own sirloins, opening a special bottle of wine, and sitting down to a juicy entree.

Dry-Rubbed Steaks with Red Wine Sauce

One hot skillet, four beautiful steaks, and you're a chef in your own home. Use whatever red wine you're drinking to make a quick shallot pan sauce.

SERVES 6

RUB AND STEAKS

1 tablespoon chili powder

1 tablespoon instant espresso powder

¼ cup brown sugar

2 teaspoons ground ginger

1 tablespoon dry mustard

1 tablespoon kosher salt

1 tablespoon ground black pepper

4 sirloin steaks or another tender cut (about 2½ to 3 pounds total)

Olive oil for sprinkling

2 tablespoons olive oil

SAUCE

1 tablespoon olive oil

1 shallot, chopped

⅔ cup dry red wine

⅔ cup beef stock

2 tablespoons unsalted butter, cut into pieces

Salt and pepper, to taste

RUB AND STEAKS

1. In a bowl, combine the chili powder, espresso powder, brown sugar, ginger, mustard, salt, and pepper. Remove 2 teaspoons of the rub and set it aside. **2.** With a fork, score both sides of each steak. With your hands, rub the steaks lightly with olive oil. Press the dry rub into the meat all over. Set the steaks aside for 20 minutes. **3.** Set the oven at 400°F. **4.** Heat a 12-inch skillet with a heatproof handle over high heat. Add 2 tablespoons of the olive oil and swirl the pan to coat it evenly. When the oil is very hot, brown the steaks for 2 to 3 minutes or until a dark crust forms on the bottom. Turn and sear the other side for 2 minutes. **5.** Transfer the steaks to the oven. Cook for 5 to 8 minutes or until a meat thermometer inserted into the thickest part of the meat registers 125°F for medium rare. Continue cooking for 5 minutes more for well-done meat. Remove the steaks from the skillet and set the meat in a warm place.

SAUCE

1. In the skillet used to sear the steaks, wipe the excess oil from the pan with a paper towel. Heat the olive oil in the skillet over medium heat. When it is hot, cook the shallot, stirring often, for 2 minutes. Add the red wine, stock, and 2 teaspoons of the reserved rub. Cook, stirring constantly, until the sauce reduces to ½ cup. Remove the pan from the heat. **2.** Reheat the sauce without boiling. Slowly whisk in the butter a little at a time until it melts. Taste for seasoning and add more salt and pepper, if you like. **3.** Thinly slice the steaks and spoon sauce over each one.

Christine Merlo

Pan-Seared Steaks with Rosemary Butter

For guests, strip steaks aren't cheap, but they do have wonderful flavor and texture. Buy less expensive London broil if you prefer. Use a heavy-based skillet (cast-iron works well) so the steaks brown nicely without burning.

SERVES 4

4 strip steaks (preferably 1½ inches thick) or London broil (2½ pounds total)

1½ teaspoons kosher salt

½ teaspoon black pepper

1 tablespoon canola or vegetable oil

2 teaspoons chopped fresh rosemary

3 tablespoons butter, cut into small pieces

1. Set the oven at 450°F. Sprinkle the steaks with 1 teaspoon of the salt and the pepper; set aside. **2.** In a 12-inch skillet with a heatproof handle, heat the oil over medium-high heat for 2 minutes or until it's shimmering hot. Add the steaks (cook in two batches if necessary) and cook, without moving them, for 3 minutes or until the bottoms are browned. Use tongs to turn the steaks and cook for 2 minutes more or until the other side browns. **3.** Sprinkle the steaks with rosemary and transfer the skillet to the oven. **4.** Cook for 5 minutes or until an instant-read meat thermometer inserted into the thickest part of the steaks registers 125°F for medium rare. Continue cooking for 5 minutes more for well-done meat. **5.** Set a couple of pieces of butter on each steak and sprinkle with the remaining ½ teaspoon salt.

Tony Rosenfeld

Braised Beef with Vegetables

Beef bottom round or chuck roast becomes meltingly tender after two hours in the oven. Partway through cooking, turnips or parsnips, yellow potatoes, and carrots go into the pan. Serve with horseradish sauce (see page 200).

SERVES 6

1 boneless beef bottom round roast or beef chuck roast (4 to 5 pounds total)

Salt and pepper, to taste

1 medium onion, quartered

2 whole cloves

2 sprigs fresh thyme

1 bay leaf

½ cup dry white wine

2 cups chicken stock or water

3 small turnips or parsnips, quartered

6 small Yukon Gold or Yellow Finn potatoes, halved

3 large carrots, cut into 1½-inch lengths

1. Turn on the broiler. Have on hand a heavy 4-quart casserole. **2.** Sprinkle the meat with salt and pepper. Place the meat in a large heavy skillet with an ovenproof handle (cast-iron works well). Broil the meat about 6 inches from the element for 5 minutes or until the surface is caramelized. Using tongs, turn the roast and broil the other side. Remove the pan from the broiler. **3.** Turn the oven down to 300°F. **4.** With the tongs, transfer the meat to the casserole. Place the onion, cloves, thyme, and bay leaf in the pan. **5.** Wipe out the excess fat from the skillet with paper towels. Set the skillet over medium heat. Add the wine and bring to a boil, scraping the bottom. Add the stock or water and return to a boil. Pour the hot liquid over the beef. **6.** Cover the casserole and transfer to the oven. Cook for 30 minutes, turn the meat, and continue cooking for 30 minutes. **7.** Turn the meat again. Add the turnips or parsnips, potatoes, and carrots to the side of the pan. Continue cooking for 1 hour or until the meat and vegetables are very tender (total cooking time is 2 hours). **8.** Transfer the meat to a cutting board. With a slotted spoon transfer the vegetables to a large deep platter. Cover loosely with foil and set aside in a warm place. **9.** Set the pan over medium-high heat and let the liquid bubble steadily, skimming the surface thoroughly to remove excess fat, for 3 minutes or until the sauce reduces and thickens. **10.** Slice the meat into ½-inch thick pieces. Arrange on the vegetables, ladle some cooking liquid on top, and serve the rest separately.

Jonathan Levitt

Beef Stew

Nothing fancy here, just stew beef, carrots, potatoes, and mushrooms, simmered with tomatoes.

SERVES 8

2½ pounds stew beef, cut into
   2-inch pieces

1 teaspoon salt

1 teaspoon pepper

¼ cup vegetable oil

2 large onions, cut into 8
   wedges each

3 garlic cloves, chopped

1 teaspoon ground cumin

½ cup red wine

6 carrots, cut into 1-inch slices

3 medium potatoes, cut into
   1-inch chunks

1 can (28 ounces) peeled Italian
   tomatoes, with their juices

1 cinnamon stick

5 cups water

1½ pounds button mushrooms,
   quartered

3 tablespoons chopped fresh
   parsley

1. In a bowl, toss the beef with salt and pepper. **2.** In a large flameproof casserole, heat the oil. Cook the onions and garlic for 5 minutes. Add the beef and cook for 8 minutes, turning often. Add the cumin and cook for 1 minute. **3.** Pour in the wine and bring to a boil. **4.** Add the carrots, potatoes, tomatoes, cinnamon stick, and water. Bring to a boil. **5.** Cover and simmer for 45 minutes. **6.** Add the mushrooms and continue cooking for 45 minutes or until the meat is very tender (total cooking time is 1½ hours). During cooking, add more water, ¼ cup at a time, if the pan seems dry. **7.** Taste for seasoning and add more salt and pepper, if you like. Sprinkle with parsley.

Debra Samuels

Baeckeoffe (Alsatian meat stew)

The classic dish baeckeoffe, which comes from France's easternmost region of Alsace, combines pork, beef, chicken, and potatoes in one pot, baked slowly for several hours. It's a hearty dish that's particularly well suited to northern climates because it warms the kitchen.

SERVES 8

1 tablespoon vegetable oil

2 onions, peeled and quartered

Salt and pepper, to taste

1½ pounds boneless pork loin,
   cut into 4-inch pieces

2 pounds boneless beef chuck,
   cut into 4-inch pieces

4 boiling potatoes (skins
   intact), cut into eighths

2 cloves garlic, crushed

1 bay leaf

1 bunch parsley stems tied with
   1 bunch fresh thyme

1 bottle dry white wine

2 large chicken breast halves,
   each halved horizontally

1. Set the oven at 325°F. **2.** In a large flameproof casserole with a tight-fitting lid, heat the oil. When it is hot, add the onions, salt, and pepper. Cook over low heat for 15 minutes. **3.** Add the pork, beef, potatoes, garlic, bay leaf, parsley tied with thyme, and wine. Add enough water to cover the meat and vegetables. **4.** Bring the mixture to a boil. Simmer for 2 minutes. **5.** Cover the pan and transfer it to the oven. Bake the mixture for 2 hours. **6.** Add the chicken, burying it in the meat mixture. Re-cover the pan and continue cooking for 1 hour or until the meats are tender and the chicken is cooked through (total cooking time is 3 hours). **7.** Serve the meat from the pot.

Sheryl Julian

New England Boiled Dinner

If you have a soup kettle and you can bring water to a boil, you can make New England boiled dinner. Simmer corned beef, then add carrots, Brussels sprouts, cabbage, potatoes, and beets. Serve with horseradish sauce (see page 200). It's a comforting, very old-fashioned dish.

SERVES 10

1 corned beef brisket (about 8 pounds)

2 whole peppercorns

2 whole cloves

14 large carrots, halved crosswise

2 pints Brussels sprouts, trimmed, with an X cut into the base of each

1 Savoy cabbage, cut into thick wedges

20 small red or white potatoes

2 bunches (8 medium) beets, peeled and quartered

1. In a soup kettle, combine the corned beef and enough water to cover it by 2 inches. Bring the liquid to a boil, skim the surface thoroughly, and reduce the heat to low. Add the peppercorns and cloves and cover the pot. **2.** Simmer the corned beef for 3 ½ hours, turning the meat halfway through cooking. **3.** Remove the meat from the cooking liquid and set it aside to cool. **4.** Add the carrots, Brussels sprouts, cabbage, and potatoes to the corned beef cooking water. Return to a boil, reduce the heat to low, and simmer the vegetables for 20 to 30 minutes or until they are very tender. **5.** Remove the vegetables from the cooking liquid and transfer them to a baking dish. Add the beets to the liquid, bring to a boil, and simmer for 20 minutes or until tender. Set them aside. **6.** Note: You can prepare up to this point in advance: Ladle the cooking liquid into a plastic container and let it cool. Refrigerate the boiled dinner in three containers: meat, vegetables, and beets. **7.** Set the oven at 325°F. **8.** Trim all the excess fat from the corned beef. Slice the corned beef against the grain. Arrange all of the vegetables and the meat in a large roasting pan, making several layers. Spoon enough cooking juices onto the mixture to moisten it. Cover with foil and transfer to the hot oven. Heat for 40 minutes or until hot.

Sheryl Julian & Julie Riven

Horseradish Sauce

Add sour cream to plain whole-milk yogurt, stir in grated bottled horseradish, raw onion, and both black and cayenne pepper, and the saucy mixture can be served with New England boiled dinner or other spoon-tender cuts of beef or lamb.

SERVES 10

1½ cups plain whole-milk
    yogurt
¾ cup sour cream
⅓ cup bottled white horseradish
2 teaspoons grated raw onion
Salt and black pepper, to taste
Pinch of cayenne pepper or
    chili powder, or to taste

1. In a small bowl, whisk the yogurt and sour cream together until they are smooth. **2.** Stir in the horseradish, onion, salt, black pepper, and cayenne or chili powder. Taste for seasoning and add more horseradish or onion if you like.

Sheryl Julian & Julie Riven

Red Flannel Hash

When you mix beets and potatoes in a skillet, the results look like red flannel, hence the name. There is no better breakfast than hash made with yesterday's New England boiled dinner, topped with a poached or soft-cooked egg. You can also use corned beef from a delicatessen and add leftover boiled potatoes. For soft-cooked eggs, see page 108.

SERVES 4

2 strips bacon
½ pound thickly sliced corned
    beef, coarsely chopped
3 cups diced leftover boiled
    potatoes
2 medium cooked beets,
    coarsely chopped
Salt and pepper, to taste
2 tablespoons butter
4 eggs, poached or soft-
    cooked

1. In a large nonstick 10-inch skillet, render the bacon over medium heat until it is golden. Set it on a plate lined with paper towels. Discard all but 1 tablespoon of fat from the pan. Set the skillet aside. **2.** Transfer the corned beef to a bowl. Add the potatoes and beets. Coarsely chop the bacon and add it to the meat mixture with salt and pepper. Mix thoroughly. **3.** Heat the fat in the skillet until it is hot. Add the butter; when it has melted, add the corned beef mixture. Press the hash down firmly with a metal spatula. Cook over medium-high heat for 10 minutes. Check the bottom of the hash by lifting the edge with the spatula. If it is browning too much, lower the heat. **4.** Use the spatula to turn the hash in pieces (it's okay if it breaks up). When it is all turned, press down again with the spatula and continue cooking for 10 minutes, pressing often, until the underside is nicely browned and crusty. Serve with eggs.

Sheryl Julian & Julie Riven

Pot Roast

Meat cooked with mustard, Worcestershire, brown sugar, and tomatoes turns dark, earthy, and delectable. Serve this spoon-tender chuck roast with buttered noodles.

SERVES 4

3 pounds boneless beef chuck roast

1 tablespoon Dijon mustard

Salt and black pepper, to taste

Pinch of crushed red pepper

1 tablespoon Worcestershire sauce

1 tablespoon brown sugar

2 cups whole peeled canned tomatoes, crushed

2 cups water

1 large Spanish onion, cut into thin wedges

1 clove garlic, finely chopped

2 tablespoons chopped fresh parsley

1. Set the oven at 350°F. Have on hand a heavy-based flameproof casserole (about 4-quart capacity). **2.** Place the beef in the casserole. **3.** In a bowl, stir together the mustard, salt, black pepper, red pepper, Worcestershire sauce, and brown sugar. Stir in the tomatoes and water. **4.** Pour the mixture over the meat. Tuck the onion and garlic around the meat. **5.** Bring the liquids to a boil. Cover the pan and transfer to the oven. Cook for 1½ hours, turning halfway through cooking, or until a fork inserted in the beef comes out easily. Remove the lid and cook for another 30 minutes (total cooking time is 2 hours). **6.** Remove the meat from the pan and transfer it to a cutting board; cover and keep warm. With a slotted spoon, remove the onions and transfer to a deep plate. Cover and keep warm. **7.** With a large spoon, skim off and discard the fat from the cooking liquid. Set the pan on a burner and bring the liquid to a boil. Let it bubble gently for 5 minutes, skimming often. Taste for seasoning and add more salt and black pepper, if you like. **8.** Slice the meat and return it to the pot. Add the onions. Sprinkle with parsley.

Sheryl Julian & Julie Riven

Sloppy Joes

Slightly sweet and sour, this sloppy Joe mixture is for spooning into soft buns. Make this during October's baseball playoffs, March's basketball games, or any weekend afternoon of football. The dish particularly suits hearty eaters.

SERVES 4

1½ pounds ground sirloin or
  other lean ground beef
1 tablespoon olive oil
1 onion, finely chopped
1 green bell pepper, cored,
  seeded, and finely chopped
1 red bell pepper, cored,
  seeded, and finely chopped
2 cloves garlic, finely chopped
⅛ teaspoon crushed red
  pepper
Salt and black pepper, to taste
1 can (15 ounces) whole
  tomatoes with their juices,
  finely chopped
2 tablespoons cider vinegar
2 teaspoons light or dark
  brown sugar
½ teaspoon dry mustard
⅛ teaspoon ground allspice
⅛ teaspoon ground cloves
2 tablespoons Worcestershire
  sauce
Dash of liquid hot sauce
4 sub rolls or other soft rolls (6
  inches each), split
Olive oil (for brushing)

1. In a large dry skillet, cook the meat over medium heat, stirring constantly, for 5 minutes or until it is broken up and turning brown. Remove it from the pan and wipe out the skillet. **2.** Add the oil, and when it is hot, cook the onion and green and red bell peppers over medium heat for 10 minutes, stirring often, or until the vegetables soften. **3.** Add the garlic, crushed red pepper, salt, and black pepper, and cook, stirring, for 1 minute. **4.** Stir the meat back into the pan. Add the tomatoes, vinegar, brown sugar, mustard, allspice, cloves, and Worcestershire and hot sauce. Bring to a boil, lower the heat, and simmer for 30 minutes. If the mixture seems dry, add water, 1 tablespoon at a time. **5.** Meanwhile, set the oven at 375°F. Set the rolls on a baking sheet. Brush the cut sides of the rolls with oil and transfer to the oven. Toast them lightly for 10 minutes or until golden. **6.** Taste the sauce for seasoning and add more salt and black pepper if you like. Set an open roll on each of four dinner plates. Spoon some of the meat mixture on each roll.

Sheryl Julian & Julie Riven

Sloppy Joe

Grilled Flank Steak Fajitas

You can also use 4 skinless, boneless chicken breast halves in place of the flank steak. Marinate the chicken for 5 minutes, and grill it for 5 minutes on a side or until cooked through.

SERVES 4

2 large onions, each cut
   lengthwise into 6 wedges
1½ tablespoons olive oil
2 green bell peppers, cored
   and halved
¼ cup lime juice
1 teaspoon salt, or to taste
1 teaspoon black pepper, or to
   taste
2 pounds flank steak
8 large flour tortillas
2 tablespoons chopped fresh
   cilantro
½ cup pico de gallo or chunky
   salsa
1 cup guacamole
1 cup sour cream (optional)

1. Light a charcoal grill or turn a gas grill to medium-high. **2.** Thread the onion wedges onto skewers and brush them with ½ tablespoon of the oil. Place the onions and bell pepper halves on the grill rack. Cook, turning occasionally, for 10 to 15 minutes (for the peppers) or 25 minutes (onions), or until both are tender and lightly charred. **3.** Transfer the vegetables to a cutting board. **4.** Meanwhile, in a shallow dish, combine the remaining 1 tablespoon of oil, lime juice, salt, and black pepper. Score the flank steak lightly on both sides. Add the steak to the marinade; turn it in the mixture. Set aside at room temperature for 10 minutes. **5.** Stack the tortillas and wrap tightly in foil. Place the bundle on the cooler part of the grill and heat for 10 minutes, turning several times, or until hot. **6.** Grill the steak for 4 to 5 minutes on a side for medium-rare meat (grill a few minutes longer for well-done meat). Transfer to a cutting board; let stand for 5 minutes. **7.** Thinly slice the meat across the grain. **8.** Cut the onions and peppers into large chunks. Place them on a serving platter and sprinkle with salt and pepper. Add the meat and any juices on the cutting board. Sprinkle with cilantro. **9.** Pass the tortillas, pico de gallo or salsa, guacamole, and sour cream (if using).

Lisa Zwirn

Carne Asada Tacos

Carne asada *(roasted meat) is a northern Mexican dish of tough, flavorful beef, which is marinated, charred on the grill, sliced thinly, and heaped onto tacos or burritos. You help yourself to salsa, guacamole, and hot sauces. At home, garnish slices of flank steak with a rustic and colorful salad of chopped tomatoes, avocado, onion, cilantro, and lime juice.*

MAKES 8

1 pound flank steak

Juice of 4 limes

2 teaspoons cayenne pepper

2 tablespoons vegetable oil

2 avocados, chopped

4 tomatoes, chopped

1 onion, chopped

16 sprigs fresh cilantro, chopped

8 soft corn tortillas, wrapped in foil

Hot sauce, to taste

1 lime, cut into 8 wedges

1. Set the meat on a board. Holding a knife blade parallel to the table, cut the meat in half, making 2 thin sheets. **2.** In a large bowl combine the lime juice, cayenne pepper, and vegetable oil. Add the beef and toss it in the mixture. Cover and refrigerate for 30 to 60 minutes. **3.** In a medium bowl combine the avocados, tomatoes, onion, and cilantro; set aside. **4.** Turn on the broiler. Set a rack on a roasting pan; set the steak on the rack. Slide the steaks under the broiler. Broil the steaks for 3 minutes on a side or until cooked through. Transfer the steaks to a board and set aside for 5 minutes. Turn the oven down to 375°F. Put the tortilla packet in the oven and cook for 8 minutes, turning the packet once. **5.** Slice the steaks against the grain into thin strips. Place beef on each tortilla. Top with the avocado mixture and hot sauce. Serve with lime wedges.

Jonathan Levitt

Italian-American Meatballs

A mixture of beef, pork, and veal forms the base of these meatballs, which are seasoned with Parmesan and pine nuts. Chopped prunes are also added; they disappear into the balls, and keep them moist. Simmer the meatballs in this simple homemade tomato sauce, and serve them over spaghetti, if you like, or eat the meatballs without pasta.

SERVES 6

SAUCE

2 cans (28 ounces each) whole peeled tomatoes

¼ cup olive oil

1 onion, finely chopped

2 cloves garlic, finely chopped

½ cup water

1 bay leaf

⅛ teaspoon salt, or to taste

¼ teaspoon crushed red pepper

MEATBALLS

3 ½ cups roughly chopped stale Italian bread

¾ cup whole milk

¼ cup ricotta cheese

¾ pound ground beef

¼ pound ground pork

¼ pound ground veal

1 clove garlic, finely chopped

2 tablespoons chopped fresh parsley

1 ½ teaspoon salt, or to taste

¼ teaspoon black pepper

¼ cup grated Parmesan

¼ cup pine nuts, toasted

5 pitted prunes, finely chopped

3 eggs, beaten well

Flour (for coating)

SAUCE

1. In a large bowl, using your hands, tear the tomatoes into pieces. **2.** In a large flameproof casserole over medium-high heat, heat the oil, add the onion and garlic, and cook, stirring occasionally, for 5 minutes or until the onion is translucent. **3.** Add the tomatoes, water, bay leaf, salt, and red pepper. Bring to a boil, lower the heat, cover the pan, and simmer for 45 minutes. Taste for seasoning and add more salt, if you like.

MEATBALLS

1. In a bowl, soak the bread in ½ cup milk to moisten it. If it is still dry, add more milk, 1 tablespoon at a time, until the crumbs are moist; set aside for 15 minutes. With your hands, break the mixture into large crumbs. Add the ricotta and mix well. **2.** In another bowl, combine the beef, pork, and veal. With a fork, break up the meats, then add the garlic, parsley, salt, black pepper, Parmesan, pine nuts, prunes, bread mixture, and eggs. Mix with your hands until combined. **3.** Roll the mixture into 12 plum-size balls, each about 2 inches in diameter. Coat each meatball lightly in flour, reshape, and slip into the tomato sauce. **4.** Return the sauce to a boil, cover the pan, and simmer for 30 minutes without moving the meatballs. Turn the meatballs gently, re-cover the pan, and continue cooking for 10 minutes. Remove the lid and simmer for 5 minutes more. Taste the sauce for seasoning and add more salt or red pepper, to taste.

Jill Santopietro

Chili Mac

A great kids' dish, this mixture of ground beef and macaroni, cooked together with tomatoes and a few spices, makes a fine weeknight meal.

SERVES 4

1 tablespoon vegetable oil
1 medium onion, chopped
3 cloves garlic, chopped
1 pound lean ground beef
8 ounces elbow macaroni
1 can (16 ounces) whole peeled
  tomatoes, crushed
2 cups chicken stock
2 teaspoons chili powder
1 teaspoon ground cumin
½ teaspoon salt, or to taste
1 cup shredded cheddar
Extra grated cheddar (for
  serving)

1. In a large skillet over medium-high heat, heat the oil, and when it is hot, cook the onion, stirring often, for 5 minutes or until lightly browned and softened. Add the garlic and cook for 1 minute more. **2.** Add the ground beef and cook, stirring constantly, for 5 minutes or until it is browned and cooked through. **3.** Add the macaroni, tomatoes, stock, chili powder, cumin, and salt. Stir well. Bring to a boil, lower the heat, and cover the pan. Simmer for 10 minutes, or until liquid is mostly absorbed and macaroni is tender but still has some bite. **4.** Add the cheese and stir just until melted. Taste for seasoning and add more salt, if you like. Serve sprinkled with extra cheddar.

Keri Fisher

Beef Stroganoff

Serve this traditional Russian dish, with sauteed beef, mushrooms, and sour cream, over noodles or potatoes. Use top-quality meat because it cooks only briefly.

SERVES 4

1½ pounds beef tenderloin
1½ tablespoons olive oil
2 medium onions, thinly sliced
10 ounces white mushrooms,
  thinly sliced
Salt and pepper
½ tablespoon butter
¾ cup sour cream
1 tablespoon Dijon mustard

1. Cut the beef into ½-inch slices, and cut each slice into ¾-inch strips. **2.** In a large skillet, heat 1 tablespoon of oil. Cook the onions, stirring often, for 8 minutes or until softened. Raise the heat to medium-high; add the mushrooms, salt, and pepper. Cook, stirring often, for 6 minutes or until the mushrooms are golden and their liquid evaporates. Transfer the vegetables to a bowl. **3.** In the same skillet, heat the butter and remaining ½ tablespoon of oil. Brown the beef over medium-high heat, stirring often, for 3 to 4 minutes. **4.** Meanwhile, in a bowl, stir together the sour cream and mustard. **5.** Return the mushroom mixture to the skillet. Add the sour cream mixture. Stir over low heat until the sauce is hot, but do not let it boil. Sprinkle with salt and pepper.

Sandrine's restaurant, Cambridge, Massachusetts

Beef Brisket

Beef brisket cooked with ketchup, vinegar, and brown sugar—for a sweet and sour sauce—is better after it has been refrigerated, so prepare this a day or two ahead, then slice it and reheat in the sauce.

SERVES 10

1 beef brisket (4–5 pounds), trimmed

2 large onions, thinly sliced

1 clove garlic, crushed

Salt and pepper, to taste

¾ cup ketchup

1 cup water

1 cup distilled white vinegar

¾ cup brown sugar

1. Set the oven at 325°F. **2.** Place the brisket in a roasting pan. Sprinkle with the onions, garlic, salt, and pepper. **3.** In a bowl, combine the ketchup, water, and vinegar. Pour the liquids over the meat. Sprinkle the brown sugar on top. **4.** Cover with foil and cook for 2½ hours or until the meat is very tender. Remove the foil and continue cooking for 15 minutes or until the meat is browned and tender when you pierce it with a fork. **5.** Scrape the onions and ketchup off the meat and stir them into the pan juices. Let the meat cool. Cover and refrigerate. **6.** Set the oven at 350°F. **7.** Remove the meat from the sauce and slice it against the grain. Discard the fat from the sauce. Return the meat to the pan. **8.** Heat the brisket in the oven for 30 to 40 minutes or until it is very hot.

Andrea Pyenson

Roast Turkey with Gravy

A large roast turkey tends to be a celebration dish. But we think families should do this once a month. You don't need to roast a holiday-size bird; a 12-pound turkey will feed you for days and there will be plenty of leftovers for sandwiches, curries, and salads.

**SERVES 6
(WITH LEFTOVERS)**

1 turkey (12–16 pounds),
    giblets removed
    from cavity

1 lemon, quartered

1 orange, quartered

Salt and pepper, to
    taste

Canola oil (for rubbing)

1 onion, quartered

2 carrots, halved

1 stalk celery, cut
    into 4 pieces

1 cup water

GRAVY

Drippings from turkey
    roasting pan

1–1 ½ cups boiling water

3 cups turkey or
    chicken stock

1 cup red or white wine,
    brandy, or port

Salt and pepper, to
    taste

3 tablespoons corn-
    starch or arrowroot
    mixed with ⅓ cup
    cold water (stir again
    just before using)

1. Set the oven at 350°F. Have on hand a roasting pan and large rack that sits snugly inside. **2.** Wipe the bird dry. Set it on the rack breast side up. Tuck the lemon and orange inside the bird. Add a generous sprinkle of salt and pepper. Tie the legs together with kitchen twine. **3.** Rub the bird all over with oil. Sprinkle with salt and pepper. **4.** Scatter the onion, carrots, and celery around the bird. Pour the water into the pan. **5.** Roast the bird for 10 minutes per pound (a 12-pound bird will take 2 hours) or until a meat thermometer inserted into the thickest part of the thigh registers 170°F. After the bird comes out of the oven, the temperature will climb 5 degrees while it rests. **6.** During cooking, if the breast is browning too much, cover the bird loosely with foil, shiny side down. If the pan is dry, add more water. **7.** Using two large spoons, remove the bird from the oven and transfer it to a large platter. Let it sit in a warm place for 20 to 30 minutes. The bird can sit for 1 hour without harm.

GRAVY

1. Remove the rack from the turkey roasting pan. Set the pan in a heatproof spot—over two burners is fine—where it will sit firmly. Add 1 cup of the boiling water and scrape the bottom of the pan to release the sediment. Add the remaining ½ cup of water, if necessary. **2.** Tip the contents of the roasting pan, including the vegetables, into a large saucepan, scraping the bottom well. Add the turkey or chicken stock and bring to a boil. **3.** Remove the pan from the heat. Tip it slightly. Use a large metal spoon to discard the fat from the surface of the liquid. There is no way to shortcut this; take your time. **4.** Return the saucepan to the heat and let it bubble steadily. As the mixture boils, notice little pools of fat on the surface. Continue skimming until the liquid is free of fat. Add the wine, brandy, or port, salt, and pepper. Simmer the mixture, stirring occasionally, for 10 minutes. **5.** Use a large slotted spoon to remove the onion, carrot, and celery from the gravy. Taste the mixture for seasoning and add more salt and pepper, if you like. **6.** Stir half the cornstarch or arrowroot mixture into the boiling gravy. Cook, stirring constantly, until the gravy thickens. If you want the gravy thicker, stir in the remaining cornstarch. Simmer the gravy for 2 minutes. **7.** Pour it into a sauce boat or bowl. **8.** Carve the turkey and serve with the hot gravy.

Sheryl Julian

Apricot-Sausage Pan Stuffing

Plump the apricots and raisins in apple juice overnight, then finish the stuffing the next day. You can fill a 14-pound turkey with this mixture or make a pan stuffing in a baking dish, as we do here.

SERVES 12

1 cup dried apricots

⅓ cup golden raisins

¾ cup apple juice

1 tablespoon apple cider
    vinegar

Butter (for the dish)

¼ cup (4 tablespoons)
    unsalted butter

1 medium onion, finely
    chopped

9 slices thickly cut whole-
    wheat bread, cut into ½-inch
    croutons

1 pound loose pork sausage

½ cup coarsely chopped
    walnuts

½ cup chopped fresh parsley

1 teaspoon dried thyme

Salt and pepper, to taste

¾ cup chicken or turkey stock

1. With scissors, snip the apricots into strips. Transfer them to a bowl and add the raisins, apple juice, and vinegar. Cover and refrigerate overnight. **2.** Set the oven at 375°F. Butter a 9 x 13-inch baking dish. **3.** In a skillet, melt the butter and cook the onion, stirring often, for 10 minutes or until it softens. **4.** Meanwhile, toast the bread in the oven for 12 minutes, turning often, until it is crisp. **5.** In a large bowl combine the onion and croutons. Toss thoroughly. **6.** Without wiping out the skillet, cook the sausage over medium-high heat, stirring constantly, for 8 minutes or until it breaks up and turns golden. **7.** With a slotted spoon, transfer the sausage to the crouton mixture. Add the walnuts, parsley, thyme, salt, pepper, and apricot mixture with its liquid. Toss thoroughly just to mix. **8.** Transfer the mixture to the baking dish. Bake for 20 minutes. Pour the chicken or turkey stock on top and continue baking for 20 minutes (total baking time is 40 minutes), or until the mixture is hot and browned on top.

Jean Safford

Turkey Pie with Apples and Biscuit Crust

You need leftover cooked turkey for this pie, so make it the day after you've roasted a bird. Or use delicatessen turkey or roast chicken.

SERVES 6

CRUST

Butter (for dish and sheet)

2 cups flour

1 tablespoon baking powder

1 teaspoon salt

2 tablespoons butter

2 tablespoons solid vegetable
   shortening

¼ cup chopped fresh parsley

1 cup whole milk

Extra flour (for rolling)

FILLING

3 tablespoons butter

3 tablespoons flour

2 tablespoons vegetable oil

1 small onion, finely chopped

1 stalk celery, finely chopped

1 leek (white part only), finely
   chopped

4 cups cooked turkey meat,
   coarsely chopped

1 tablespoon chopped fresh
   sage or parsley

2 Granny Smith apples, peeled,
   cored, and coarsely chopped

¼ cup apple cider

2 cups turkey or chicken stock

Salt and pepper, to taste

CRUST

1. Set the oven at 350°F. Have on hand a deep 10-inch baking dish. Butter it lightly. Line a baking sheet with parchment paper or butter it lightly. **2.** In a bowl, mix together the flour, baking powder, and salt. Add the butter and shortening. With your fingers or the tines of a fork, work the mixture together until it resembles sand. Add the parsley and milk and use a fork to work the liquids into the flour mixture to form a moist dough. **3.** Transfer the dough to a floured counter and knead it lightly, adding a little more flour to make it manageable but not dry. **4.** Roll the dough into an oblong or rectangle (it should be the same shape as the baking dish). Carefully lift the dough onto the baking sheet. **5.** Bake the dough in the hot oven for 10 minutes. Set it aside to cool.

FILLING

1. In a small skillet, melt the butter and whisk in the flour. Cook over medium heat, stirring, for 5 minutes or until it is golden brown. **2.** In a large saucepan, heat the oil. Add the onion, celery, and leek. Cook the vegetables over medium heat, stirring often, for 10 minutes or until they soften. **3.** Stir in the turkey, sage or parsley, apples, and cider. Lower the heat and cook for 10 minutes. Transfer to the baking dish. **4.** In another saucepan, bring the stock to a boil. Lower the heat to a simmer. Whisk in the browned butter-flour mixture with salt and pepper. When the sauce is smooth and thickened, pour it into the turkey and vegetables. The filling should be thick. **5.** Cover it with the baked crust. **6.** Bake the pie for 35 to 45 minutes or until the mixture is bubbling at the edges and the crust turns golden brown.

Dorset Inn, Dorset, Vermont

Curry Sauce

Private chef German Lam, who teaches in the Boston, Massachusetts, area, offers this recipe to his students. Add leftover roast chicken or turkey and sauteed vegetables. Simmer them in the sauce just to reheat them, and serve with rice.

MAKES 3 PINTS

3 tablespoons olive oil

1 small onion, cut into strips

1 piece (2 inches) fresh ginger, peeled and chopped

4 cloves garlic, halved

2 tablespoons sliced lemongrass

Salt, to taste

3 tablespoons curry powder

1 teaspoon ground cumin

1 teaspoon ground coriander

1 quart chicken stock

1 can (8 ounces) coconut milk

1 cup apple juice

Juice of 1 lime

1. In a large skillet over medium heat, heat the oil. Add onion, ginger, garlic, lemongrass, and salt. Cook, stirring often, for 8 minutes or until softened. **2.** Add the curry powder, cumin, and coriander. Cook, stirring, for 2 minutes, until you can smell the spices. **3.** Stir in the chicken stock. Bring to a boil, lower the heat, and simmer for 15 minutes. **4.** Add the coconut milk and apple juice. Simmer for 15 minutes more. Set aside to cool. **5.** In a blender, puree the sauce. Add the lime juice.

German Lam

Turkey Chili

Ever since ground turkey meat has become available, we've been making chili with a mixture of dark and light meat. Here, bell and poblano peppers, tomatoes, and white beans simmer with the chili.

SERVES 6

2 tablespoons vegetable oil

1 red onion, finely chopped

1 green bell pepper, cored, seeded, and coarsely chopped

1 red bell pepper, cored, seeded, and coarsely chopped

1 poblano or other mild chili pepper, cored, seeded, and chopped

1 teaspoon salt, or to taste

1 clove garlic, finely chopped

1 pound each light and dark-meat ground turkey

1 teaspoon dried oregano

1 can (15 ounces) whole peeled tomatoes (with their juices), crushed in a bowl

2 cups chicken stock

1 cup water

2 cans (16 ounces each) white beans, drained and rinsed

Black pepper, to taste

4 scallions, trimmed and thinly sliced (for garnish)

1. In a large, heavy-based casserole, heat the oil. Add the onion, green and red bell peppers, chili pepper, and salt. Cook over medium heat, stirring often, for 15 minutes or until the vegetables soften. Add the garlic and cook, stirring, for 30 seconds. **2.** Add the turkey and cook over medium heat, stirring constantly, until the meat breaks up and no longer looks raw. **3.** Stir in the oregano, tomatoes, stock, water, and beans. Bring to a boil and turn the heat to medium-low. **4.** Cover the pot and simmer the mixture for 30 minutes. Taste for seasoning, and add black pepper, if you like. Ladle into bowls and sprinkle with scallions.

Sheryl Julian & Julie Riven

Butterflied Herb-Roasted Turkey

To butterfly a turkey, you need heavy-duty kitchen shears, a roasting pan large enough to hold the flattened bird, and an instant-read meat thermometer. This bird roasts on a bed of stuffing. Season the turkey the day before so the salt has a chance to penetrate the meat.

SERVES 10

14-pound turkey (reserve neck
   and gizzard for gravy)
2 ½ tablespoons kosher salt
1 ½ tablespoons chopped fresh
   thyme
1 ½ tablespoons chopped fresh
   sage
1 ¼ teaspoons coarsely ground
   black pepper
1 recipe Fennel and Apple
   Stuffing (see page 217)
3 tablespoons unsalted butter,
   melted

1. Set the oven at 425°F. Position an oven rack on the lower shelf.
2. Remove any giblets from the vent and neck end of the bird. Set the turkey skin side down on a cutting board. With a small sharp knife, make a ¼-inch-deep cut along both sides of the backbone. Using kitchen shears, follow the lines to remove a strip about 2 inches wide (save this for soup). Turn the bird over so the skin side is up. **3.** With your hands, press down as hard as you can on the center of the breastbone to flatten the meat. Be forceful. Wipe the bird with damp paper towels and pat it dry. **4.** In a small bowl, combine the salt, thyme, sage, and pepper. Sprinkle the mixture all over the turkey. Using your fingers to make a pocket between the skin and breast meat and the skin and leg meat, rub some of the herb mixture in the pockets.
5. Spread the stuffing in the roasting pan. Set the bird, skin side up, on top. Tuck up the drumsticks so the legs overlap the breast. Tuck the wing tips behind the wings. Brush the skin with some of the butter.
6. Roast the turkey for 30 minutes. Lower the oven temperature to 375°F. Brush with more butter. Continue roasting, brushing occasionally, until a thermometer inserted into the thickest parts of the thigh registers 170°F (total cooking time is about 2½ hours). **7.** Transfer the turkey to a cutting board; let it rest in a warm place for 30 minutes.
8. Return the stuffing in the pan to the oven. Raise the temperature to 425°F. Bake the stuffing for 20 minutes or until it is brown and crisp.
9. With clean shears, cut the turkey up the center. Snip the legs from the breast. With a long knife, carve the breast meat off the bone and arrange on a platter. Set the drumsticks on the platter. Carve the thigh meat off the bone and arrange on the platter.

Tony Rosenfeld

Fennel and Apple Stuffing

**MAKES ENOUGH TO
GO UNDER OR INSIDE
A 14-POUND BIRD**

2 tablespoons unsalted butter

1 medium bulb fennel (about
    1 pound), quartered, cored,
    and cut in ¼-inch dice

1 Spanish onion, cut in ¼-inch
    dice

1 teaspoon kosher salt

1½ pounds crusty country
    bread or baguette, cut into
    1-inch cubes (about 10 cups)

1 cup coarsely chopped dried
    apple

¼ cup dried cranberries

¾ cup chicken stock

¾ cup grated fresh Parmesan

2 tablespoons chopped fresh
    sage

1 tablespoon chopped fresh
    thyme

1. In a large skillet over medium heat, melt the butter. Add the fennel, onion, and salt. Cook, stirring often, for 6 minutes or until the vegetables soften. **2.** Transfer the mixture to a large bowl. Add the bread cubes, apple, cranberries, stock, Parmesan, sage, and thyme. Toss well. Bake under the turkey (as directed on page 216).

Turkey Salad with Mayfair Dressing

On the day following a festive turkey meal, here's what to do with the meat. This lightly curried dressing was originally served at the Roberts Mayfair Hotel, a historic property in St. Louis. The flavors are similar to many British mayonnaise-style dishes, which are also favorites all over New England. Add the dressing to cooked turkey, along with red grapes and shelled pistachios.

SERVES 4

½ stalk celery, chopped

½ medium onion, chopped

1 large clove garlic

½ tin (2 ounces) anchovies, drained

Juice of ½ lemon

½ teaspoon curry powder

Salt and pepper, to taste

2 tablespoons yellow mustard

½ teaspoon sugar

1 egg plus 1 extra yolk

½ cup olive oil

½ cup vegetable oil

½ bunch parsley (leaves only)

8 cups (2 pounds) chopped cooked turkey

1 ½ cups red seedless grapes, cut in half

1 cup shelled pistachios

1. In a blender, combine the celery, onion, garlic, anchovies, and lemon juice. Blend into a puree. **2.** Add the curry powder, salt, pepper, mustard, and sugar; blend well. **3.** Remove the cap in the blender lid, and with the motor running on medium speed, add the egg and extra yolk, then slowly drizzle in the olive and vegetable oils. **4.** Add the parsley and blend until it is coarsely chopped. Chill the dressing for 30 minutes. **5.** In a large bowl, combine the turkey, grapes, and pistachios. Add enough dressing to moisten the mixture well. Taste for seasoning and add more salt and pepper, if you like.

Karoline Boehm Goodnick

Stuffed Cabbage Rolls

Boston Globe *food writer Debra Samuels's grandmother, Bess Greenberg, made her stuffed cabbage rolls with ground beef and some unusual ingredients (a glass of ginger ale and several spoons of grape jelly among them). Samuels replaced the beef with ground turkey, and the ginger ale with fresh ginger. She still adds grape jelly.*

MAKES 16

FILLING

2 small heads Savoy cabbage

2 pounds ground turkey

½ cup raw white rice

1 onion, finely chopped

1 egg, lightly beaten

2 teaspoons kosher salt

1 teaspoon pepper

1 can (16 ounces) tomato sauce

SAUCE

1 can (16 ounces) tomato sauce

Remaining tomato sauce from
    making the filling

1 can (28 ounces) whole
    tomatoes, crushed in a bowl

¼ cup brown sugar

1 tablespoon cider or distilled
    white vinegar

2 tablespoons lemon juice

¾ cup raisins

1 ½ inch piece fresh ginger,
    peeled and thickly sliced

2 tablespoons grape jelly

FILLING

1. Bring a large pot of water to boil. Core the cabbages and place one head in the boiling water, cored side down. Simmer for 5 minutes. Remove the head from the water and repeat with the other head. Carefully pull the largest cabbage leaves from the heads. Some may have already come loose. You will need 16 leaves. Submerge the heads again, if necessary, so you have enough leaves. Trim away the tough stem from the bottom of each leaf; set aside. **2.** In a mixing bowl, combine the ground turkey, rice, onion, egg, salt, pepper, and ½ cup of the tomato sauce. Mix until thoroughly combined; set aside.

SAUCE

1. In a large Dutch oven, combine the tomato sauce with the sauce that remains from the filling. Add the crushed tomatoes, sugar, vinegar, and lemon juice. Bring to a boil and lower the heat. Add the raisins, ginger, and grape jelly. Taste for seasoning and add more brown sugar or lemon juice, if you like. Keep the sauce simmering over very low heat. **2.** Lay a cabbage leaf vein side up on a cutting board. Shape ¼ cup of the turkey mixture into a thick oval cylinder. Lay it on the lower portion of the leaf, near the cored end. Bring the core side up over the cylinder. Fold the sides of the leaves over the turkey. Roll up the cylinder and secure with a toothpick. **3.** Repeat with remaining leaves and filling. Carefully lay the stuffed cabbage rolls seams side down in the sauce, packed tightly next to each other. Lower the heat and cover the pan. Simmer over low heat for 2½ hours. Halfway through cooking, turn the rolls and spoon sauce over them. **4.** To serve: Arrange 2 rolls, seams down (without toothpicks), over noodles, and spoon the sauce on top.

Debra Samuels

Turkey Tetrazzini

SERVES 8

Butter (for the dish)

1 pound farfalle (bow-tie) pasta

10 tablespoons unsalted butter

1 large Spanish onion, chopped

8 ounces button mushrooms, sliced

1 red bell pepper, cored, seeded, and chopped

Salt and black pepper, to taste

½ cup flour

4 cups chicken stock

1 cup shredded Asiago cheese

1 tablespoon chopped parsley

1 cup frozen peas

3 cups cooked diced turkey

1. Set the oven at 400°F. Butter a 9 x 13-inch baking dish. **2.** Bring a large pot of salted water to a boil. Add the pasta and cook, stirring occasionally, for 8 minutes or until the pasta is almost tender. Drain into a colander. **3.** Meanwhile, in a large skillet over medium heat, melt 2 tablespoons of the butter and add the onion, mushrooms, bell pepper, salt, and black pepper. Cook, stirring often, for 8 minutes. Remove them from the pan. **4.** Wipe out the skillet and return it to the stove. Add the remaining 8 tablespoons of butter. When it melts, whisk in the flour. Cook, stirring constantly, for 2 minutes. Slowly pour the stock into the pan and continue whisking until the sauce comes to a boil and thickens. Remove from the heat. Whisk in ¾ cup of cheese, parsley, and plenty of salt and black pepper. Stir in the peas, mushroom mixture, turkey, and pasta. Mix gently. **5.** Transfer the mixture to the dish; sprinkle with the remaining ¼ cup cheese. Cover with foil and bake for 10 minutes. Remove the foil and continue baking for 15 minutes or until the top is lightly browned.

Christine Merlo

Roast Chicken

Roast Chicken

Roast chickens are in many markets now, and you're charged a handsome price for them. Buy a whole chicken and do it yourself. The bird starts cooking breast side down, then finishes breast side up.

SERVES 6

1 whole chicken (3½–4 pounds)

Salt and pepper, to taste

1 onion, quartered

½ lemon

1 teaspoon butter

1 tablespoon olive oil

1. Set the oven at 400°F. Have on hand a roasting pan. **2.** Remove the chicken giblets. Pat the chicken dry. Sprinkle the inside with salt and pepper and add the onion and lemon. **3.** Butter a 6-inch piece of parchment paper. Set it buttered side up in the roasting pan. Set the chicken on the paper. Rub it all over with the olive oil. Sprinkle the bird with salt and pepper. Set the bird in the pan breast side down on the parchment paper. **4.** Roast the chicken for 30 minutes. **5.** Use a wooden spoon inserted into the cavity to turn the bird breast side up. Baste it with the juices in the pan. **6.** Turn the oven temperature down to 375°F. **7.** Continue roasting the chicken for 20 minutes or until a meat thermometer inserted into the thickest part of the thigh registers 175°F (total roasting time is 50 minutes). **8.** Transfer the chicken to a platter and let it stand for 10 minutes before carving.

Sheryl Julian

Chicken in a Pot

To simmer the chicken, you will need a heavy-based pot that will comfortably hold a large chicken. Many manufacturers now make enamel-coated cast-iron Dutch ovens in appealing colors that work well and will also go to the table. In this dish, the chicken is browned in the pot, then simmered on the stove top until tender. Serve with crusty bread or steamed potatoes.

SERVES 6

1 whole chicken (3½–4 pounds)

Salt and pepper, to taste

1 bunch fresh thyme

2 tablespoons butter

2 onions, quartered

2 plum tomatoes, quartered

1 cup white wine

1 cup water

1. Rinse and dry the chicken. Season the cavity with salt and pepper. Tuck a few of the sprigs of thyme into the cavity. Sprinkle salt and pepper onto the flesh of the bird. **2.** In a heavy-based flameproof casserole with a tight-fitting lid, melt the butter. Brown the chicken well all over, first on the breast, then on each side. Use two wooden spoons to turn the chicken. It should sit on its side without falling over. The browning will take at least 5 minutes. **3.** While the chicken is browning on the first side, add the onions and tomatoes to the pan. If they slip under the chicken when you turn it to brown the other side, that's okay. **4.** Set the chicken on its back. Pour in the wine and water. Tuck the remaining thyme into the pan at the side. Bring the liquids to a boil. **5.** Cover the pan, turn the heat to low, and let the chicken cook in the simmering liquid for 2 hours or until it is cooked through and a meat thermometer inserted into the thickest part of the thigh registers 170°F. Check several times to make sure there is enough liquid in the pot. The chicken will add juices, but if the lid isn't tight, they can boil away. **6.** Transfer the chicken to a cutting board. Cover loosely with foil and let it rest for 5 minutes in a warm place. **7.** Carve the chicken into 8 pieces: 2 wings with some breast meat attached, 2 breasts, 2 thighs, and 2 legs. Serve the chicken in deep plates with lots of cooking juices.

Sheryl Julian

Chicken Kebabs

A lemony marinade is used for this skewered chicken. When you grill it, be sure the fire isn't so hot that the chicken chars and dries out. Sear it first, then set the chicken around the edge of the coals until it cooks through but stays moist.

SERVES 4

4 whole skinless, boneless chicken breasts

½ cup olive oil

1 lemon, cut into slices

2 bay leaves, halved

3 cloves garlic, crushed

Salt and freshly ground black pepper, to taste

½ teaspoon cayenne pepper

1 teaspoon ground cumin

1. Soak eight bamboo skewers in a bowl of water for 30 minutes. **2.** Remove any sinew from the chicken and divide the breasts in half, if this hasn't been done already. Cut the chicken into 1½-inch cubes and pile them into a bowl with the oil, lemon, bay leaves, garlic, salt, black and cayenne pepper, and cumin. **3.** Cover the chicken with plastic wrap and refrigerate it for one day, turning the contents of the bowl several times so the chicken marinates evenly. **4.** Thread the chicken pieces onto the skewers, dividing them evenly. **5.** Heat a charcoal fire or gas grill. When the coals are hot, grill the chicken, turning the skewers often so that the meat cooks evenly. Set the skewers toward the edge of the grill, cover the grill, and cook the chicken for 10 minutes or until it is cooked through in the middle of the skewers. **6.** Serve two skewers per person on a bed of rice pilaf.

Sheryl Julian

Chicken Legs with Indian Spices

The drumsticks and thighs on a bird can stand up to longer cooking than the breasts. Make a quick broth with the poultry pieces and water. While the chicken cooks, mellow the spices and aromatics. Stir in the chicken meat, broth, yogurt, and potatoes to make a dish redolent with Indian spices. To finish, add lime juice and fresh cilantro.

SERVES 4

3 pounds chicken legs and
  thighs

4 cups water

2 teaspoons salt

2 tablespoons butter

2 teaspoons cumin seeds

1 teaspoon black pepper

1 onion, finely chopped

4 cloves garlic, finely chopped

1 piece (2 inches) of ginger
  root, finely chopped

1 tablespoon ground coriander

1 teaspoon ground turmeric

4 green chili peppers, seeded
  and finely chopped

¼ cup plain yogurt

5 small potatoes, cut into small
  wedges

Juice of 2 limes

½ cup chopped fresh cilantro

1. In a large flameproof casserole, combine the chicken, water, and 1 teaspoon of the salt. If the water does not cover the meat, add more. Bring to a boil, skim the surface thoroughly, lower the heat, and partially cover the pan. Simmer for 40 minutes or until the chicken is cooked through. Remove the chicken pieces from the pot. Tip the broth into a bowl. **2.** Rinse and dry the pot. Add the butter. When it melts, add the cumin seeds, black pepper, onion, garlic, and ginger. Partially cover and cook, stirring occasionally, for 8 minutes. **3.** Add the coriander, turmeric, remaining 1 teaspoon salt, and chili peppers. Cook, stirring, for 1 minute. **4.** Set the pan aside. Pull the chicken meat off the bones. Measure 3 cups of the broth. **5.** Stir the yogurt and broth into the onion mixture. Add the chicken and potatoes. Bring to a boil, lower the heat, and cover the pan. Simmer for 25 minutes or until the potatoes are tender. **6.** Add the lime juice and cilantro. Taste for seasoning and add more salt and black pepper, if you like.

Jonathan Levitt

Chicken Nuggets

Add your favorite dipping sauce—ketchup, mayonnaise, honey mustard, barbecue sauce, or Chinese duck sauce—to these sauteed nuggets.

SERVES 4

1½ pounds skinless, boneless
    chicken breasts, cut into
    1-inch squares

Salt and pepper, to taste

2 cups flour

3 eggs

3 cups unseasoned panko
    (Japanese bread crumbs) or
    regular white bread crumbs

3 tablespoons olive oil

1. Set the oven at 375°F. Have on hand a rimmed baking sheet. **2.** Set up an assembly line for breading the chicken in this order: Place the chicken on a plate; sprinkle it with salt. **3.** In three bowls beside the plate, place the flour, the eggs, and the crumbs. Beat the eggs with a fork for just a few seconds. Place a clean plate at the end of the line. Dip a piece of chicken into the flour to coat it, dip it into the eggs, roll it in the crumbs, dip it back into the eggs, and finally roll it in the crumbs again to coat it thoroughly with crumbs. Place the breaded chicken on the clean plate. Repeat with the remaining pieces. **4.** In a large nonstick skillet, heat the olive oil over medium heat. Fry the chicken pieces, a few at a time, turning often, for 2 to 3 minutes or until they are golden all over. Use tongs to transfer the chicken to the baking sheet. **5.** Cook them for 10 minutes more or until they are cooked through. Drain on paper towels, and sprinkle with salt and pepper.

Jonathan Levitt

Chicken Nuggets

Sauteed Chicken with Mushrooms

Some combinations are unbeatable. Chicken, white wine, and mushrooms is one of those. Simmer the pieces of poultry in the wine sauce and serve this classic French dish for an elegant dinner.

SERVES 4

1 chicken (3½ pounds), cut into 8 pieces

Salt and pepper, to taste

2 tablespoons olive oil

12 ounces crimini or white button mushrooms, halved or quartered

4 large portobello mushrooms, stems removed, caps cut into ¼-inch pieces

1 large Spanish onion, cut into thin wedges

2 tablespoons flour

1 cup white wine

1 cup chicken stock

¼ cup heavy cream

2 tablespoons chopped fresh parsley

1. Sprinkle the chicken all over with salt and pepper. **2.** In a large flameproof casserole, heat the oil. When it is hot, add the chicken pieces skin side down. It's okay to crowd the pan, but they should make only one layer. Cook, without moving, for 5 minutes. **3.** Turn the chicken and cook the other sides for 5 minutes. Remove all the chicken from the pan. **4.** Add the crimini or white button mushrooms, the portobellos, and onion with salt and pepper. Cook over medium-low heat, stirring often, for 8 minutes or until the mixture releases the liquid in the mushrooms. **5.** Turn up the heat and continue cooking, uncovered, stirring often, for 5 minutes or until the liquid evaporates. **6.** Sprinkle the mixture with flour and cook, stirring, for 2 minutes. **7.** Add the wine and stock and cook, scraping the bottom of the pan, until the liquids come to a boil. Return the chicken to the pan, skin side up. Cover with the lid and simmer for 45 minutes or until the chicken is cooked through. **8.** Remove the chicken from the pan. **9.** Taste the sauce for seasoning, add more salt and pepper, if you like, and add the cream. Let the mixture return to a boil. Return the chicken to the pan. Sprinkle with parsley.

Sheryl Julian

Creamed Chicken on Toast

Creamed mixtures can contain milk or heavy cream—or neither, as in this version. To achieve this creaminess, chicken stock is thickened with a butter-flour paste; the mixture is a little like the filling for chicken potpie.

SERVES 4

4 cups chicken stock

2 chicken breast halves (1½ pounds total), skin removed

½ teaspoon salt, or more to taste

1 onion, coarsely chopped

2 carrots, peeled and cut into ¼-inch cubes

2 stalks celery, cut into ¼-inch pieces

4 tablespoons butter, at room temperature

4 tablespoons flour

1 cup frozen peas

Pinch of grated nutmeg, to taste

¼ teaspoon pepper, or more to taste

2 tablespoons chopped fresh parsley

4 thick slices challah or other soft eggy bread, toasted and halved

1. In a large flameproof casserole, combine the stock and chicken breasts. Add ½ teaspoon salt and bring to a boil. Skim the surface, lower the heat, cover pan, and simmer the chicken for 10 minutes. **2.** Add the onion, carrots, and celery to the chicken. Cover the pan and continue cooking for 20 minutes or until the chicken and vegetables are cooked through. **3.** Remove the chicken from the liquid and set it aside until the chicken is cool enough to handle. Use a slotted spoon to remove the vegetables from the stock. **4.** On a plate with a fork, mash together the butter and flour until they form a smooth paste; set it aside. **5.** Remove the chicken from the bones and cut the meat into ½-inch pieces. **6.** Return the chicken cooking liquid to a boil. Using a whisk, scoop up half of the butter-flour paste and whisk it into the simmering liquid. Add the remaining paste and let the sauce simmer, stirring occasionally, for 5 minutes. **7.** With a large metal spoon, stir the chicken, vegetables, and peas into the sauce. Continue cooking for 5 minutes or until the meat and vegetables are very hot. Taste for seasoning, add nutmeg, pepper, and more salt, if you like, and the parsley. **8.** Arrange two pieces of toast on each of four dinner plates. Ladle the creamed chicken mixture on top.

Sheryl Julian & Julie Riven

Chicken Pie with Biscuit Topping

A hearty one-pan pie, serve this to weekend guests in chilly weather. It will warm the house with aromas of a time gone by.

SERVES 6

FILLING

3½ cups chicken stock

8 chicken thighs

Salt and pepper, to taste

5 tablespoons unsalted butter

2 carrots, peeled and thinly sliced

1 large Spanish onion, chopped

2 celery stalks, thinly sliced

⅓ cup flour

½ teaspoon thyme, chopped

½ cup frozen peas

TOPPING

1½ cups flour

2 teaspoons baking powder

¼ teaspoon salt

1 teaspoon chopped fresh thyme

5 tablespoons unsalted butter

1 cup milk

FILLING

1. In a large flameproof casserole, combine the chicken stock, chicken thighs, salt, and pepper. Bring to a boil, skim the surface, lower the heat, and cover the pan. Simmer for 15 minutes or until the chicken is cooked through. **2.** Remove the chicken from the broth. When it is cool enough to handle, remove the meat from the bone, discard the skin and bones; shred the meat. **3.** Have on hand a 10-inch skillet with a heatproof handle or a baking dish of the same size. **4.** In a saucepan, melt 2 tablespoons of the butter. Add the carrots, onion, and celery. Cook, stirring often, for 8 minutes or until they soften. Remove the vegetables from the pan. **5.** Add the remaining 3 tablespoons of butter. Whisk in the flour. Cook the mixture, whisking constantly, for 2 minutes. Whisk in the chicken stock slowly. When the mixture comes to a boil, let it bubble gently for 2 minutes. Return the vegetables to the pan with the chicken. Add the thyme and peas. Simmer 2 minutes more. Taste for seasoning and add more salt and pepper, if you like. Set aside.

TOPPING

1. Set the oven at 400°F. **2.** In a bowl, combine the flour, baking powder, salt, and thyme. Whisk well to combine them. Add 4 tablespoons of the butter. With 2 blunt knives or a pastry blender, work the mixture until it looks like coarse crumbs. **3.** Stir the milk into the dry ingredients and use a rubber spatula to form a dough. **4.** Using a large metal spoon, drop the dough in spoonfuls on the chicken mixture. Gently spread the dough to cover the top of the skillet. Dot the top of the dough with the remaining 1 tablespoon of butter. **5.** Bake for 30 minutes until the top is golden and the filling is bubbly.

Christine Merlo

Chicken Pie with Biscuit Topping

Helena's Chicken

Lilian Cheung, a nutritionist at the Harvard School of Public Health in Boston, Massachusetts, says that her mother's Chinese-inspired recipe for chicken, bell peppers, mushrooms, and curry powder can be served as a tortilla filling or over whole grain pasta or brown rice. She also stuffs it inside pita bread with honey mustard and slices of ripe avocado.

SERVES 4

2 skinless, boneless chicken breasts (about 1 pound total), cut into thin slices

Salt and pepper, to taste

1 tablespoon cornstarch

1 teaspoon water

2 tablespoons canola oil

½ pound button mushrooms, thinly sliced

1 each red, green, and yellow bell pepper, cored, seeded, and thinly sliced

1 large onion, thinly sliced

1 carrot, cut into matchsticks

2 teaspoons mayonnaise

2 teaspoon ketchup

1 teaspoon curry powder

1 teaspoon sugar

1. In a bowl, combine the chicken, salt, pepper, cornstarch, and water. Stir well, cover, and refrigerate for 1 hour. **2.** In a wok, heat 1 tablespoon of the oil over high heat. Cook the mushrooms, stirring constantly, for 8 minutes or until they release their liquid. Turn up the heat and continue cooking, stirring constantly, until the mushroom liquid evaporates. Remove the mushrooms from the pan. **3.** Add the remaining 1 tablespoon of oil to the pan. Add the peppers, onion, and carrot. Cook, stirring often, for 8 minutes or until they are almost tender. Remove the vegetables from the pan. **4.** Add the chicken and cook, stirring constantly, for 5 minutes or until it is cooked through. Remove the pan from the heat and stir in the mayonnaise, ketchup, curry powder, and sugar. Return the mushrooms and bell pepper mixture to the pan. Return the pan to the heat. Cook over medium heat just until the mixture is hot and thickens slightly.

Helena Cheung

Chicken Scaloppine with Lemon, Tomatoes, and Capers

Sweet Basil of Needham, Massachusetts, offers this garlicky dish with pounded chicken breasts and a sauce made with lemon, tomatoes, and capers.

SERVES 4

4 skinless, boneless chicken
    breast halves

Salt and pepper, to taste

3 tablespoons flour

3 tablespoons olive oil

3 tablespoons unsalted butter

3 cloves garlic, finely chopped

½ cup white wine

Juice of 2 lemons

2 cups chicken stock

2 plum tomatoes, seeded and
    diced

2 tablespoons capers, rinsed

¼ cup chopped fresh parsley

1. Place the chicken breasts, two at a time, between two large sheets of plastic wrap. Use the smooth side of a meat mallet to pound them to about ½-inch thickness. Sprinkle the chicken with salt and pepper. Spread the flour on a plate and dip the chicken into it to coat both sides, shaking off the excess. **2.** In a heavy 12-inch skillet, heat the olive oil over medium-high heat. When it is hot, add 1 tablespoon of the butter. When the butter melts, add the chicken to the skillet. Cook for 4 to 5 minutes or until golden on the bottom. Turn and cook for 2 minutes more. Transfer the chicken to a plate. (It is not cooked through at this point.) **3.** Add the garlic and cook, stirring, for 30 seconds. Add the wine and lemon juice. Simmer, scraping up the browned bits on the bottom of the pan, for a few minutes or until almost all the liquid is gone. **4.** Add the stock, tomatoes, and capers. Turn the heat to high, and bring the liquid to a boil. Simmer steadily for 6 minutes or until the liquid is reduced by about a third. **5.** Stir in the remaining 2 tablespoons of butter. Return the chicken to the pan and simmer for 2 minutes or until the sauce thickens slightly and the chicken is cooked through. Taste for seasoning and add more salt and pepper, if you like. Sprinkle with parsley.

Sweet Basil, Needham,
Massachusetts

Chicken Cacciatore

When this recipe ran in The Boston Globe, *readers told us for months afterward how much they liked it. What sets this version apart from other cacciatore dishes is oven roasting (far easier than browning the chicken in batches on top of the stove) and roasted red peppers and balsamic vinegar, which add depth to the sauce.*

SERVES 6

2 pounds boneless, skinless chicken thighs

Salt and pepper, to taste

2 tablespoons olive oil

3 cloves garlic, finely chopped

2 carrots, chopped

2 medium onions, chopped

3 stalks celery, chopped

10 mushrooms, quartered

1 cup chopped bottled roasted red peppers

2 cups chicken stock

1¾ cups port

¾ cup balsamic vinegar

1 can (28 ounces) imported whole tomatoes, crushed in a bowl

1 bay leaf

1 pound farfalle (bow-tie) pasta, cooked until tender and drained

¼ cup of grated Parmesan or Asiago cheese

2 tablespoons chopped fresh basil

1. Set the oven at 400°F. In a large ovenproof dish, arrange the thighs in one layer, skinned side up. Sprinkle with salt and pepper. Roast the chicken for 20 minutes. **2.** In a large skillet, heat the oil. Cook the garlic, carrots, onions, celery, mushrooms, and roasted peppers over medium heat, stirring often, for 20 minutes. **3.** Add the stock, port, balsamic vinegar, crushed tomatoes, and bay leaf to the skillet. Bring to a boil. Pour this over the chicken thighs, cover with foil, and return the dish to the oven. Cook the cacciatore for 1 hour or until the meat is cooked through (total cooking time is 1 hour and 20 minutes). **4.** After draining the pasta, return it to its pan. Toss the pasta with some of the cacciatore cooking liquid. Arrange the pasta on each of six deep plates. Add chicken and more sauce. Sprinkle with cheese and basil.

Sweet Basil,
Needham, Massachusetts

Pilav (Armenian chicken with rice)

A classic Armenian dish, this chicken and rice is made by poaching a bird, then using the stock to make rice pilaf. Browned orzo also goes into the rice, a tradition that dates back centuries. Modern Armenian cooks use orzo or angel hair pasta.

SERVES 4

CHICKEN

1 chicken (3½ pounds), cut into 8 pieces

1 quart water

1 teaspoon salt

RICE

2 teaspoons canola oil

¼ cup orzo

2 cups basmati rice

¼ teaspoon salt

4½ cups chicken stock (see above)

¼ cup water

CHICKEN

1. In a soup pot, combine the chicken, water, and salt. Bring to a boil, skim the surface thoroughly, lower the heat, cover the pan, and simmer the chicken for 45 minutes or until it is cooked through. **2.** Remove the chicken from the liquid. Tip the liquid into a heatproof bowl. Leave both to cool completely. Cover the broth and refrigerate it. Remove the skin and bones from the chicken and transfer the chicken to a container; cover and refrigerate. **3.** Skim off and discard the fat from the stock. Measure 4½ cups.

RICE

1. In a large flameproof casserole, heat the oil. When it is hot, add the orzo. Cook the orzo, stirring often, for 5 minutes or until it browns. **2.** Add the rice and salt. Stir well, then stir in the stock. **3.** Bring the mixture to a boil, lower the heat, cover the pan, and simmer the rice for 17 minutes or until the grains are tender and the liquid is absorbed. **4.** Meanwhile, in a saucepan, combine the chicken and water. Reheat the chicken, turning it in the pan, until it is hot. **5.** Spoon the rice onto serving plates and top with chicken.

Emeline Aroush

Grilled Chicken Breast on Vegetables

Grilled Chicken Breasts on Vegetables

When the grill is lit, cook zucchini, red peppers, and scallions with boneless breasts for a quick supper.

SERVES 4

4 skinless, boneless chicken
   breasts
2 tablespoons olive oil, plus
   more for sprinkling
2 teaspoons chopped fresh
   thyme
1¼ teaspoons kosher salt
½ teaspoon black pepper
2 medium zucchini, thinly sliced
2 red peppers, cored and cut in
   4 pieces
1 bunch scallions, left whole
   but trimmed
2 teaspoons balsamic vinegar

1. Prepare a medium-hot charcoal fire or heat a gas grill to medium-high. **2.** Set the chicken on a plate, sprinkle with enough oil to barely coat it, add 1 teaspoon thyme, ½ teaspoon salt, and ¼ teaspoon pepper; set aside. **3.** In a bowl, toss the zucchini, red peppers, and scallions with 1 tablespoon oil, ½ teaspoon salt, and the remaining ¼ teaspoon pepper. Let sit at room temperature while the grill heats. **4.** Grill the chicken and vegetables without turning them for 3 minutes or until they have good grill marks. With tongs, flip the meat and vegetables. Continue cooking for 5 minutes or until the chicken is firm to the touch and just cooked through (check by slicing into a thick spot), and the vegetables are all browned and tender. **5.** Divide the vegetables among four plates and set a piece of chicken on top. Sprinkle with the balsamic vinegar, the remaining ¼ teaspoon salt, the remaining 1 teaspoon thyme, and the remaining 1 tablespoon olive oil.

Tony Rosenfeld

Pulled Chicken Sandwiches

Substitute chicken leg quarters for the split breasts, if you like; cook the legs an additional 10 to 15 minutes.

SERVES 6

1½ cups ketchup
¼ cup cider vinegar
2 tablespoons Worcestershire
   sauce
2 tablespoons Dijon mustard
¼ cup brown sugar
2 cloves garlic, finely chopped
2 tablespoons vegetable oil
1 teaspoon chili powder
Dash of hot sauce, or to taste
Salt and pepper, to taste
6 chicken leg quarters (about 6
   pounds)
6 soft hamburger buns

1. Light the grill. **2.** In an old skillet (it will go directly onto the grill rack), combine the ketchup, vinegar, Worcestershire, mustard, brown sugar, garlic, vegetable oil, chili powder, hot sauce, salt, and pepper. Stir well. **3.** Season the chicken generously with salt and pepper. **4.** Grill the chicken over medium-high heat for about 20 minutes on a side, or until a meat thermometer registers 170°F. Set it aside to cool slightly. **5.** Meanwhile, set the skillet of sauce on a warm section of the grill (if using a gas grill, turn off the grill first). Let the sauce cook, stirring occasionally, for 5 minutes, or until it is hot and bubbling. **6.** When the chicken is cool enough to handle, discard the skin and bones. Using two forks, shred the chicken. Add the chicken to the ketchup sauce and stir well. Serve on the buns.

Keri Fisher

Chicken Legs Bonne Femme

Legs have more flavor than the breasts of a chicken (the whole legs are also a bargain in the supermarket). Here they're simmered with white wine, chicken stock, mushrooms, and onions, and served with small yellow potatoes. Bonne Femme, literally "good woman" in French, is a very appealing and homey way to cook.

SERVES 8

8 whole chicken legs (thighs attached to drumsticks)

3 medium onions, quartered

Olive oil (for sprinkling)

Salt and pepper, to taste

2 tablespoons butter

½ pound button mushrooms, quartered

1 clove garlic, crushed

2 cups white wine

2 cups chicken stock

16 fingerling or other small yellow potatoes

2 tablespoons chopped fresh thyme

2 tablespoons chopped fresh parsley

1. Set the oven at 500°F. In a large roasting pan, arrange the chicken, skin side up, and tuck the onions around the edges. They should all fit snugly. Sprinkle with oil, salt, and pepper. **2.** Roast the chicken for 25 minutes or until the onion tips are starting to brown (the chicken will not be cooked through). **3.** Meanwhile, in a large flameproof casserole, heat the butter. Add the mushrooms, garlic, salt, and pepper. Cook over medium-high heat, stirring often, for 8 minutes or until they start to soften. **4.** Pour the wine and stock into the pan, scraping the bottom. Add the chicken pieces and onions. Bring to a boil, partially cover with the lid, and simmer gently for 15 minutes or until the chicken is cooked through. **5.** In a saucepan fitted with a steamer insert, steam the potatoes over high heat for 8 minutes or until tender. Halve or quarter them. **6.** Remove the chicken legs from the pan and halve them. Return them to the pan with the potatoes. Simmer for 2 minutes. Taste for seasoning and add more salt and pepper, if you like. Sprinkle with thyme and parsley.

Sheryl Julian

Chicken Provencal

The sunny flavors of Provence, in the south of France, are in this pot, and perfectly suit our region. Serve it in summer, when you want something light, or in winter, when you need a sunny dish.

SERVES 4

2 tablespoons olive oil

1 whole chicken (3½–4 pounds), cut into 8 pieces

1 clove garlic, crushed

1 cup dry white wine

1 cup chicken stock

1 cup pitted black or green olives

Grated rind of 1 orange

1 cup canned tomatoes, crushed

1 tablespoon chopped fresh basil

Salt and pepper, to taste

1. In a large flameproof casserole, heat the oil over medium-high heat. Brown the chicken in batches, skin side down at first, letting each piece sit for a few minutes before you move it. Remove the browned chicken from the pan and transfer to a plate while you brown the remaining chicken. **2.** Return all the pieces to the pan. Add the garlic, wine, stock, olives, orange rind, tomatoes, half the basil, salt, and pepper. **3.** Bring the mixture to a boil. Turn down the heat, cover the pan, and simmer the chicken for 35 minutes, or until the meat is cooked through. Sprinkle with the remaining basil. Serve in deep plates with plenty of the cooking liquid and steamed yellow potatoes.

Sheryl Julian

Chicken with Polenta

In this dish, red gravy is a deeply flavored mixture of red wine and tomatoes in which chicken thighs simmer. Polenta sticks to the bottom of the pan, so don't be alarmed by the mess or put off by the attention polenta requires. It's all worth it.

SERVES 6

CHICKEN

6 bone-in chicken thighs
  (2 pounds total)
Salt and black pepper, to taste
Flour (for sprinkling)
2 tablespoons canola oil
2 medium onions, sliced
1 green bell pepper, cored,
  seeded, and sliced
5 cloves garlic, finely chopped
2 teaspoons dried thyme
1 teaspoon dried oregano
1 cup red wine or water
1 can (28 ounces) diced
  tomatoes

POLENTA

5 cups water
1 tablespoon salt
1 1/2 cups coarse polenta flour
1/4 cup Parmesan (optional)
2 tablespoons butter, cut up
  (optional)

CHICKEN

1. Sprinkle the thighs all over with salt, pepper, and flour. **2.** In a large flameproof casserole, heat the canola oil over high heat. Brown chicken thighs and remove them from the pan. **3.** Reduce the heat to medium-high. Add the onions, green pepper, garlic, and salt. Cook, stirring often, for 10 minutes or until softened. **4.** Add the thyme and oregano and cook, stirring, for 1 minute more. Pour in the wine or water and cook, scraping the bottom, for 2 minutes. Stir in the tomatoes and bring to a boil. Return the chicken to the pan, and lower the heat. Set the cover on askewed. Simmer for 1 hour, stirring occasionally. Taste for seasoning and add more salt and black pepper.

POLENTA

1. In a large saucepan, bring the water and salt to a boil. Stirring constantly with a wooden spoon, add the polenta in a slow, steady stream. Reduce the heat to medium-low. Simmer, stirring often, for 20 minutes. **2.** Stir in Parmesan and butter, if using. Taste for seasoning and add more salt, if you like. Spoon the polenta into 6 deep plates and add the chicken and some sauce to each one.

Karoline Boehm Goodnick

Chicken Paprikas

Real Hungarian paprika makes a big difference in this creamy classic. Serve the dish over wide noodles.

SERVES 4

2 tablespoons butter

4 skinless, boneless chicken
  breasts

2 onions, finely chopped

Salt and pepper, to taste

2 tablespoons sweet paprika

1 tablespoon flour

½ cup chicken stock

½ cup sour cream

2 tablespoons chopped fresh
  parsley

1. In a large flameproof casserole, heat the butter and cook the chicken breasts, without touching them, for 5 minutes. Turn and cook the other side for 3 minutes more. Remove the chicken from the pan. Add the onions, salt, and pepper. Cook, stirring often, for 10 minutes or until the onions soften. **2.** Sprinkle the paprika into the pan and cook, stirring, for 2 minutes. Sprinkle the flour into the pan and continue cooking, stirring, for 2 minutes more. **3.** Stir the stock into the mixture and continue stirring until the liquid starts bubbling and the sauce is smooth. **4.** Return the chicken to the pan. Turn it in the sauce. Cover and cook for 10 minutes or until the chicken is cooked through. **5.** Remove a large ladle of the liquid from the pan and transfer to a bowl. **6.** Stir the sour cream into the liquid. Stir the sour cream mixture back into the pan. Turn the chicken in the sauce. Taste for seasoning and add more salt and pepper, if you like. Reheat without boiling. Sprinkle with parsley.

Pork Loin on a Bed of Apples, Fennel, and Potatoes

For fall entertaining, this boneless loin, which roasts on onions, sliced fennel, crisp apples, and small potatoes, is stunning to bring to the table.

SERVES 8

3 tablespoons butter

1 Spanish onion, thinly sliced

2 bulbs fresh fennel, trimmed
   and thinly sliced

Salt and pepper, to taste

4 apples (Ginger Gold,
   Baldwin, Macoun), unpeeled,
   cored, and thickly sliced

10 small new potatoes,
   scrubbed and thickly sliced

Olive oil (for the dish)

3 tablespoons chopped fresh
   thyme

2 tablespoons olive oil

1 boneless pork loin (about 3½
   pounds)

2 tablespoons chopped fresh
   parsley

1. In a large skillet, melt the butter over medium heat. Cook the onion and fennel with salt and pepper, stirring often, for 5 minutes. Add the apples to the pan and continue cooking for 5 minutes more. **2.** Meanwhile, in a steamer over cold water, set the potatoes, cover the pan, and steam over high heat for 10 minutes or until the potatoes are almost tender. **3.** Set the oven at 375°F. Have on hand a baking dish long enough to hold the meat with room around the sides. Lightly oil the baking dish. In the dish, layer the fennel mixture with the potatoes and thyme. Set the dish aside. **4.** Wipe out the skillet. Heat the oil over medium-high heat. Sprinkle the loin with salt and pepper. Brown it in the skillet. When it is golden all over, set the meat on the fennel mixture. Transfer to the oven. Roast the meat for 1 hour or until a meat thermometer inserted into the meat registers 145°F. Set in a warm place while the temperature rises 5 degrees. **5.** Arrange the vegetables on each of eight dinner plates. Carve the meat into slices and set them on the vegetables. Sprinkle with parsley.

Sheryl Julian

Pork Tenderloins Wrapped in Bacon

Begin these bacon-wrapped pork tenderloins in a skillet, then finish cooking them in the oven. Pork tenderloins are often sold two to a package, and they're often different sizes. If one is done before the other, pull it from the oven when it's done and keep it warm until the other one is finished cooking.

SERVES 4

1 pound (16 strips) thick-sliced
   smoked bacon, at room
   temperature
2 pork tenderloins (2 pounds
   total), trimmed of excess fat
Salt and pepper, to taste
2 tablespoons canola oil

1. Set the oven at 375°F. Lay 8 slices of bacon on a cutting board so the strips are touching. Set 1 tenderloin across the bacon in the middle of the slices. Fold the bacon strips around the tenderloin and secure with toothpicks. (Pin the toothpicks flat and close to the meat.) Repeat with the remaining bacon and tenderloin. Sprinkle with salt and pepper. **2.** In a heavy 12-inch skillet with a heatproof handle and high sides, heat the oil over medium-high heat. Add the bacon-wrapped tenderloins, toothpicks down. Cook without disturbing for about 4 minutes or until the bacon at the bottom is browned. **3.** Using tongs, give the tenderloins a quarter turn and brown the next section for about 4 minutes. Do this two more times, turning the meat and cooking the bacon for a total of 16 minutes. Spoon off some of the fat as the bacon renders. **4.** Transfer the skillet to the oven and cook the tenderloins for 6 to 10 minutes longer or until a thermometer inserted into the thickest part reaches 145°F. Remove the skillet from the oven and transfer the tenderloins to a cutting board. Set in a warm place while the temperature rises 5 degrees. **5.** Remove the toothpicks and cut the meat into 1-inch slices.

From Sauce on Main,
Cambridge, Massachusetts

Pork Chops with Apple Cider

For weeknight meals, these quick boned pork loin chops are pan-seared and served with an apple-cider vinegar sauce.

SERVES 6

2 tablespoons canola oil

6 boneless pork loin chops
   (2½ to 3 pounds)

Salt and pepper, to taste

½ small onion, chopped

2 cloves garlic, finely chopped

1½ cups apple cider

1 teaspoon each chopped fresh
   oregano and thyme

1 teaspoon apple cider vinegar

1. Set the oven at 400°F. **2.** In a skillet with a heatproof handle, heat 1 tablespoon of the oil. Sprinkle the chops with salt and pepper. Brown the chops on both sides. Transfer to the oven and cook for 10 minutes or until an instant-read thermometer registers 145°F. **3.** Remove the chops from the pan, cover with foil, and keep warm. Add the remaining 1 tablespoon of olive oil. Cook the onion and garlic, scraping the bottom of the pan, for 8 minutes or until softened. **4.** Add the apple cider, oregano, and thyme. Bring the liquid to a boil. Let the sauce simmer steadily until the liquid reduces by half. Stir in the vinegar, taste the sauce for seasoning, and add more salt and pepper, if you like. Return the chops to the pan to reheat slightly.

Christine Merlo

Maple-Glazed Pork Ribs

The Fireplace restaurant in Brookline, Massachusetts, serves its ribs with green apple slaw, a creamy combination of shredded cabbage and green apples.

SERVES 6

1 jar or can (12 ounces) roasted
   red peppers, drained and
   coarsely chopped
2 cups ketchup
1 cup pineapple juice
⅓ cup dark brown sugar
⅓ cup pure maple syrup
2 racks (5½–6 pounds total)
   St. Louis–style pork ribs,
   trimmed of excess fat
Salt and black pepper, to taste

1. In a food processor, work the peppers until they are coarsely pureed. Add the ketchup, pineapple juice, sugar, and maple syrup. Puree until smooth. **2.** Turn on the broiler and set a rack about 5 inches below the heat source. Sprinkle the ribs with salt and pepper and transfer to a rimmed baking sheet. Broil for 5 to 8 minutes on a side or until they are lightly browned. **3.** Turn the oven to 325°F. Pour enough water into a large roasting pan to make a ½-inch layer. Generously brush the ribs on both sides with the sauce. Place the ribs, meaty sides up, in one layer in the pan. **4.** Cover the pan tightly with foil and cook the ribs for 2½ hours or until a knife inserted into the meat shows no resistance and the ribs are very tender. (Make up to 2 days ahead. Cool, wrap in foil, and refrigerate with remaining sauce.) **5.** Turn the oven to 400°F. Brush the ribs all over with more sauce. Cook them for 15 to 20 minutes or until they are hot and the sauce is glazed. Meanwhile, in a small saucepan, bring the remaining sauce to a boil. **6.** Transfer the ribs to a cutting board and cut them into 3-rib pieces. Serve with the remaining sauce.

From The Fireplace restaurant,
Brookline, Massachusetts

Layered Franks, Sauerkraut, and Potatoes

A four-layered dish, which includes sauerkraut, all-beef hot dogs, and tart apples, can be made and served in one large skillet. Creamy mashed potatoes form the top crust.

SERVES 6

1 cup water

2 tablespoons brown sugar

1 tablespoon cider vinegar

1 clove garlic, chopped

½ teaspoon salt

½ teaspoon pepper

1 can or jar (14 ounces) sauerkraut, rinsed well and drained

3 medium (2 pounds) russet potatoes, peeled and cut into small chunks

¾ cup milk, heated until hot

2 tablespoons butter

Salt and pepper, to taste

1 pound all-beef frankfurters, halved lengthwise, cut into 1½-inch chunks

2 apples (Cortland, Granny Smith), cored and thickly sliced

1. Set the oven at 350°F. Have on hand a deep 10-inch skillet with a heatproof handle. **2.** In a small bowl, combine the water, brown sugar, vinegar, garlic, salt, and pepper; set aside. **3.** In the skillet, heat the sauerkraut over medium-high heat for 1 minute. Add the brown sugar mixture, stir well, and continue cooking for 10 minutes or until the liquid evaporates; set aside. **4.** Meanwhile, in a large saucepan, combine the potatoes with cold water to cover and a generous pinch of salt. Bring to a boil and simmer the potatoes for 10 minutes or until they are tender. **5.** Drain the potatoes and return them to the pan. With a potato masher, beat in the milk a little at a time with 1 tablespoon of the butter, salt, and pepper. Mash until smooth. **6.** Lay the frankfurters, cut sides down, in one layer on the sauerkraut. Add the apples, overlapping them to fit, if necessary. Spread the mashed potatoes on top in an even layer. **7.** Dot with the remaining 1 tablespoon of butter and sprinkle with salt and pepper. Bake the skillet for 30 minutes or until the top is golden brown.

Christine Merlo

Pork and Beef Meat Loaf

A rich mixture made with both pork and beef, this loaf also contains anchovy paste and soy sauce. It comes from Martha's Vineyard, Massachusetts, cook Alice Berlow.

SERVES 4

Butter (for the pan)

³/₄ pound ground beef

³/₄ pound ground pork

1 egg, lightly beaten

¼ cup dry white bread crumbs

2 cloves garlic, finely chopped

1 medium onion, finely chopped

1 tablespoon Worcestershire sauce

1 teaspoon anchovy paste

¼ cup ketchup or barbecue sauce

1 tablespoon soy sauce

1 teaspoon salt

1 teaspoon ground black pepper

1. Set the oven at 350°F. Lightly butter an 8½ x 4½ x 2½-inch loaf pan. **2.** In a large bowl combine the beef, pork, egg, bread crumbs, garlic, onion, Worcestershire sauce, anchovy paste, ketchup or barbecue sauce, soy sauce, salt, and pepper. With your hands, mix the meat and seasonings thoroughly. **3.** Fill the pan with the meat mixture. Set it on a rimmed baking sheet. **4.** Bake the meat loaf for 1 to 1½ hours or until the meat is bubbling at the edges and a meat thermometer inserted in the center of the loaf registers 160°F. Carefully tip the loaf to pour off the excess fat. **5.** Let the loaf stand for 10 minutes before cutting into thick slices.

Alice Berlow

All-Beef Meat Loaf

Great meat loaf paired with mashed potatoes is a real treat. The following day, meat loaf sandwiches are almost as good (and they're great for breakfast too).

SERVES 6

2½ pounds (85 percent lean) ground beef

2 medium carrots (or use turnips or parsnips), grated

1 can (6 ounces) tomato paste

1 medium onion, finely chopped

1 cup fresh bread crumbs

2 eggs

1 clove garlic, crushed

2 teaspoons salt

½ teaspoon black pepper

½ tablespoon dried oregano

½ cup ketchup

1. Set the oven at 400°F. Have on hand a 12-inch baking dish. **2.** In a large bowl, combine the beef, carrots (or turnips or parsnips), tomato paste, onion, bread crumbs, eggs, garlic, salt, pepper, and oregano. Mix well. **3.** Place the meat mixture in the dish and shape it into a mound that is about 2½ inches high and 11 inches long. **4.** Cover the dish with foil and cook it for 30 minutes. Reduce the oven temperature to 350°F, remove the foil, and brush meat loaf all over with ketchup. **5.** Continue baking, uncovered, for about 30 minutes more or until a meat thermometer inserted into the center of the loaf registers 165°F (total cooking time is 1 hour). Tilt the pan to spoon out the fat. Cut into thick slices.

From Deluxe Town Diner,
Watertown, Massachusetts

Meat Loaf with Rolled Oats

Using oats in place of some of the bread crumbs yields a lighter texture to this all-beef meat loaf.

SERVES 8

1 medium onion, chopped

1 small green bell pepper, cored, seeded, and chopped

1½ cups dry bread crumbs

½ cup quick-cooking rolled oats

½ cup marinara sauce

1 teaspoon adobo seasoning

1 teaspoon salt

½ teaspoon black pepper

1½ teaspoons fresh sage, finely chopped

2 cloves garlic, crushed

½ cup whole milk

2 eggs, beaten

2½ pounds ground chuck (85 percent lean)

1. Set the oven at 350°F. Line a rimmed baking sheet with parchment paper. **2.** In a large bowl, combine the onion, bell pepper, bread crumbs, oats, marinara sauce, adobo seasoning, salt, black pepper, sage, and garlic. Stir in the milk and eggs. **3.** With your hands, gradually add the meat, mixing gently. **4.** Spoon the meat into mounds in the center of the baking sheet. Form one loaf about 10 inches long by 5 inches. **5.** Bake for 1 hour and 45 minutes, turning the sheet from back to front during cooking, or until a meat thermometer inserted into the center registers 160°F. **6.** Remove the meat loaf from the oven and set aside to rest for 10 minutes.

St. Alphonzo's Kitchen,
Boston, Massachusetts

Moroccan Lamb Stew

Lamb goes especially well with cinnamon, coriander, and other Moroccan spices. In this stew, which has a slightly sweet taste, carrots, zucchini, chickpeas, and raisins are also in the pot.

SERVES 6

2 pounds boneless lamb shoulder, trimmed and cut into 2-inch pieces

3 tablespoons olive oil, or more if necessary

3 large onions, cut into 1-inch wedges

Salt and pepper, to taste

3 cloves garlic, finely chopped

1 cinnamon stick

2 teaspoons ground coriander

3 ½ cups water, or more if necessary

8 carrots, cut on the diagonal into ¾-inch pieces

3 small zucchini, cut on the diagonal into ¾-inch pieces

1 can (15 ounces) chickpeas, rinsed and drained

½ cup raisins

1. Pat the lamb dry with paper towels. **2.** In a large flameproof casserole, heat 2 tablespoons of the olive oil. Brown the meat in two or three batches over medium heat for about 4 minutes. Use a slotted spoon to transfer the meat to a bowl. **3.** Use paper towels to wipe out any fat from the pan. **4.** Heat the remaining 1 tablespoon of olive oil. When it is hot, add the onions, salt, and pepper. Cook, stirring often, for 5 minutes, or until the onions start to brown. **5.** Stir in the garlic, cinnamon stick, and coriander. **6.** Return the lamb to the pan. Pour in enough water to cover the lamb. Bring to a boil, scraping the bottom of the pan to release the browned bits. Lower the heat and cover the pan. Simmer for 45 minutes. **7.** Use a spoon to skim the fat from the liquid. **8.** Add the carrots, re-cover the pan, and simmer for 15 minutes. **9.** Stir in the zucchini and re-cover the pan. Simmer for 15 minutes or until the lamb and vegetables are both tender. (Total cooking time is 1 hour and 15 minutes.) **10.** Add the chickpeas and raisins and heat for a few more minutes or until they are hot. Taste for seasoning and add more salt and pepper, if you like.

Lisa Zwirn

Pan-Roasted Lamb Chops

Lamb rib chops are the succulent little nuggets on a bone that some butchers call "lamb lollipops." Brown them over high heat until the chops are golden on the outside and pink inside. Scatter lots of fresh herbs on top. They couldn't be easier.

SERVES 8

8 lamb rib chops

Salt and pepper, to taste

2 tablespoons olive oil

2 tablespoons chopped
    mixed rosemary, thyme, and
    oregano

1. With a small sharp knife, remove the fat from the bones beginning at the ends and stopping at the round piece of meat. The chops should look like meat on sticks. Sprinkle with salt and pepper. **2.** In a large nonstick skillet, heat the oil, swirling the pan around so it coats the bottom. When it is hot, add 4 lamb chops. Cook without moving for 3 minutes. Turn and cook the other sides for 3 minutes more. Repeat with the remaining chops. They should be cooked through but pink in the center. **3.** Arrange on a plate and sprinkle with the rosemary mixture.

Sheryl Julian

Desserts

Old-fashioned desserts have been a hallmark of New England cooks for centuries. This is the region where the wives of sea captains packed their men tins of spicy hermits to take on long voyages, where Boston cooking teacher Fannie Farmer first codified American measurements into the cups and tablespoons we now use, where Ruth Wakefield invented the Toll House cookie, where blueberry picking season meant weeks of beautiful pies cooling on kitchen windows in farmhouses across the countryside.

Whatever trends come and go, good bakers here mostly stick to tried-and-true confections made with pure ingredients. A sugar cookie must be buttery and crisp, a bar cookie tender, brownies rich, gingerbread dark and moist, shortbread melting. If you're looking for a stunning glazed chocolate cake, spicy frosted carrot cake, thumbprint cookies filled with dabs of jam, or Boston cream pie, it's all here. (Muffins, quick breads, and other baked treats traditional for breakfast and brunch start on page 107.) Serve these sweets as a homey ending to an elegant dinner, set a tempting dessert buffet with a few of these treats in a row, or put on the kettle, steep the tea, and imagine a time when things weren't quite so hectic and everyone stopped for a hot cup in the mid-afternoon.

It's enough to bring back that fine tradition.

Notes for baking

❖ Good bakers measure every ingredient and prepare the baking pan before they begin mixing, so assembling a cake or cookie is quick and efficient.

❖ Read a recipe to the end before you begin to bake, so you understand what you're about to make and know if you need to allow time to cool or refrigerate ingredients.

❖ In all these recipes, we used King Arthur all-purpose flour for testing, and the dip and scoop method of measuring. That is, we stir the top of the flour bin so the flour isn't densely packed, then dip the measuring cup into the bin, and level off the top with a flat-bladed dull knife.

❖ Instead of sifting flour, we suggest whisking flour, salt, leavening agents, and spices in a bowl to distribute them evenly.

❖ Eggs are always Grade A Large size. Ad campaigns sometimes suggest that only brown eggs are local eggs, but both white and brown can be local.

❖ Save one wooden spoon just for baking, so when a recipe calls for using a mixing bowl and wooden spoon, you're not using a spoon that made tomato sauce yesterday.

❖ A heat-resistant rubber spatula, a metal offset spatula, and a large metal spoon are three simple tools that are indispensable in the baking kitchen.

❖ Oven heat varies and many ovens have a hot spot, which means that one side is a higher temperature than the other. Bake all items in the middle of the oven, unless a recipe states otherwise, and rotate the confection from back to front halfway through baking unless a recipe says not to open the oven door.

❖ For most cookies, we prefer using parchment paper rather than greasing the baking sheets. Parchment allows you to remove the cookies easily after baking. Scrape off any crumbs that adhere to it and reuse the papers for other cookies in that recipe.

❖ After baking, wash cake pans and baking sheets with hot soapy water and a sponge. Don't use anything abrasive.

❖ Most cookies keep for a week in an airtight container, or can be frozen, well wrapped, for several months. To defrost, unwrap the confection and allow several hours for it come to room temperature.

Carrot Cake with Cream Cheese Frosting

Packed with grated carrots, walnuts, and raisins, this cake is flavored with orange juice and rind, cinnamon, nutmeg, and ginger. The classic cream cheese frosting is just right with the dense, moist cake. You need a one-piece straight-sided tube pan, or an angel food cake pan with a solid, not detachable, base (www.lacuisineus.com). This batter is made in a bowl with a wooden spoon.

MAKES 1 LARGE CAKE

CAKE

Butter (for the pan)

Flour (for the pan)

2 cups flour

2 teaspoons baking soda

½ teaspoon salt

1 tablespoon ground cinnamon

½ teaspoon ground nutmeg

½ teaspoon ground ginger

1½ cups vegetable oil

2 cups granulated sugar

4 eggs

¼ cup orange juice

1 teaspoon grated orange rind

1 pound (4 cups) freshly grated
   carrots

1 cup walnuts, coarsely
   chopped

¾ cup dark raisins

FROSTING

1 large package (8 ounces)
   cream cheese, at room
   temperature

½ cup (1 stick) unsalted butter,
   at room temperature

1¾ cups confectioners' sugar,
   sifted

1 teaspoon vanilla extract

1 teaspoon grated orange rind

CAKE

1. Set the oven at 350°F. Butter a one-piece tube pan. Line the bottom with parchment paper. Butter the paper. Dust the pan with flour, tapping out the excess. **2.** In a bowl, whisk the flour, baking soda, salt, cinnamon, nutmeg, and ginger. **3.** In another, larger, bowl with a wooden spoon, stir together the oil, sugar, eggs, orange juice, and orange rind until the mixture is smooth. **4.** Stir the flour mixture into the egg mixture. Gently fold in the carrots, walnuts, and raisins. **5.** Pour the batter into the pan. Tap it gently on the counter to remove any air bubbles. **6.** Bake the cake for 65 minutes or until the edges are starting to brown and the top springs back when gently pressed with a fingertip. **7.** Transfer the pan to a wire rack to cool. Turn the cake out onto the rack and set it right side up. Leave to cool completely.

FROSTING

1. In a mixer, beat the cream cheese and butter until smooth. **2.** Gradually add the confectioners' sugar, beating until it is all incorporated. Beat in the vanilla and orange rind. **3.** Set the cake on a cake plate. With an offset spatula, spread the frosting all over the top and sides. Set aside in a cool place for several hours for the cake to mellow and the frosting to set.

Cary Wheaton

Boston Cream Pie

There is endless speculation about the origins of this cake, which was first made at the Parker House hotel in the nineteenth century. Some say it might have been baked originally in a pie pan. It's definitely a cake, which is cut in half and sandwiched with an eggy custard, then glazed with chocolate. It's part of Boston's quirky culinary past. We use the batter for Hot-Milk Cake (see page 262), adapted to fit into a springform pan.

MAKES ONE 9-INCH CAKE

CAKE

Butter (for the pan)

Flour (for the pan)

1½ cups flour

1 teaspoon baking powder

¼ teaspoon salt

3 eggs

1¼ cups sugar

¾ cup whole milk

1½ tablespoons butter

1 teaspoon vanilla extract

FILLING

3 tablespoons granulated
    sugar

2 tablespoons flour

¼ teaspoon salt

½ cup whole milk

1 egg

½ teaspoon vanilla

1 tablespoon butter, cut up

CAKE

1. Set the oven at 350°F. Butter a 9-inch springform pan. Line the bottom with a round of parchment paper cut to fit it. Butter the paper and dust it with flour, tapping out the excess. **2.** In a bowl, whisk the flour, baking powder, and salt. **3.** In an electric mixer, beat the eggs and sugar at medium speed for 5 minutes or until thickened and the mixture ribbons onto itself when the beaters are lifted. **4.** In a small saucepan, heat the milk and butter to scalding; set aside. **5.** With the mixer set on low, beat the vanilla into the batter, then beat in the flour mixture. It's okay if there are still pockets of flour. Scrape down the sides of the bowl. **6.** Beat the hot milk mixture into the batter just until it is well combined. This thins the batter. **7.** Pour the batter into the pan. Bake the cake for 30 minutes or until the top springs back when pressed with a fingertip. Set it on a rack to cool.

FILLING

1. In a saucepan off the heat, combine the sugar, flour, and salt. Whisk in the milk a little at a time until it is all added. Use a rubber spatula to incorporate flour in the corners of the pan. **2.** Set the pan over low heat. Cook, whisking constantly, until mixture comes to a boil and thickens. Simmer 2 minutes. Remove the pan from the heat. **3.** In a bowl, beat the egg just to mix it. Stir a few spoonfuls of the milk mixture into the egg. Keep adding milk until half the mixture is added. Gradually whisk the egg mixture back into the saucepan. Return to low heat. Cook, stirring constantly, for 2 minutes. Do not let the mixture come to a boil. **4.** Remove from the heat. Add the vanilla and butter and stir until the butter melts. Transfer to a bowl. Press a piece of plastic wrap directly on the surface of the custard. Leave to cool; refrigerate until cold.

GLAZE

1 ounce unsweetened
   chocolate, coarsely chopped

1 cup confectioners' sugar,
   sifted

1 tablespoon hot water

GLAZE

1. In a bowl over hot but not boiling water, melt the chocolate. Remove the bowl from the heat and wipe the bottom. **2.** Stir the sugar and water into the chocolate. If necessary, to make a thinner glaze that will spread more easily, add a few more drops of hot water. **3.** To assemble the cake: Unsnap the side of the pan and slip the cake off the bottom. Transfer it to a platter. **4.** With a serrated knife, cut the cake horizontally in half. Lift off the top layer. Tuck strips of waxed paper under the cake all around to catch the drips. **5.** Spread the filling on the bottom layer. Set the top layer on the filling. **6.** Pour the glaze on the top of the cake. Refrigerate for 1 hour. Cut into wedges.

Hot-Milk Cake

The original recipe for this simple, rich, fine-textured cake came from Peter Kelly's great-grandmother. Kelly is on the staff of Johnson & Wales University culinary school in Providence, Rhode Island. His great-grandmother gave it to her daughter-in-law, Kelly's grandmother. She gave it to Kelly's mother, Kathryn, who made it for every occasion while Peter was growing up in Valatie, New York, in the Hudson River Valley. This recipe uses a one-piece tube pan (www.lacuisineus.com); the thin batter will leak out of a regular angel-food pan (the one with a removable bottom). When you add the hot milk to the batter, it makes the mixture very thin. Don't worry; it's fine.

MAKES ONE 10-INCH CAKE

Butter (for the pan)

Flour (for the pan)

3 cups flour

2 teaspoons baking powder

1/2 teaspoon salt

6 eggs

2 1/2 cups sugar

1 1/2 cups whole milk

3 tablespoons butter

2 teaspoons vanilla extract

Confectioners' sugar (for sprinkling)

1. Set the oven at 325°F. Butter a one-piece 10-inch tube pan. Line the bottom with a circle of parchment paper cut to fit. Butter the paper and dust the pan with flour, tapping out the excess. **2.** In a bowl, whisk the flour, baking powder, and salt. **3.** In an electric mixer, beat the eggs and sugar at medium speed for 5 minutes or until thickened and the mixture ribbons onto itself when the beaters are lifted. **4.** In a small saucepan, heat the milk and butter to scalding; set aside. **5.** With the mixer set on low, beat the vanilla into the batter, then beat in the flour mixture. It's okay if there are still pockets of flour. Scrape down the sides of the bowl. **6.** Beat the hot milk mixture into the batter just until it is well combined. **7.** Pour the batter into the prepared pan. Bake the cake for 60 minutes or until a skewer inserted into the middle of the cake comes out clean. **8.** Let the cake cool in the pan for 20 minutes, and then turn it out, peel off the parchment paper, and set it right side up on a wire rack to cool completely. Sprinkle with confectioners' sugar. **9.** Cut the cake into thick slices for serving.

Peter Kelly

Hot-Milk Cake

Aunt Selma's Chocolate Cake with Espresso Glaze

Aunt Selma's Chocolate Cake with Espresso Glaze

No one remembers whose aunt Selma is. Holly Safford of The Catered Affair in Hingham, Massachusetts, got the recipe years ago from someone who also had it secondhand. The name Helen Daly always comes up as having first made this light and luscious cake.

MAKES 1 LARGE CAKE

CAKE

Butter (for the pan)

Flour (for the pan)

1 cup cool black coffee

6 ounces semisweet chocolate, coarsely chopped

2 cups flour

1 tablespoon baking powder

1 teaspoon salt

1 cup (2 sticks) unsalted butter, at room temperature

2 cups granulated sugar

4 eggs, separated

1 teaspoon vanilla extract

GLAZE

⅓ cup heavy cream

1 tablespoon instant espresso powder

2 ounces semisweet chocolate, coarsely chopped

CAKE

1. Set the oven at 350°F. Have on hand a 10-inch Bundt pan. Butter the pan and dust it with flour, tapping out the excess. **2.** In a saucepan over low heat, combine the coffee and chocolate. Cook, stirring often, until the chocolate melts. The liquid should not boil. Set aside to cool. **3.** In a bowl, whisk the flour, baking powder, and salt. **4.** In an electric mixer, cream the butter and sugar until well combined. **5.** Add the egg yolks, one at a time, beating well after each addition and scraping down the sides of the bowl often. **6.** Stir in chocolate mixture and vanilla. **7.** With the mixer set on its lowest speed, beat in the flour mixture. **8.** In another bowl, beat the egg whites until they form stiff peaks. Stir a large spoonful of whites into the chocolate mixture to lighten it. Fold in the remaining whites until no white patches show. **9.** Pour the batter into the pan. Bake the cake for 45 minutes or until the top is firm and the cake pulls away from the sides of the pan. Let the cake cool in the pan. **10.** Turn the cake out onto a rack. Set the rack on a rimmed baking sheet.

GLAZE

1. In a saucepan, scald the cream and espresso powder. Add the chocolate and cook, stirring, just until the chocolate melts and the mixture is smooth. Do not boil. **2.** Cool the glaze for 15 minutes, stirring occasionally. Spoon it over the cake.

Helen Daly

Chocolate-Walnut Zucchini Cake

Make this cake when your garden is overflowing with zucchini. The shreds disappear in this chocolate-flavored batter but lend it a wonderful moist texture, which makes a light, handsome cake. To prepare the zucchini, halve it, scoop out the seeds, and shred only the skin and flesh.

MAKES 1 LARGE CAKE

Butter (for the pan)

Flour (for the pan)

2½ cups flour

½ cup unsweetened cocoa
   powder

2 teaspoons baking powder

1½ teaspoons baking soda

1 teaspoon ground cinnamon

1 teaspoon salt

¾ cup (1½ sticks) unsalted
   butter, at room temperature

1½ cups granulated sugar

3 eggs

2 teaspoons vanilla extract

½ cup whole milk

2 medium zucchini, seeded and
   grated (to make 2 cups)

1 cup chopped walnuts

Confectioners' sugar (for
   sprinkling)

1. Set the oven at 350°F degrees. Butter a 10-inch Bundt pan, and dust it with flour, tapping out the excess. **2.** In a bowl whisk the flour, cocoa powder, baking powder, baking soda, cinnamon, and salt. **3.** In an electric mixer, cream the butter and sugar. Add the eggs, one at a time, beating well after each addition. Blend in the vanilla. **4.** With the mixer set on its lowest speed, add the flour mixture to the batter alternately with the milk, beginning and ending with flour, until it is thoroughly blended. Remove the bowl from the mixer stand. **5.** With a rubber spatula, stir in the zucchini and walnuts. **6.** Transfer the batter to the pan. Bake the cake for 45 to 50 minutes or until a skewer inserted into the middle of the cake comes out clean. **7.** Let the cake cool in the pan. Turn it out onto a wire rack to cool completely. Sprinkle with confectioners' sugar.

Elaine Kennard

Chocolate-Walnut Zucchini Cake

Yellow Cake with Chocolate Frosting

If you're inclined to make a children's birthday cake, this yellow cake, baked in a rectangular pan and spread with chocolate frosting, is easy to assemble. You can make clusters of colored balloons with M&M candies as the rounds, and gel from the baking section of the supermarket as the strings.

MAKES 1 LARGE CAKE

CAKE

Butter (for the pan)

Flour (for the pan)

3 cups flour

2 teaspoons baking powder

¼ teaspoon salt

6 tablespoons unsalted butter, at room temperature

1½ cups granulated sugar

3 eggs

2 teaspoons vanilla extract

¼ cup canola oil

1 cup whole milk

FROSTING

¼ cup (½ stick) unsalted butter, cut up

2 ounces unsweetened chocolate, coarsely chopped

1 to 2 tablespoons whole milk, or more if necessary, heated until just warm

1½ cups confectioners' sugar, sifted

CAKE

1. Set the oven at 325°F. Butter a 9 x 13-inch baking pan. Dust it with flour, tapping out the excess; set aside. **2.** In a bowl, whisk the flour, baking powder, and salt. **3.** In an electric mixer, beat the butter at medium speed for 1 minute or until creamy. Gradually beat in the sugar and continue beating for 3 minutes, scraping down the sides of the bowl several times. **4.** Beat in the eggs, one at a time, beating well after each addition. Beat in the vanilla, then the oil in a thin, steady stream. **5.** With the mixer on low speed, beat the flour mixture into the batter alternately with the milk, beginning and ending with flour. **6.** Transfer the batter to the pan. Bake the cake for 45 minutes or until the top springs back when pressed lightly with a fingertip. Transfer the pan to a wire rack to cool.

FROSTING

1. In a heatproof bowl over a saucepan of hot water, melt the butter. Add the chocolate and stir until the chocolate melts. Remove the bowl from the water; dry the bottom. **2.** With a wooden spoon, beat in 1 tablespoon of the milk. Then beat in the sugar, a few spoonfuls at a time, to make a frosting that holds its shape. Beat in 1 tablespoon more of milk, if necessary, until the frosting is smooth. **3.** With an offset spatula, spread the frosting on the cake in a smooth layer. Set the cake aside for several hours to mellow.

Sheryl Julian & Julie Riven

Pumpkin Breads

With brown sugar, lots of spices, molasses, pumpkin puree, and an oil base, this light and moist quick bread has a fine taste and beautiful texture. The breads freeze well.

MAKES 2 LOAVES

Butter (for the pan)

Flour (for the pan)

3¼ cups flour

1 teaspoon salt

2 teaspoons baking soda

2 teaspoons ground cinnamon

1 teaspoon ground nutmeg

½ teaspoon ground cloves

1 cup canola oil

1⅔ cups light brown sugar

4 eggs

1 can (16 ounces) pumpkin puree

2 tablespoons molasses

1 teaspoon vanilla extract

1. Set the oven at 350° degrees. Butter two 8½ x 4½ x 2½-inch loaf pans. Dust them with flour, tapping out the excess. **2.** In a bowl, whisk the flour, salt, baking soda, cinnamon, nutmeg, and cloves. **3.** In an electric mixer, beat the oil and sugar at medium-high speed for 3 minutes or until the mixture thickens. **4.** Add the eggs, one by one, beating well after each addition. **5.** Beat in the pumpkin, molasses, and vanilla. **6.** With the mixer set on its lowest speed, beat the dry ingredients into the batter until smooth. **7.** Divide the mixture between the pans. Bake them for 45 minutes or until the tops are firm and a skewer inserted into the breads comes out clean. **8.** Cool the loaves in the pans for 20 minutes. Turn them out onto a rack and leave them right side up to cool completely.

Andrea Pyenson

Cranberry-Orange Walnut Bread

Fresh cranberries are available from late September through December, but since the berries freeze well, stash a few bags in your freezer so you have them on hand for baking the rest of the year. Make this quick bread in a bowl with a wooden spoon.

MAKES 1 LOAF

Butter (for the pan)

Flour (for the pan)

2 cups flour

1 teaspoon baking powder

½ teaspoon baking soda

¾ teaspoon salt

½ teaspoon ground cinnamon

½ cup (1 stick) unsalted butter, melted and cooled

1 cup granulated sugar

¾ cup orange juice

Grated rind of 1 orange

1 egg, lightly beaten

1 cup fresh cranberries

⅔ cup chopped walnuts

1. Set the oven at 350°F. Butter a 9 x 5-inch loaf pan, and dust the pan with flour, tapping out the excess. **2.** In a bowl, whisk together the flour, baking powder, baking soda, salt, and cinnamon. **3.** In a large bowl with a wooden spoon, stir together the butter, sugar, orange juice and rind, and egg. **4.** Stir the flour mixture into the egg mixture just until smooth. Stir in the cranberries and walnuts. **5.** Transfer the batter to the pan. Bake for 55 minutes or until a toothpick inserted into the center of the cake comes out clean. Cool in the pan for 15 minutes, then turn the bread out onto a rack and set it right side up to cool completely.

Lisa Zwirn

Dark Gingerbread Cake

This old-fashioned recipe includes instructions to pour boiling water into the finished batter before transferring it to the cake pan. It thins the batter so dramatically you'll think you've ruined the cake. But you haven't. The gingerbread is quite light and moist and loaded with spices. Serve it with softly whipped cream.

MAKES ONE 9-INCH CAKE

Butter (for the pan)

2 1/2 cups flour

1 1/2 teaspoons baking soda

1/2 teaspoon salt

2 teaspoons ground ginger

2 teaspoons ground cinnamon

1/2 teaspoon ground cloves

1/2 teaspoon ground nutmeg

1 cup (2 sticks) butter, at room temperature

1 cup firmly packed light or dark brown sugar

2 eggs

1 cup molasses

1/2 cup boiling water

1. Set the oven at 375°F. Butter a 9 x 13-inch baking pan. **2.** In a bowl, whisk the flour, baking soda, salt, ginger, cinnamon, cloves, and nutmeg. **3.** In the bowl of an electric mixer, cream the butter and sugar until they are light and fluffy. Add the eggs and beat for 1 minute after each addition. **4.** Beat in the molasses until blended. With the mixer set on its lowest speed, add the dry ingredients to the batter just until they are combined. Then add the boiling water in a thin stream. Mix just until smooth. **5.** Pour the batter into the pan and transfer it to the hot oven. Bake the cake for 50 minutes or until it is firm and set in the center. **6.** Leave the cake to cool to lukewarm, then cut it into large squares.

Sheryl Julian

Individual Molten Chocolate Cakes

Individual Molten Chocolate Cakes

These cakes have a tender crust and an oozing, fudgy center. Dorian McCarron, executive chef of Delfino in Roslindale, Massachusetts, uses 6-ounce metal baba molds, also called dariole *(cooking.com or amazon.com). You can also use other 6-ounce tapered individual baking dishes. Don't overcook the cakes or let them sit too long in their cups after baking. Prepare the batter ahead, if you like; it will sit at room temperature for up to 2 hours. Fill the cups and bake them at the last minute.*

SERVES 4

Butter (for the cups)

Sugar (for the cups)

¹⁄₂ cup (1 stick) unsalted butter, cut up

5 ounces bittersweet chocolate, chopped

¹⁄₂ cup granulated sugar

2 eggs

1 cup minus 2¹⁄₂ tablespoons sifted flour

1. Set the oven at 350°F. Butter four 6-ounce, tapered ramekins, custard cups, or baba molds. Coat with sugar, shaking out the excess. **2.** In a heatproof bowl set over, but not touching, a pan of simmering water, place the butter and chocolate. Stir often until the mixture is melted and smooth. Remove the bowl from the water. Wipe the bottom. Cool for 2 minutes. **3.** Whisk in the sugar, then the eggs, beating for 30 seconds or until the batter thickens. Add the flour and stir until blended. **4.** Spoon the batter into the cups. Set them on a baking sheet. Bake metal cups for 12 minutes, porcelain cups for 14 minutes, or until the tops are just set and the centers soft. Let the cups sit for 2 minutes. Using a dish towel to hold the cups, run a dull knife around the inside of each cup and invert the cakes onto plates. Garnish with raspberries, if you like.

Delfino restaurant,
Roslindale, Massachusetts

Ricotta Cheesecake

After baking a buttery bottom crust, mix ricotta and cream cheese with lemon and orange rind, and lots of eggs, and bake the mixture until it sets. Before you begin, let the ricotta drain for several hours so it's not watery in the filling.

MAKES ONE 9-INCH CAKE

CRUST

¼ cup sliced almonds

¼ cup flour

2 tablespoons granulated sugar

¼ teaspoon salt

5 tablespoons cold unsalted butter, cut up

1 egg yolk

1 teaspoon vanilla extract

Grated rind of 1 lemon

CAKE

Butter (for the pan)

1 pound whole-milk fresh ricotta

1 pound cream cheese, at room temperature

¾ cup plus 1 tablespoon granulated sugar

5 eggs, separated

Grated rind of 1 lemon

Grated rind of 1 orange

Pinch of salt

CRUST

1. Set the oven at 325°F. Have on hand a 9-inch springform pan. **2.** In a food processor, pulse the almonds, flour, sugar, and salt. Add the butter and pulse until the mixture is the texture of coarse meal. Add the yolk, vanilla, and lemon rind. Pulse just until a dough begins to form. **3.** With your hands, press the dough on the bottom of the pan. Prick it well with a fork and bake for 25 minutes. The dough will be soft and pull away from the edges of the pan. Cool on a wire rack.

CAKE

1. Butter the sides of the cool pan. **2.** Set a fine-meshed strainer over a bowl. Add the ricotta cheese, cover with plastic wrap and a heavy weight, and refrigerate for several hours. **3.** Set the oven at 375°F. Discard all the liquid in the bowl of ricotta. Force the cheese through the sieve. **4.** In an electric mixer, beat the ricotta and cream cheese on medium speed for 1 minute or until fluffy. Turn the mixer to medium-low and add ¾ cup of the sugar, then the egg yolks, one at a time. **5.** Turn the speed to medium-high and beat the mixture for 5 minutes or until fluffy. Transfer to a wide mixing bowl. Fold in the lemon and orange rinds. **6.** Wash and dry the mixer bowl. Beat the egg whites and salt. When they start to foam, sprinkle in the remaining 1 tablespoon of sugar. Beat on medium speed until they form soft peaks (they should not be stiff). **7.** Stir a large spoonful of the whites into the ricotta batter. Fold in the remaining whites as lightly as possible. Transfer the batter to the pan. Bake for 1 hour or until the cake is golden. Run a knife around the top edge to loosen it. Cool on a wire rack. The cake will deflate a little. Unsnap the side of the pan and transfer the cake to a platter. Chill for several hours. Serve at room temperature.

Jill Santopietro

Linzer Torte

Boston-based clarinetist Richard Stoltzman studied cooking at the Cordon Bleu Cookery School in London. This jam-filled tart in cinnamon-flavored pastry has become his specialty.

MAKES ONE 9-INCH TORTE

1 cup (2 sticks) cold butter, cut into chunks

½ cup granulated sugar plus 1 tablespoon

1 egg, separatd

1 extra yolk

2 cups whole almonds

1 scant cup flour

½ tablespoon ground cinnamon

1 teaspoon ground cloves

2 tablespoons unsweetened cocoa powder

6 ounces raspberry jam

1 cup heavy cream, softly whipped (for serving)

1. Have on hand a 9-inch tart pan with removable base and a pastry bag fitted with a ½-inch plain round tip. **2.** In an electric mixer, cream the butter. Add ½ cup sugar and the 2 egg yolks, mixing just until incorporated. **3.** In a food processor, work the almonds until ground. **4.** With the mixer set on low speed, gradually add the almonds and flour to butter mixture. Mix in the cinnamon, cloves, and cocoa, taking care not to overmix. **5.** Using your fingers or an offset spatula, press some of the dough into the tart pan to form a ¼-inch-thick layer. **6.** In a bowl, stir the jam to soften it. Spread it on the pastry, leaving a ¼-inch border around the edge. Scoop the remaining dough into the pastry bag. Pipe two strips of dough across the torte in one direction; working across them, pipe two more strips to make a large cross-hatch. Pipe a ring of dough around the edge. Alternatively, roll pieces of the dough under your palms to form the crosshatch and the rim pieces. **7.** In a bowl, whisk the egg white until light and foamy. Whisk in the remaining 1 tablespoon sugar. With a pastry brush, brush the exposed parts of the crust with the egg mixture. Refrigerate the torte for at least 30 minutes. **8.** Set the oven at 300°F. **9.** Bake the torte for 1 hour. It will appear soft at the end of baking, but will firm up as it cools. Serve with whipped cream.

Richard Stoltzman

Chocolate-Chip Brownies

Award-winning author Lisa Yockelson (Baking by Flavor *and* ChocolateChocolate *are two of her books*), *a regular contributor to* The Boston Globe, *makes these cake-y brownies with fudgy centers. We think they're wonderful.*

MAKES 16

Butter (for the pan)

Flour (for the pan)

3 ounces unsweetened chocolate, melted and cooled

1 ounce bittersweet chocolate, melted and cooled

1¼ cups flour

½ teaspoon baking powder

¼ teaspoon salt

2 tablespoons unsweetened cocoa powder

¾ cup miniature semisweet chocolate chips

12 tablespoons (1½ sticks) unsalted butter, at room temperature

1 cup granulated sugar

3 eggs

2 teaspoons vanilla extract

Confectioners' sugar (for sprinkling)

1. Set the oven at 350°F. Butter an 8- or 9-inch square baking pan. Dust the pan with flour, tapping out the excess. **2.** In a bowl over hot but not boiling water, melt the unsweetened and bittersweet chocolates. Remove the bowl from the water, wipe the bottom of the bowl, and set the chocolate aside to cool. **3.** In another bowl, whisk the flour, baking powder, salt, and cocoa powder. **4.** In a smaller bowl, toss the chocolate chips with 1 teaspoon of the flour mixture. **5.** In an electric mixer, cream the butter at medium speed for 3 minutes. Add the sugar and beat 1 minute more. Beat in the eggs, one at a time, blending well after each addition. **6.** With the mixer set on its lowest speed, blend in the chocolate mixture, vanilla, and flour mixture. Beat only until blended. **7.** Remove the bowl from the mixer stand. With a large metal spoon, stir in the chocolate chips. **8.** Transfer the batter to the baking pan, spreading it evenly and smoothing the top. **9.** Bake the brownies for 30 minutes or until the top is just set. Transfer the pan to a wire rack to cool completely. **10.** Cut the brownies into quarters, then cut each quarter into 4 squares. Use a small offset spatula to remove the brownies from the pan. Store in an airtight container for up to 1 week. Just before serving, dust the tops of the brownies with confectioners' sugar.

Lisa Yockelson

Chocolate-Chip Brownies

Bittersweet-Chocolate Brownie Cookies

These have the same texture as a dense brownie—rich and deeply chocolatey and studded with chips—only in cookie form. Before baking, refrigerate the batter for 30 minutes or until it is firm enough to scoop.

MAKES 26 LARGE COOKIES

1 cup flour

1 teaspoon baking powder

1/4 teaspoon salt

1/2 cup (1 stick) unsalted butter, cut up

8 ounces semisweet chocolate, coarsely chopped

4 ounces unsweetened chocolate, coarsely chopped

4 eggs

1 cup light brown sugar

1/2 cup granulated sugar

1 teaspoon vanilla extract

1 cup semisweet chocolate chips

1. Line two baking sheets with parchment paper. **2.** In a bowl, whisk the flour, baking powder, and salt. **3.** In a double boiler over boiling water, combine the butter and semisweet and unsweetened chocolates. Cook over low heat until melted and smooth. Remove the mixture from the heat; set aside to cool slightly. **4.** In an electric mixer, beat the eggs with the brown and granulated sugars on medium speed for 1 minute. Beat in the chocolate mixture and vanilla. Beat the flour mixture into the batter just until the dry ingredients are thoroughly combined. Remove the bowl from the mixer stand. Fold in the chocolate chips. **5.** Refrigerate the batter for 30 minutes, stirring the mixture several times, or until the batter just holds its shape. **6.** Set the oven at 350°F. **7.** With a soup spoon, scoop mounds of batter onto the baking sheets, leaving 1½ inches between the mounds, and setting about 8 on each sheet. **8.** Bake the cookies for 18 to 20 minutes or until the tops are just firm when pressed lightly with a fingertip. **9.** Let the cookies cool on the sheets for 20 minutes. Carefully transfer the parchment paper to wire racks to cool the cookies completely. To store: Layer the cookies with waxed paper in an airtight container and store for up to 4 days.

Julie Riven

Chocolate Crinkle Cookies

Chocolate cookies are a messy project. After chilling the dough overnight, you roll it into balls in your palms, then drop them into confectioners' sugar. When the cookies bake, the powdery sugar forms a crinkly top. There are many versions of this old-fashioned cookie, including recipes that call for adding mini chocolate chips to the batter.

MAKES 2¹⁄₂ DOZEN

2 ounces unsweetened
　　chocolate, coarsely chopped
1¹⁄₄ cups flour
1 teaspoon baking powder
¹⁄₄ teaspoon salt
¹⁄₄ cup canola oil
1 cup granulated sugar
2 eggs
1 teaspoon vanilla extract
¹⁄₂ cup confectioners' sugar, or
　　more (for rolling)

1. In the top pan of a double boiler set over, but not touching, simmering water, heat the chocolate, stirring occasionally, until it melts. Remove the double boiler from the heat. Wipe the bottom of the pan dry. **2.** In a bowl, whisk the flour, baking powder, and salt. **3.** In an electric mixer, combine the oil and granulated sugar. Beat for 1 minute. The mixture will look granular. **4.** Add the eggs and beat well. Beat in the vanilla, then the chocolate, until the batter is smooth. With the mixer on low, beat in the flour mixture just until combined. **5.** Remove the bowl from the mixer stand. With a rubber spatula, scrape up the bottom of the dough. Cover the bowl with plastic wrap and refrigerate overnight. **6.** Set the oven at 350°F. Line two baking sheets with parchment paper. **7.** Place the confectioners' sugar in a shallow bowl. Scoop up heaping teaspoons of dough and shape them into balls in your palms. **8.** Roll the balls in confectioners' sugar to coat them all over. Set them on a baking sheet about 1 inch apart. Continue until all the dough is used. **9.** Bake the cookies for 14 minutes or until the tops crack and set. Remove the cookies from the oven and set aside for 5 minutes. Transfer them on the parchment paper to wire racks to cool completely. **10.** Store in an airtight container, layered with waxed paper, for up to 1 week.

Cheryl Rubin

Chocolate Crinkle Cookies

Giant Chocolate-Chip Cookies

To make these very large chocolate-chip cookies, use a ¼ cup ice cream scoop or measure. Each baking sheet will hold 5 mounds. The Coach House of Edgartown, Massachusetts, began with the recipe on the Toll House chocolate chip package and adapted it to turn them into this giant version with chopped dark chocolate. You need to refrigerate the dough after making the batter.

MAKES 15

2¼ cups flour

1 teaspoon baking soda

1 teaspoon salt

1 cup (2 sticks) unsalted butter, at room temperature

1 cup granulated sugar

⅔ cup packed light brown sugar

2 eggs

1 teaspoon vanilla extract

12 ounces bittersweet or semisweet chocolate, chopped into chunks

1. Line two large baking sheets with parchment paper. **2.** In a bowl, whisk the flour, baking soda, and salt. **3.** In an electric mixer, beat the butter and granulated and brown sugars until light and fluffy. Beat in the eggs one at a time, followed by the vanilla. **4.** With the mixer set on low speed, blend in the dry ingredients. Stir in the chocolate. Scrape down the sides of the bowl, cover with plastic wrap, and refrigerate for at least 30 minutes. **5.** Set the oven at 350°F. **6.** Scoop the batter, placing 5 evenly spaced mounds on each sheet. Do not flatten. **7.** Bake for 15 to 17 minutes or until the cookies are golden all over and the center is firm. Transfer to a rack to cool. Scoop and bake the remaining batter in the same way.

The Coach House,
Edgartown, Massachusetts

Crisp Chocolate-Chip Cookies

Made with chopped bittersweet chocolate, rather than chips, these have less flour than regular chocolate chip cookies and become crisper in the oven. For perfectly round cookies, use a small (2-tablespoon) ice cream scoop. Set the mounds 3 inches apart because the cookies spread during baking.

MAKES ABOUT 30

2 cups flour

1 teaspoon kosher salt

1 teaspoon baking soda

1 cup (2 sticks) unsalted butter, at room temperature

¾ cup granulated sugar

1 cup light brown sugar

1 egg

1 teaspoon vanilla extract

1 ½ tablespoons water

1 ½ cups finely chopped bittersweet chocolate

1. Set the oven at 375°F. Line two baking sheets with parchment paper. **2.** In a bowl whisk the flour, salt, and baking soda. **3.** In an electric mixer on medium speed, cream the butter and granulated and brown sugars for 5 minutes or until fluffy. **4.** Beat in the egg, vanilla, and water. **5.** With the mixer set on low speed, beat in the flour mixture until combined. Remove the bowl from the mixer stand. With a spatula, fold in the chocolate. **6.** With a small ice cream scoop or a metal spoon, spoon golf-ball-size mounds of dough onto the baking sheets 3 inches apart. Bake the cookies for 12 minutes or until the edges are golden and crisp. **7.** Cool on the sheets until firm. Transfer to wire racks to cool completely. Store for up to 3 days in an airtight container.

Jonathan Levitt

My Mother's Sugar Cookies

My Mother's Sugar Cookies

Like many women of her generation, Sheryl Julian's mother, Doris, used recipes from the backs of food boxes. This recipe came with her Spritz cookie press, which she bought decades ago and used for years, before adapting the formula to make without the press. The batter is rolled into balls and stamped with a glass dipped in granulated sugar and baked until they're quite crisp on the outside.

MAKES ABOUT 4 DOZEN

1 cup (2 sticks) unsalted butter, at room temperature

²/₃ cup granulated sugar

1 egg, lightly beaten

1 teaspoon vanilla extract

2¹/₂ cups flour

Pinch of salt

Extra granulated sugar (for rolling)

1. In an electric mixer, cream the butter until soft. Add the sugar and beat until it is incorporated. **2.** Beat in the egg, followed by the vanilla. With the mixer set on its lowest speed, beat in the flour and salt. **3.** Scrape down the sides of the bowl and press a piece of plastic wrap directly onto the batter. Refrigerate for 10 minutes. **4.** Set the oven at 350°F. Line two baking sheets with parchment paper. **5.** Spread enough sugar on a deep plate to make a thin layer. Using a teaspoon, scoop up a mound of dough and roll it in your hands into a ball. Drop it onto the sugar and roll it around to coat it all over. With the bottom of a glass dipped into the sugar, press the ball to flatten it. Turn it over in the sugar and press again. Transfer to a baking sheet. Continue rolling and pressing batter into cookies (you'll need to use the sheets again). **6.** Bake the cookies for 14 minutes or until the edges are just beginning to color. Check the baking sheets after 12 minutes to make sure cookies at the edges have not browned. Transfer to a wire rack to cool. Store in an airtight container for up to 2 weeks.

Sheryl Julian

Molasses Sugar Cookies

Crisp, sugary, thin, and addictive, these traditional molasses cookies will become your cookie jar standby. Solid vegetable shortening now comes trans-fat free, which is the best choice for baking.

2 cups sifted flour

2 teaspoons baking soda

1 teaspoon salt

1 teaspoon ground ginger

1 teaspoon ground cinnamon

¾ cup solid vegetable
   shortening (trans-fat free)

1 cup granulated sugar

1 egg

¼ cup molasses

Extra granulated sugar (for
   flattening)

1. Set the oven at 350°F. Line two large baking sheets with parchment paper. Have on hand a glass that is completely flat on the bottom. **2.** In a bowl, whisk the flour, baking soda, salt, ginger, and cinnamon. **3.** In an electric mixer, cream together the shortening and sugar. When they are fluffy, add the egg and beat thoroughly, then add the molasses and beat just to blend it in. **4.** With the mixer set at its lowest speed, add the flour mixture to the batter just until it is thoroughly incorporated. **5.** Remove the beaters and roll the dough into balls, making them about 1 inch across and dropping them 2 inches apart on the baking sheets. Put a layer of sugar on a small plate and repeatedly dip the glass into the sugar, then onto the cookies, flattening them to about a ⅛-inch thickness. **6.** Bake the cookies for 10 to 12 minutes or until they are just set. Change the position of the baking sheets from top to bottom and back to front halfway through cooking to ensure even baking. **7.** Remove the baking sheets from the oven, let the cookies cool for a minute, then transfer them to wire racks to cool completely. **8.** Store the cookies in an airtight tin for up to 1 week.

Alice Read

Hermits

Hermits are soft gingerbread-raisin cookies that do not contain ginger. Centuries ago, they were taken to sea in tins by North Atlantic fishermen because they kept well. When The Boston Globe ran a cookie contest some years ago, this was entered by a Brookline, Massachusetts, reader who got the recipe from a cousin in Nova Scotia. The instructions produced bar cookies, but we adapted the recipe to shape the batter into logs, which you cool, then slice, to make the traditional hermit shape. Each piece has chewy and crisp edges.

MAKES 40

3½ cups flour

½ teaspoon baking powder

1 teaspoon baking soda

1 teaspoon salt

1 teaspoon ground cinnamon

1 teaspoon ground allspice

½ cup (1 stick) butter, at room temperature

1 cup granulated sugar

1 cup molasses

3 eggs

1 cup raisins

Extra granulated sugar (for sprinkling)

1. Set the oven at 350°F. Line two large baking sheets with parchment paper. **2.** In a bowl, whisk the flour, baking powder, baking soda, salt, cinnamon, and allspice. **3.** In an electric mixer, cream the butter and sugar. Add the molasses and beat well. Add the eggs, one by one, until the mixture is smooth. It will look curdled; that's okay. **4.** With the mixer set on its lowest speed, beat the dry ingredients into the batter until it is smooth. Remove the bowl from the mixer. **5.** Use a spoon to stir in the raisins. The dough is quite sticky. **6.** Spoon the dough onto the sheets in 4 log shapes (2 on each sheet). Use an offset spatula dipped often into cold water to smooth the tops and sides. Don't worry about wetting the dough too much. Each log should be 12 inches long and no wider than 2½ inches. **7.** Sprinkle the logs generously with sugar. Bake them for 25 to 30 minutes or until they are firm when pressed with a fingertip. The logs spread and flatten during baking. **8.** Transfer the logs on the parchment paper to wire racks to cool completely. Set the logs, one at a time, on a cutting board and cut each log into 10 slices. Store in an airtight container.

Elaine "Cookie" McGinn

Hermits

Date and Nut Bars

Date and Nut Bars

Dense, chewy date and nut bars are traditional in New England, probably because they keep well. Begin with whole pitted dates, and after chopping them, let them soak in boiling water to soften. They're much better than packaged chopped dates, which tend to be too dry.

MAKES 32

8 ounces (2 cups) whole pitted dates, coarsely chopped

½ cup boiling water

1½ cups flour

1 teaspoon baking soda

½ teaspoon salt

1 cup (2 sticks) unsalted butter, at room temperature

½ cup granulated sugar

½ cup light brown sugar

2 eggs

1 teaspoon vanilla extract

2 cups walnut pieces, coarsely chopped

1. Set the oven at 350°F. Butter a 9 x 13-inch baking pan. **2.** In a bowl, combine the dates and water. Set aside for 15 minutes or until cool. **3.** In a bowl, whisk the flour, baking soda, and salt. **4.** In an electric mixer, cream the butter until light. Add the granulated and brown sugars and beat until well blended. Beat in eggs, one by one, followed by the vanilla. **5.** Stir in cooled dates and water. **6.** With the mixer set on its lowest speed, blend in the flour mixture. **7.** Remove the bowl from the mixer stand. With a large metal spoon, fold in the nuts. **8.** Transfer the batter to the baking pan. Smooth the top. **9.** Bake the bars for 30 minutes or until the top is firm to the touch. Set the pan on a wire rack to cool completely. **10.** Make 3 lengthwise cuts and 7 crosswise cuts to form 32 bars. Store in an airtight container.

Oatmeal-Raisin Cookies

Karoline Boehm Goodnick, a Boston Globe writer and food stylist, got this recipe from her father's sister, who was not known for her cuisine. She once cooked and carved a turkey upside down, says her niece. But Aunt Carol makes the best oatmeal-raisin cookies Karoline has ever tasted. These are crispy on the outside, moist and chewy inside.

MAKES 36

1½ cups flour

1 teaspoon baking soda

1 teaspoon salt

¼ teaspoon nutmeg

¼ teaspoon cinnamon

1 cup (2 sticks) unsalted butter,
    at room temperature

1 cup granulated sugar

1 cup light brown sugar

2 eggs

1 teaspoon vanilla extract

3 cups quick-cooking oats

1 cup dark raisins

Extra granulated sugar (for
    sprinkling)

1. Set the oven at 375°F. Line two baking sheets with parchment paper. **2.** In a bowl, whisk flour, baking soda, salt, nutmeg, and cinnamon. **3.** In an electric mixer, cream the butter with the granulated and brown sugars on medium-high speed until light and fluffy. Scrape down the sides of the bowl occasionally. **4.** Beat in the eggs, one at a time, followed by the vanilla. **5.** With the mixer set on low speed, add the flour mixture until just incorporated. **6.** Remove the bowl from the mixer stand. Stir in the oats and raisins. **7.** Use a teaspoon to drop heaping mounds of batter on the baking sheets, setting them about 1½ inches apart. Flatten slightly and sprinkle with sugar. **8.** Bake for 15 minutes or until the edges are lightly golden but the centers are still pale. Cool on the sheets for 1 minute, then transfer to wire racks to cool completely. Store in an airtight container for up to 1 week.

Karoline Boehm Goodnick

Oatmeal-Raisin Cookies

Macaroons

Macaroons

These macaroons puff, then deflate slightly when cool. Macaroons have always been popular in New England. When Boston, Massachusetts, department stores had bakeries, a store called Gilchrist sold large chewy macaroons in individual waxed papers. Everyone lined up to buy one or one dozen.

MAKES 28

1 roll (7 ounces) almond paste
¼ cup egg whites
½ cup granulated sugar
¼ cup sliced almonds (for garnish)

1. Set the oven at 325°F. Line a baking sheet with parchment paper. **2.** Break off small pieces of the almond paste and put them into the bowl of an electric mixer. Measure 1 tablespoon of egg whites and pour over almond paste to soften it. Stir with a spoon to coat the pieces. Let them stand for 2 minutes. **3.** With a paddle attachment on medium speed, beat the sugar into the paste for 1 minute or until it resembles coarse crumbs. **4.** Increase speed to medium high and gradually add the remaining egg whites. Beat for 3 minutes to form a smooth, sticky paste, scraping down the sides of the bowl. **5.** Using a 1-teaspoon measuring spoon, drop mounds of batter onto the baking sheet, spacing them 1 inch apart. Gently press 1 sliced almond on each cookie. **6.** Bake one sheet at a time in the center of the oven for 12 to 14 minutes or until the macaroons are golden. Rotate the sheet from front to back halfway through baking to ensure even baking. **7.** Remove the macaroons from the oven and let them cool on the sheet for 1 minute. Slide the macaroons, still on the parchment, onto a wire rack to cool completely. **8.** Bake the remaining macaroons the same way. When they are cool, carefully peel them off the paper and store in an airtight container for up to several days.

The Country Club, Brookline, Massachusetts

Almond Squares

Elegant and professional-looking, these thin, crisp squares came from Boston Globe *reader Jillian Greene's late great-grandmother. Jillian and her mother, Nancy, cut the bars into diamonds. Here are instructions for cutting squares, which are easier.*

MAKES 48

Butter (for the pan)

1 cup (2 sticks) unsalted butter, at room temperature

1 cup granulated sugar

1 egg, separated

2 teaspoons vanilla extract

2 cups flour

1 cup sliced almonds

1. Set the oven at 350°F. Grease an 11 x 16-inch jelly roll pan. **2.** In an electric mixer, cream the butter and sugar until light. Add the egg yolk and vanilla. **3.** With the mixer set on its lowest speed, beat in the flour. **4.** Pat the batter into the prepared pan, pressing it into the corners. **5.** In a bowl with a fork, beat the egg white until frothy. Spread the white on the batter and sprinkle it with almonds. Press the almonds into the dough with your fingertips. **6.** Bake the mixture for 15 to 18 minutes or until it is golden brown. **7.** Transfer the pan to a wire rack to cool for 5 minutes. Make 5 lengthwise cuts and 7 horizontal cuts to form 48 squares. Let the mixture cool completely before using a wide metal spatula to lift the squares out of the pan. Store in an airtight container for up to 1 week.

Jean Fine

Almond Squares

Shortbread Triangles

There used to be stories told of Scottish women who made shortbread so quickly and easily that if they saw someone coming up the lane for tea, they could put the dough together and slip the shortbread into the oven by the time the guest was at the door. This is impossible, of course, but nevertheless a wonderful notion.

MAKES 24

1 cup (2 sticks) unsalted butter, at room temperature

1 cup confectioners' sugar, sifted

2 cups flour

¼ teaspoon salt

Granulated sugar (for sprinkling)

Extra flour (for cutting)

1. Set the oven at 350°F. Line two baking sheets with parchment paper. Use a pie pan or plate and a pencil to draw three 6-inch rounds on the papers. Turn the papers over. **2.** In an electric mixer, beat the butter at medium speed for 1 minute. Add the confectioners' sugar and beat until the mixture is creamy. **3.** Add the flour and salt. Continue beating, scraping down the sides of the bowl, until the mixture is smooth. Remove the bowl from the mixer stand. **4.** Set one-third of the dough in the center of each round. With your fingertips, smooth the dough evenly. **5.** Sprinkle the dough generously with granulated sugar. Dipping a large straight-edged knife repeatedly into flour, cut the rounds evenly into 8 triangles. **6.** Bake the rounds for 20 minutes or until they are just starting to turn brown (they're pale when done), turning the sheets from back to front halfway through baking. **7.** Slide the parchment papers onto wire racks and let the rounds sit for a few minutes to cool. Carefully transfer the papers to a board. Use a clean knife to cut the rounds along the same lines you made before baking. Set the triangles on a wire rack to cool completely. Store in an airtight container for up to 1 week.

Sheryl Julian

Shortbread Slice-and-Bake Cookies

Rather than shaping the classic triangles, these cookies are formed into a log, chilled, then sliced and baked in rounds.

MAKES 36

½ cup (1 stick) unsalted butter, at room temperature

¼ cup granulated sugar

1 teaspoon vanilla extract

⅛ teaspoon salt

1 ¼ cups flour

Granulated sugar (for sprinkling)

1. In an electric mixer, beat the butter and sugar until creamy. Beat in the vanilla and salt. **2.** With the mixer set on low speed, mix in the flour just until incorporated. **3.** Remove the bowl from the mixer stand. With your fingers, blend the ingredients completely to form a soft dough. **4.** Tear off a long sheet of plastic wrap. Set the dough on the wrap and shape it into a log, using the wrap to help you. The log should be about 9 inches long and 1½ inches in diameter. Enclose the log in the wrap and refrigerate overnight. **5.** Set the oven at 350°F. Line two baking sheets with parchment paper. **6.** Slice the log into ¼-inch rounds and place them on the sheets. Sprinkle the rounds with sugar. **7.** Bake the cookies for 16 to 18 minutes or until they begin to brown at the edges and are still pale in the center. Cool on the sheets for a few minutes then transfer to a wire rack to cool completely.

Lisa Zwirn

Peanut Butter Cookies

The butter in this mixture is melted first, which makes the batter come together easily with just a bowl and a wooden spoon. Refrigerate the batter for several hours or overnight until it is firm enough to roll into balls. If you do leave it overnight, let it soften on the counter for an hour before you shape it. Chunky peanut butter makes a big difference in this recipe; it gives the cookies a nice crunch.

MAKES ABOUT 40

1⅓ cups flour

½ teaspoon baking soda

1 teaspoon salt

½ cup (1 stick) butter, melted and cooled

½ cup granulated sugar

½ cup light brown sugar

1 egg

1 teaspoon vanilla extract

1 cup chunky or crunchy peanut butter

Extra granulated sugar (for pressing)

1. In a bowl whisk the flour, baking soda, and salt. **2.** In another bowl with a wooden spoon, stir together the butter and granulated and brown sugars. Beat in the egg, vanilla, and peanut butter until the mixture is smooth. Blend in the flour mixture until well incorporated. **3.** Scrape down the batter, cover the bowl with plastic wrap, and refrigerate the dough for several hours or overnight. **4.** Set the oven at 375°F. Line two baking sheets with parchment paper. **5.** Pinch off walnut-size pieces of dough. With your hands, shape them into balls and place them 2 inches apart on the baking sheets. **6.** Put enough sugar on a plate to make a thin layer. Dip the tines of a fork repeatedly in the sugar and press it down once on each ball. Then press in a perpendicular direction to make a cross-hatch pattern. **7.** Bake the cookies for 12 to 14 minutes or until they are beginning to brown at the edges. **8.** Transfer the parchment sheets to wire racks to cool. Store in an airtight container for up to 1 week.

Jonathan Levitt

Peanut Butter Cookies

Thumbprint Cookies

To make thumbprint cookies, you roll dough into balls, press your thumb into them to make a little indentation, and fill the hollow with jam before baking. They are as charming as their name suggests. These are fun to do with children. Allow 30 minutes for the dough to chill before shaping.

MAKES 4 DOZEN

1 cup (2 sticks) butter, at room
   temperature
½ cup granulated sugar
2 egg yolks
2⅔ cups flour
½ cup jam, jelly, or preserves,
   or more if necessary
Confectioners' sugar (for
   sprinkling)

1. Line two baking sheets with parchment paper. **2.** In an electric mixer, cream the butter and granulated sugar until light. Add the yolks, one by one, and beat well. **3.** With the mixer set on its lowest speed, beat in the flour just until the mixture is smooth. **4.** With your hands, shape the dough into smooth walnut-size balls no larger than 1 inch wide. Press each one with your thumb to make an indentation. Fill the indentation with jam, jelly, or preserves. **5.** Refrigerate the baking sheets for 30 minutes. **6.** Set the oven at 350°F. **7.** Bake the cookies for 15 to 18 minutes or until they are just beginning to brown. Cool completely on the baking sheets. Sprinkle with confectioners' sugar. Store in an airtight container.

Helene Feigen

Kourambiethes (*Greek sugar cookies*)

Greek celebration cookies are rich and buttery, completely covered with powdered sugar. The dough is made short-bread style, with very little sugar. After rolling into balls and baking, they're dusted generously with more powdered sugar while warm. They melt in your mouth. Allow 1 hour for the dough to chill before shaping.

MAKES 36

1 cup (2 sticks) unsalted butter,
   at room temperature
1¼ cup confectioners' sugar
1 teaspoon vanilla extract
2½ cups flour

1. Set the oven at 350°F. Line two baking sheets with parchment paper. **2.** In an electric mixer, beat the butter until creamy. Add ¼ cup of the sugar and vanilla. **3.** With the mixer set on low speed, beat in the flour until combined. Remove the bowl from the mixer stand. **4.** With a rubber spatula, stir the dough to make sure the crumbs on the bottom are mixed in. Press the dough down in the bowl, cover with plastic wrap, and refrigerate for 1 hour. **5.** Pinch off small pieces of dough and roll them into 1-inch balls. Set them on the sheets. Bake for 20 to 25 minutes or until they are sand colored. **6.** Place the remaining 1 cup of confectioners' sugar in a wide shallow bowl. **7.** Use a metal spatula to transfer several cookies from the baking sheets to the bowl of sugar. With two forks, roll the warm cookies in the sugar until they are coated all over. Transfer to a rack to cool.

The former Zesto Cafe, Framingham, Massachusetts

Kourambiethes

Pie Pastry

When making berry or other fruit pies, use orange juice instead of the vinegar. For more delicate tarts, substitute lemon juice for the vinegar. This mixture is made in a food processor. It should not form a ball in the machine, but rather make large moist clumps. Finish shaping on a lightly floured counter. Make the whole recipe and divide it in half. If you only need one crust, freeze the other half in foil. Defrost it completely before rolling out.

**MAKES ENOUGH FOR
1 DOUBLE-CRUST PIE**

2½ cups flour

½ teaspoon baking powder

½ teaspoon salt

¼ cup solid vegetable
   shortening (trans-fat free),
   cut into several pieces

½ cup (1 stick) unsalted butter,
   cut up

3 tablespoons granulated
   sugar

1 tablespoon distilled white
   vinegar

1 egg

2 tablespoons ice water

Extra flour (for sprinkling)

1. In a food processor, combine the flour, baking powder, and salt. Pulse for several seconds just to sift them. Add the shortening and butter. Pulse again until the mixture resembles coarse crumbs. **2.** Remove the processor lid. Sprinkle the sugar over the mixture and pulse quickly just to mix it in. **3.** In a small bowl, whisk the vinegar, egg, and ice water. Sprinkle the liquids over the flour mixture. Pulse several times, or just until the dough comes together in large moist clumps. Do not let it form a ball. **4.** Turn the dough out onto a lightly floured counter. Gently, patting the dough with flour, work it into a neat ball. **5.** Divide it in half and shape each half into a flat disk. Wrap them separately in foil and refrigerate for 20 minutes. Use as directed.

Sheryl Julian

Blueberry Pie

The amount of blueberries here fills a deep 9-inch glass pie pan with a fluted rim. Pans that are shallow—plain round glass pans, for instance—will take 6 cups of blues (use 5 frozen, 1 fresh), ½ cup sugar, and 4 tablespoons tapioca. Heap the berries in the crust so you'll have a domed pie when the fruit cooks down.

MAKES 1 DEEP DOUBLE-CRUST PIE

Flour (for sprinkling)

1 recipe Pie Pastry (see page 299)

Flour (for rolling)

1 pint (2 cups) fresh blueberries, rinsed, left to dry, and picked over for stems

6 cups frozen wild Maine blueberries (use three 10-ounce bags without thawing)

¾ cup granulated sugar

6 tablespoons instant tapioca

Pinch of salt

1½ tablespoons lemon juice

1 tablespoon unsalted butter, cut into 6 pieces

2 tablespoons milk (for brushing)

Extra sugar (for sprinkling)

1. Have on hand a deep 9-inch pie pan and rimmed baking sheet lined with parchment paper. **2.** On a generously floured counter, roll one disk of dough to an 11-inch round. Lift it onto the rolling pin, brush off the excess flour, and ease the dough into the pie pan, letting the excess hang over the edges. Use scissors to trim the edges of the pastry so there is an even ½-inch overhang. Turn the overhang under to form a hem all around. **3.** In a bowl, combine the berries, sugar, tapioca, salt, and lemon juice. Transfer the fruit to the pie pan. Dot the top with butter. Refrigerate the pie. **4.** Set the oven at 400°F. **5.** Roll out the other piece of dough to an 11-inch round. Brush off the excess flour. Lift the round onto the rolling pin, and ease the dough into the pie pan. Turn the top edges under all around the rim. Dip a fork into flour and press the edges together with the fork to seal them. **6.** Brush the pastry with milk and sprinkle it with sugar. Set the pie on the baking sheet. Use the tip of a knife to make 6 vents in the pie. **7.** Bake the pie for 20 minutes. Turn the oven temperature down to 375°F. Continue baking for 20 minutes or until the pastry is golden brown (total baking time is 40 minutes). **8.** Cool the pie for 15 minutes. Serve warm with ice cream.

Note: to make a lattice topped pie follow the instructions on page 302.

Sheryl Julian

Blueberry Pie

Strawberry-Rhubarb Pie with Easy Lattice Top

These instructions tell you how to make a quick lattice by first setting strips on the pie in one direction, then laying a second set over the first. It avoids weaving.

MAKES ONE 9-INCH PIE

8 stalks (1 pound) rhubarb, ends trimmed, stalks cut into ½-inch pieces

¼ cup instant tapioca

1 cup granulated sugar

Flour (for sprinkling)

1 recipe Pie Pastry (see page 299)

Flour (for rolling)

1 pint strawberries, hulled and quartered

1 egg white, lightly beaten

1 tablespoon sugar (for sprinkling)

1. Have on hand a 9-inch pie pan. **2.** In a bowl, combine the rhubarb, tapioca, and ½ cup of the sugar. Let the fruit sit while you roll out the pastry. **3.** On a generously floured counter, roll one disk of dough to an 11-inch round. Lift it onto the rolling pin, brush off the excess flour, and ease the dough into the pie pan, letting the excess hang over the edges. Use scissors to trim the edges of the pastry so there is an even ½-inch overhang. Turn the overhang under to form a hem all around. **4.** Refrigerate the pan while you prepare the lattice. **5.** Set the oven at 375°F. Roll out the remaining dough on a lightly floured board to a 10-inch round. Using a fluted pastry wheel or a long, straight-edged knife, cut the edges of the dough so they are straight. Slice the dough at 1-inch intervals into 10 strips. **6.** Remove the pie pan from the refrigerator. Stir the strawberries into the rhubarb mixture. Fill the pastry with fruit. Sprinkle the remaining ½ cup of sugar on top of the fruit. **7.** Set 5 pastry strips on the pie, so they're parallel and evenly spaced. Then set the 5 remaining strips perpendicular to the first set, also evenly spaced, so they form a lattice pattern. Using scissors, trim the lattice so it is even with the overhang. **8.** Turn the edge up over the lattice and pinch the edge all around to flute it. Or use the tines of a fork to make impressions around the edge to seal the top and bottom. Brush the pastry lattice with beaten egg white and sprinkle it with sugar. Set the pie on a rimmed baking sheet. **9.** Bake the pie in the center of the oven for 50 to 55 minutes or until the crust is golden brown and the filling is bubbling and thickened. Cool the pie for 15 minutes.

Sheryl Julian & Julie Riven

Pumpkin Pie

Boston's celebrated restaurateur Lydia Shire, owner of Locke-Ober and Scampo in Boston, and Blue Sky in York Beach, Maine, makes this spice-filled, smooth, and rich pumpkin pie for her own table. Serve thick slices with whipped cream.

MAKES ONE 9-INCH PIE

Flour (for sprinkling)

½ recipe Pie Pastry (see page 299)

1 can (15 ounces) solid-pack pumpkin puree

1 teaspoon ground cinnamon

1 teaspoon ground ginger

½ teaspoon ground allspice

¼ teaspoon ground cloves

¼ teaspoon ground nutmeg

1 teaspoon salt

⅓ cup granulated sugar

⅓ cup dark brown sugar

1 cup light cream

3 eggs, lightly beaten

1. Set the oven at 375°F. Have on hand a deep 9-inch pie pan. **2.** On a generously floured counter, roll one disk of dough to an 11-inch round. Lift it onto the rolling pin, brush off the excess flour, and ease the dough into the pie pan, letting the excess hang over the edges. Use scissors to trim the edges of the pastry so there is an even ½-inch overhang. Turn the overhang under to form a hem all around. **3.** Prick the dough well all over, line it with a piece of foil, pressing it down firmly onto the crust, then fill it with dried beans. Bake the shell for 15 minutes. Lift out the foil and beans and continue baking for 5 minutes. **4.** In a large bowl, whisk together the pumpkin, cinnamon, ginger, allspice, cloves, nutmeg, and salt. Stir in the granulated and brown sugars with the cream. **5.** Add the eggs. When the mixture is smooth, pour it into the partially baked shell. **6.** Bake the pie for 40 minutes or until the filling is set around the edges and jiggles slightly in the middle. **7.** Set on a wire rack to cool completely.

Note: Most supermarkets sell 9-inch glass baking dishes. In general, the ones that are fluted are deeper than the ones with the plain rims. If a recipe calls for a deep 9-inch pie pan, use the fluted version. Kitchen supply stores sell pie pans that are even deeper.

Lydia Shire

Apple Pie

The traditional way to eat apple pie is with strong cheddar cheese or ice cream. In this recipe, rather than cutting the apples into slices, they're cut crosswise too, which makes the filling more compact so you can get lots of apples into the crust.

MAKES ONE 9-INCH PIE

¾ cup granulated sugar

2 tablespoons flour

¾ teaspoon ground cinnamon

½ teaspoon ground nutmeg

Pinch of salt

Flour (for sprinkling)

1 recipe Pie Pastry (see page 299)

6 baking apples, peeled, quartered, and sliced both lengthwise and crosswise (see box on next page)

2 tablespoons butter

1 tablespoon lemon juice

2 tablespoons milk (for brushing)

Extra granulated sugar (for sprinkling)

1. In a bowl, combine the sugar, flour, cinnamon, nutmeg, and salt; set aside. **2.** On a generously floured counter, roll one disk of dough to an 11-inch round. Lift it onto the rolling pin, brush off the excess flour, and ease the dough into the pie pan, letting the excess hang over the edges. Use scissors to trim the edges of the pastry so there is an even ½-inch overhang. Turn the overhang under to form a hem all around. **3.** In a large bowl, toss the apples with the sugar mixture. Pile them into the crust. Dot the apples with butter and sprinkle them with lemon juice. Refrigerate. **4.** Set the oven at 400°F. **5.** Roll out the other piece of dough to an 11-inch round. Brush off the excess flour. Lift the round onto the rolling pin, and ease the dough into the pie pan. Turn the top edges under all around the rim. Dip a fork into flour and press the edges together with the fork to seal them. Brush the pastry with milk and sprinkle it with sugar. Set the pie on the baking sheet. Use the tip of a knife to make 6 vents in the pie. **6.** Bake the pie for 20 minutes. Turn the oven temperature down to 375°F. Continue baking for 30 minutes or until the pastry is golden and the apples are tender when pierced with a skewer (total baking time is 50 minutes). **7.** Cool the pie for 15 minutes.

Sheryl Julian & Julie Riven

Not every apple is good in pie

Because McIntosh apples are so readily available and people like their winey flavor, they're often used to make apple pies, but they're not suitable baking apples; they turn watery and pulpy in the oven.

A good baking apple keeps its shape during cooking, doesn't release too much water, and has enough flavor so that spices are not really necessary.

Old-fashioned Gravenstein, an early tart apple, makes a fine pie, particularly when mixed with another variety. Cooks who lean toward Gravenstein also like Rhode Island Greening and Northern Spy. Cortland and Golden Delicious apples are in many supermarkets at the height of the season; Cortland stays white when peeled, which many cooks like (it makes them ideal in salads, too). Other good bakers are Pippin, Paula Red, Ida Red, Baldwin, Jonagold, and Rome Beauty.

Strawberry Shortcake

When local strawberries come into the markets in June, they beg for a sweet little cake and some cream. This simple round is made in an ordinary layer cake pan, and served with whipped cream and macerated ripe berries.

SERVES 6

SHORTCAKE

Butter (for the pan)

Flour (for the pan)

2 cups flour

¼ teaspoon salt

1½ teaspoons baking powder

¾ cup (1½ sticks) unsalted
   butter, cut up

½ cup granulated sugar

1 cup heavy cream

1 egg, lightly beaten

Extra granulated sugar (for
   sprinkling)

Confectioners' sugar (for
   sprinkling)

STRAWBERRIES

1 pint strawberries, trimmed
   and halved or sliced

1 tablespoon granulated sugar

½ cup heavy cream, softly
   whipped

SHORTCAKE

1. Set the oven at 375°F. Butter an 8-inch layer cake pan. Line the bottom with a circle of parchment paper cut to fit it. Butter the paper and dust the pan with flour, tapping out the excess. **2.** In a bowl, whisk the flour, salt, and baking powder. **3.** Add the butter and use a pastry blender or two blunt knives to work the butter into the dry ingredients until the mixture resembles crumbs. **4.** Stir the granulated sugar into the flour mixture. **5.** In a bowl mix the cream and egg. With a rubber spatula, stir the cream mixture into the flour mixture just until it forms a moist batter. Do not overmix. **6.** Spoon the batter into the pan and smooth the top. Sprinkle with granulated sugar. Bake the shortcake for 35 minutes or until the top is golden and a skewer inserted into the middle comes out clean. Let the shortcake cool in the pan on a rack for 20 minutes. Turn it out onto a plate, then turn it right side up onto a flat cake platter. Sprinkle with confectioners' sugar.

STRAWBERRIES

1. In a bowl, layer the berries and sugar. Set them aside for 15 minutes. Stir gently. **2.** Cut the cake into 6 triangles and set them on dessert plates. Spoon berries and cream on the wedges.

Sheryl Julian

Peach Crisp

Ripe peaches, brown sugar, lemon, almonds, cinnamon, and butter—all in one dish, with the fruit on the bottom and the crispy part on top. On a warm summer night, what more could you want?

SERVES 6

FILLING

Butter (for the dish)

6 large peaches

Grated rind of ½ lemon rind

1½ tablespoons lemon juice

¼ cup brown sugar

TOPPING

½ cup flour

½ cup chopped almonds, toasted

½ cup brown sugar

¼ teaspoon ground cinnamon

¼ teaspoon salt

6 tablespoons unsalted butter, chilled and cut into small pieces

FILLING

1. Set the oven at 375°F. Butter an 8-inch-square baking dish. **2.** Bring a large saucepan of water to a boil. With a paring knife, score a small x at the base of each peach. With a slotted spoon, lower the peaches into the water. Let them sit for 30 seconds, then lift them out and transfer to a bowl of very cold water. Let cold tap water run into the bowl to keep the water cold. **3.** When the peaches are cool enough to handle, use a paring knife to peel off the skin. Quarter the peaches, discard the pits, and cut the peaches into ½-inch-thick slices. **4.** In a bowl, toss the peaches with the lemon rind and juice, and the brown sugar. Spread the mixture in the baking dish.

TOPPING

1. In a bowl, combine the flour, almonds, brown sugar, cinnamon, and salt. Mix well. With your fingertips, work in the butter until the mixture is crumbly but not quite sandy. **2.** Crumble the almond mixture evenly over the peaches. Bake the crisp for 50 to 55 minutes or until the topping is golden brown. Serve warm with ice cream.

Jonathan Levitt

Blueberry Cobbler

Blueberry Cobbler

Cobblers do not take their name from the village shoemaker but rather from the polished, slightly bumpy surface of cobblestones. When this dessert comes out of the oven—berries on the bottom, a golden, sugary, biscuit-like topping covering them—you'll see the resemblance. The filling is a little runny which makes a saucy mixture for the tender topping.

SERVES 8

DOUGH

Butter (for the dish)

2 cups flour

2 teaspoons baking powder

½ teaspoon salt

8 tablespoons butter, cut up

3 tablespoons granulated
    sugar

¾ cup whole milk

Extra flour (for sprinkling)

FILLING

3 pints fresh blueberries,
    picked over

¼ cup granulated sugar

2 tablespoons instant tapioca

Grated rind and juice of ½
    lemon

Whole milk (for brushing)

Extra granulated sugar (for
    sprinkling)

DOUGH

1. Set the oven at 375°F. Butter a deep 2½-quart baking dish. **2.** In a bowl, whisk the flour, baking powder, and salt. **3.** Add the cut-up butter, and with a pastry blender or two blunt knives, cut through the pieces until the mixture resembles coarse crumbs. **4.** Stir in the sugar. Sprinkle ½ cup of the milk over the dough and work it with a fork until the dough starts to form large clumps. Add more milk, 1 tablespoon at a time, until all of the dough forms clumps. **5.** Turn them out onto a lightly floured counter and knead them very gently once or twice until the mixture forms a dough. Flatten the dough into a flat round cake. Refrigerate on a plate for 5 minutes. **6.** On a floured counter, roll the dough to the same size and shape as the dish. With a ½-inch plain round or star cutter, stamp a circle or star in the middle of the dough for an air vent.

FILLING

1. In a bowl, combine the blueberries, sugar, tapioca, lemon rind, and juice; stir gently. Transfer the berries to the prepared dish. **2.** Pick the dough up onto the rolling pin and lay it over the berries. If the dough seems too large for the dish, tuck in the edges. Brush the dough with milk and then sprinkle it with sugar. **3.** Bake the cobbler for 45 to 50 minutes or until the pastry is golden brown all over. Set the cobbler on a rack and let it settle for 10 minutes.

Sheryl Julian & Julie Riven

Blueberry Slump

A slump is an old-fashioned bread and fruit pudding. Here challah or brioche is layered and baked with blueberries until the bread slices are soaked with berry juices.

SERVES 6

¼ cup (½ stick) unsalted
   butter, melted

3 pints fresh blueberries

½ cup granulated sugar

Grated rind and juice
   of 1 lemon

3 tablespoons water

12 slices eggy white bread such
   as challah or brioche

Extra granulated sugar (for
   sprinkling)

1. Set the oven at 375°F. Using some of the melted butter, butter a deep 2 ½-quart baking dish. **2.** In a saucepan, combine the blueberries, sugar, lemon rind and juice, and water. Cook over medium heat, stirring often, for 5 minutes or until some berries collapse. Remove from the heat. **3.** With a brush, dab the butter on one side of each slice of bread. Halve the slices on the diagonal. **4.** Layer the blueberries and bread in the dish, beginning and ending with bread. As you layer, press down on the bread with a spoon. On the top layer, overlap the remaining bread slices buttered side up to form a pattern. Sprinkle generously with sugar. **5.** Bake the slump 25 minutes or until the top is golden. Watch it carefully so it does not burn. **6.** Cool for 5 minutes.

Sheryl Julian

Baked Apples with Maple Syrup

Moisten baking apples with cider and maple syrup and bake them until they're meltingly tender. Drench the dish in heavy cream and more maple syrup and serve right away. They're soft, comforting, and warm.

SERVES 4

4 baking apples (see page
   305), cored

½ cup apple cider

¼ cup maple syrup, plus more
   for sprinkling

1. Set the oven at 350°F. In an 8-inch square baking dish, place the apples in one layer. **2.** In a small bowl combine the cider and ¼ cup maple syrup. Pour the mixture over the apples. Bake the apples for 45 minutes or until tender when pierced with a skewer. During baking, baste the apples often with the juices at the bottom of the dish.

Jonathan Levitt

Baked Apples with Maple Syrup

Strawberry-Rhubarb Compote

Lightly sweetened rhubarb and strawberries, simmered together for an hour, turn into a soft pink-colored compote, which tastes dreamy with a little cold heavy cream. Serve it with a plate of simple cookies.

SERVES 8

8 thick stalks of rhubarb, trimmed and cut into 2-inch pieces

1 quart fresh strawberries, hulled and quartered

⅓ cup granulated sugar

1 navel orange

1 cup heavy cream (for serving)

1. In a heavy-based flameproof casserole, combine the rhubarb, strawberries, and sugar. **2.** Grate the orange rind into the pot. Halve the orange and squeeze the juice of one half into the fruit. With your fingers pull the squeezed orange membranes off the rind and add them to the pot. **3.** Cook over medium heat, stirring often, until the juices run. Cover and let the mixture bubble steadily over low heat, stirring often, for 30 minutes. **4.** Uncover, turn the heat to medium, and continue simmering for 30 minutes or until the juices reduce and the mixture thickens. **5.** Divide the mixture among eight small bowls and pour the cold cream around the edges of each bowl.

Sheryl Julian

Indian Pudding

One of the oldest recipes in New England, Indian pudding is a molasses-flavored mixture made with cornmeal, eggs, and milk. Indian pudding is probably an acquired taste, but a favorite among New Englanders. This recipe comes from the famous Durgin-Park restaurant in Boston, Massachusetts, which began offering the formula in 1948. We updated it to make it lighter. Serve hot with scoops of vanilla ice cream.

SERVES 6

Butter (for the dish)

½ cup molasses

¼ cup (½ stick) butter, melted

¼ cup granulated sugar

2 eggs, lightly beaten

1 cup yellow cornmeal

¼ teaspoon baking soda

¼ teaspoon salt

3 cups whole milk

1. Set the oven at 275°F. Butter a 2-quart shallow baking dish. **2.** In a bowl, combine the molasses, butter, and sugar. With a spoon, mix it thoroughly. **3.** Stir in the eggs, cornmeal, baking soda, and salt. **4.** In a saucepan or microwave, scald the milk. Gradually stir the milk into the cornmeal mixture. Transfer the batter to the baking dish. **5.** Bake the pudding for 2 hours or until it is set in the middle. Spoon into bowls and serve hot.

From Durgin-Park, Boston, Massachusetts

Cinnamon Rice Pudding

In the lineup of comfort dishes, rice pudding has to be near the top of the list. This pudding, made with short-grain white rice, simmers slowly with cinnamon sticks for 50 minutes.

SERVES 4

2 quarts whole milk

¾ cup short-grain white rice
   (such as arborio)

2 whole cinnamon sticks

1 cup granulated sugar

Ground cinnamon (for
   sprinkling)

1. In a medium saucepan, combine the milk, rice, and cinnamon sticks. Bring to a boil over medium heat, stirring often to prevent the rice from sticking. Reduce heat to low and simmer gently, stirring occasionally, for 20 minutes. **2.** Stir in the sugar and continue cooking, stirring often, for 30 minutes or until the rice is cooked through and has absorbed most of the milk. **3.** Discard the cinnamon sticks. Serve the rice pudding hot or cold, sprinkled with ground cinnamon.

Jonathan Levitt

Hot Fudge Sauce

Boston, Massachusetts, is ice cream country. Even during the darkest, snowiest winters, people adore cones and hot fudge sundaes. Buy premium ice cream and use this dark, luscious, fudgy sauce to spoon over it.

MAKES 2 CUPS

½ cup (1 stick) unsalted butter,
   cut up

6 tablespoons unsweetened
   cocoa powder

4 ounces bittersweet
   chocolate, chopped

1 cup granulated sugar

1 cup evaporated milk

1 teaspoon vanilla extract

1. In a saucepan, melt the butter over medium heat. Add the cocoa and mix until smooth. Stir in the chocolate, sugar, and evaporated milk. **2.** Bring to a boil, and cook, stirring constantly, for 5 minutes. **3.** Remove from the heat. Stir in the vanilla. Use hot or transfer to a plastic container and refrigerate. Reheat over medium-low heat until liquid and hot again.

Virginia's Fine Foods,
Brookline, Massachusetts

Metric Conversion Table

Approximate U.S. Metric Equivalents

LIQUID INGREDIENTS

U.S. MEASURES	METRIC	U.S. MEASURES	METRIC
¼ TSP.	1.23 ML	2 TBSP.	29.57 ML
½ TSP.	2.36 ML	3 TBSP.	44.36 ML
¾ TSP.	3.70 ML	¼ CUP	59.15 ML
1 TSP.	4.93 ML	½ CUP	118.30 ML
1¼ TSP.	6.16 ML	1 CUP	236.59 ML
1½ TSP.	7.39 ML	2 CUPS OR 1 PT.	473.18 ML
1¾ TSP.	8.63 ML	3 CUPS	709.77 ML
2 TSP.	9.86 ML	4 CUPS OR 1 QT.	946.36 ML
1 TBSP.	14.79 ML	4 QTS. OR 1 GAL.	3.79 LT

DRY INGREDIENTS

U.S. MEASURES		METRIC	U.S. MEASURES	METRIC
17³/₅ OZ.	1 LIVRE	500 G	2 OZ.	60 (56.6) G
16 OZ.	1 LB.	454 G	1¾ OZ.	50 G
8⅞ OZ.		250 G	1 OZ.	30 (28.3) G
5¼ OZ.		150 G	⅞ OZ.	25 G
4½ OZ.		125 G	¾ OZ.	21 (21.3) G
4 OZ.		115 (113.2) G	½ OZ.	15 (14.2) G
3½ OZ.		100 G	¼ OZ.	7 (7.1) G
3 OZ.		85 (84.9) G	⅛ OZ.	3½ (3.5) G
2⁴/₅ OZ.		80 G	1/16 OZ.	2 (1.8) G

Index

About the Author

Sheryl Julian is Food Editor of *The Boston Globe*. She trained at the Cordon Bleu schools in London and Paris and was deputy director of L'Ecole de Cuisine La Varenne in Paris, a bilingual cooking school. Her *Boston Globe* magazine food column, written with Julie Riven, ran for more than 20 year; they are co-authors of *The Way We Cook*. She is co-founder of The Women's Culinary Guild of New England, the first organization in America for women in the food business, and a founding member of the Culinary Historians of Boston, a group dedicated to the history of the table. Her food writing has won several national awards.